D0848928

THE RISE OF RAWLINS LOWNDES

TRICENTENNIAL STUDIES, NUMBER 12

This volume is part of a series of *Tricentennial Studies*, published by the University of South Carolina Press on behalf of the South Carolina Tricentennial Commission, to commemorate the founding of South Carolina in 1670.

THE RISE OF RAWLINS LOWNDES, 1721–1800

by Carl J. Vipperman

Published for the
South Carolina Tricentennial Commission
by the
UNIVERSITY OF SOUTH CAROLINA PRESS
Columbia, South Carolina

Copyright © University of South Carolina 1978
FIRST EDITION
Published in Columbia, South Carolina, by the
University of South Carolina Press, 1978
Manufactured in the United States of America

Library of Congress Cataloging in Publication Data

Vipperman, Carl J., 1928–
    The rise of Rawlins Lowndes, 1721–1800.

   (Tricentennial studies ; no. 12)
   Includes bibliographical references and index.
      1. Lowndes, Rawlins, 1721–1800. 2. Legislators—South
Carolina—Biography. 3. South Carolina—History—
Colonial period, ca. 1600–1775. 4. South Carolina—
History—Revolution, 1775–1783. I. Title. II. Series:
South Carolina Tricentennial Commission. Tricentennial
studies ; no. 12.
F272.L87V56   975.7′03′0924 [B]   78–17353
ISBN 0-87249-259-1

To
BERNARD MAYO
with sentiments of the most profound respect;
and to
MIKE LASSITER
DAN QUINN
R. TODD WILLIAMS
PROCTOR CHAMBLESS, JR.
and
WAYNE WATSON,
former students in my undergraduate history course on the Old South offered at the University of Georgia, who conceived a plan to finance this volume when rising costs delayed publication of the series, and established a fund for the purpose with the University of Georgia Alumni Foundation. Their generous offer was refused, the gesture alone having repaid the author for all his efforts.

CONTENTS

PREFACE

IN A MOOD characteristically virulent, Charles Woodmason, the celebrated Anglican itinerant of the South Carolina backcountry, summed up the career of Rawlins Lowndes: "He was originally a Parish Orphan Boy, nor knows his own Origin—Taken from the Dunghill by our late Provost Marshal—Made his Valet—then learn'd to read and write—then became Goaler—Then Provost Marshal—Got Money—Married Well—Settled Plantations—became a Planter—A Magistrate—A Senator—Speaker of the House and now Chief Judge."[1] That was in 1769. Woodmason himself was a former merchant and planter, who had in recent years taken up the cross and carried the gospel of Jesus Christ into the half-civilized backsettlements only to return a few years later the best hater in South Carolina, possessed of a personality so curiously blending passion with prejudice that he could simultaneously love and despise his neighbor with equal zest. The Anglican missionary had known Rawlins Lowndes for almost twenty years, since long before the former got religion and the latter got wealth.[2]

Considering the time and circumstances, Woodmason had reason enough to bear enmity against the wealthy lowcountry judge, for in the 1760s they faced each other across a burning sectional issue, the South Carolina Regulator Movement. Yet the minister, for all his want of charity toward Lowndes, was nonetheless hon-

1. *The Carolina Backcountry on the Eve of the Revolution: The Journal and Other Writings of Charles Woodmason, Anglican Itinerant*, ed. Richard J. Hooker, (Chapel Hill, 1953), p. 269.
2. In 1752 Woodmason operated a store at the corner of Church and Tradd streets, Charles Town, S.C., *South Carolina Gazette*, August 10, 1752.

est; and his sketch, except for the nonsense concerning Lowndes' unknown origins, was essentially correct. Woodmason's short, sharp phrases fairly exclaim the fact that the entire career of Rawlins Lowndes had been a courageous struggle upward from personal misfortune to a position of prominence in South Carolina's political, social, and economic life. The theme is classic, and the story is well worth telling in detail.

Perhaps I ought to confess that my decision to write this book was made well after the task was under way. On completing graduate work, I intended to follow the usual procedure and revise for publication my dissertation on William Lowndes, son of Rawlins and Congressman from South Carolina from 1811 to 1822. To this end I began to broaden the original cursory treatment of the Lowndes family background and history, and, to use the phrase of Governor James Glen, commenced "turning over" the old journals. As is often the case in such projects, I soon became absorbed in something I had not planned to devote nearly so much attention to, the long and distinguished public career of Rawlins Lowndes. Except for a few receipts, bills of sale and the like, perhaps two dozen private letters, the fragment of a journal and his final will, Rawlins Lowndes had left no personal papers. But I was pleasantly surprised to discover how much of his career could be pieced together from the public records. Weeks became months and the months a year and I had not yet reached the event of William's birth. At about this point, on a suggestion of George C. Rogers, Jr., editor of the *Papers of Henry Laurens*, I decided to abandon the unborn son for the time being and write this book on his father.

The dearth of personal papers and sources of information on his private affairs has been the principal factor in determining the nature of this study and the limits of its scope. What I attempt here is simply to reconstruct the circumstances of his early years and to trace his public career, offering an occasional opinion on his conduct and motives. As might be expected, there are still areas in the life of Rawlins Lowndes where I was unable to discover what he was doing, to say nothing of why he was doing it. This is particularly true of the years of his minority. For this period consequently, I have given more attention to his father and to other

persons who had an important influence on his life than to Rawlins himself. If I seem to have explained the office of provost marshal in more detail than the standards of narrative biography
would normally require, the neglect of this office by historians
and its importance not only to Lowndes personally but also to the
sectional history of colonial South Carolina must plead my excuse.
Otherwise I have tried not to sally out too far or too frequently
into the surrounding historical landscape. In following Lowndes'
public career I have made a conscious effort to stay as close to his
elbow as the sources permitted, although this was often no closer
than the door of the Commons House, and to regard events from
his vantage point.

A word of explanation concerning certain usages that appear
in the text and notes may be helpful. Respect for form and propriety so characteristic of South Carolina colonials did not always
extend to spelling and syntax, as if these were areas reserved for individual creativity. I have chosen not to dilute the original flavor
of their composition nor to call attention to deviations from the
modern norm in either case except in rare instances where clarity
seemed questionable. For essentially the same reason I have retained the colonial spelling of Charles Town as long as it was
used in fact, changing over to Charleston with the Act of Incorporation of 1783. My use of the antiquated spelling of "gaol,"
or even "goal," rather than the more modern "jail" has been deliberate, seeming more appropriate to the narrative in the early
chapters. Colonial dates appearing in the sources have been simplified by dating each new year from January 1, rather than carrying the old year along with the new down to March 25, the
contemporary practice. Similarly, early issues of the weekly *South
Carolina Gazette*, which list both the opening and closing dates
of the week covered, are cited under the closing date only. Crown,
Council, Commons House of Assembly and variations thereof,
and Speaker have been capitalized throughout while king, governor, lieutenant governor, and certain other offices have been arbitrarily denied that distinction. Original punctuation has been
left undisturbed for the most part except for the occasional deletion of a superfluous comma or semicolon.

My scholarly debts have accumulated in numbers far too great for more than a few to be acknowledged here. Joseph H. Parks first introduced me to the fascinating realm of the American past, inspiring as much by his humanity as by the high standards of his scholarship. Bernard Mayo, the breadth and depth of whose erudition has been the joy and the despair of more than one generation of graduate students, stimulated my interest in the Lowndes family. If my judgments lack the generosity and independence of either, it is no fault of theirs. I am greatly indebted to George C. Rogers, Jr., and Robert M. Weir of the University of South Carolina, both authorities on the history of colonial South Carolina and equally generous in sharing with me their knowledge of the period. Each gave the manuscript a critical reading, contributing in distinctively different ways to its substantial improvement. Phinizy Spalding, my colleague at the University of Georgia, in addition to reading a portion of the manuscript, has become something of an authority on my subject through sheer patience if not genuine interest in his friend's favorite topic.

One debt I cannot hope to repay. It was my great good fortune to serve three years on the faculty of the College of Charleston with the late Samuel Gaillard Stoney, whose particular delight was to rouse a sleepy colleague with a Saturday morning call for a tramp through the lowcountry wilderness over the grounds of abandoned baronial estates. With a knowledge of the trackless jungle worthy of Ben Gunn himself, a high aristocratic forehead and a mastery of Carolina lore behind it, he pointed the way back to lowcountry grandeur of the eighteenth century. Under his penetrating gaze the tangled undergrowth melted away and spacious lawns, stately groves, and capital mansions came into view, including Crowfield up in the Goose Creek area and the Horseshoe far out on Chessey Creek west of the Edisto, both long since returned to wilderness with hardly a trace of civilization left behind. The day always ended in appropriate fashion, over a glass of madeira in his eighteenth-century quarters. If this study contains a trace of his feel for the historical era he loved far better than his own, the credit must go to Mr. Sam.

Retracing the steps of a historical figure becomes a journey in the literal sense, ranging far beyond the paths the subject trod. This one, covering a span of several years, has taken the author to the principal port cities of colonial America, from Charleston to Boston with varying interludes of research at some seventeen major repositories along the way. For the authors whose scholarship has lighted the way before me, the appended bibliographical note may be examined. Among the small army of professional and uniformly gracious archivists and librarians whose assistance was essential to this study, the directors and staffs of two South Carolina repositories deserve special mention. Mrs. Granville T. Prior and the staff at the South Carolina Historical Society in Charleston took a genuine interest in my project and could hardly have done more to make my repeated visits there both profitable and pleasant. Charles E. Lee and the staff have made the South Carolina Archives in Columbia a researcher's delight, and for this author, a most rewarding summer retreat over the past few years.

The enlightened policy of the University of Georgia, which permits the arrangement of teaching schedules to provide for regular periods of sustained research and writing free from the responsibilities of the classroom, is highly prized and justly praised not merely by this author but throughout the faculty. Graduate research assistants whose intelligent initiative and dependability will not be forgotten are Roger Martin, Von Pittman, and Theda Perdue. As one who has never mastered the typist's art, I fully appreciate the services that Gloria Davis, Linda Green, and Nancy Heaton have performed in translating my scrawl into readable prose.

To the South Carolina Historical Society, who published the essay I contributed on Charles Lowndes, much of which appears again in the first chapter of this book, I am grateful for allowing me to repeat myself.

Upcountry South Carolina, in the author's judgment, made the most treasured contribution of all. My wife, the former Reginald Graham of Seneca, has constantly aided and encouraged me through the slow and halting progress toward completion of this book. Only she knows how deeply I value her counsel and support.

CHAPTER I

The Prodigal Father

OUT OF THE BRITISH WEST INDIES bound for Carolina in the spring of 1730, a sailing ship approached the end of her voyage, a thin broken line of horizon away northwestward. The vessel kept her course through mile after mile of offshore ground-swells as the thin gray line gradually thickened and darkened into recognizable features of the Carolina coast. Just off the bar that lay athwart the harbor mouth she dropped anchor to await the pilot boat, while the children aboard marveled at the white beaches, the mysterious groves of live oak, and the green belt of salt marsh stretching in lone and level vastness beyond. Now turning her prow northward into the coastwise channel, the ship coasted along Morris Island until Sullivan's Island loomed dead ahead, then swung gracefully westward between them into the broad blue bay of Charles Town harbor. In due course the vessel sailed up the bay and into the Cooper River, moved alongside a wharf jutting out below the bustling port city's eastern wall, and here deposited her passengers and cargo. In the busiest port on the Atlantic seaboard south of Philadelphia such arrivals had become commonplace, and this one would have excited little more than passing interest among casual dockside observers.

Among the passengers who disembarked from this particular vessel, however, the Charles Lowndes family deserved, and probably received, something more than mere passing notice. Charles Lowndes was a man of substance and property, a member of the slave-holding, sugar-planting aristocracy of the British West Indies with important family connections in the islands and the mother country. The family name was already familiar to colonial officials who had had occasion to correspond with his distant relatives, William Lowndes of Westminster in the treasury office at Whitehall, and Thomas Lowndes of Overton, who held the patent of provost marshal for South Carolina. Moreover, Charles Lowndes was connected with the prominent Rawlins family of St. Christopher, more commonly called St. Kitts, second largest of the Leeward Islands, and had served on the governor's council there before departing for Carolina.[1] He doubtless shared in the official attention extended to immigrants of his class by Governor Robert Johnson, an enthusiastic promoter of immigration to Carolina.[2] His arrival was not a pretentious display of wealth or property, however. He brought with him only his wife Ruth and their three young sons. All their slaves and virtually all their moveable property had been left behind, to be sent on after the family had got established here.[3]

Within this family of five immigrants now going about the strange routine of entry into a new colony, two were destined for extraordinary careers; so extraordinary, in fact, that together they illustrate the extremes of success and failure which life in colonial South Carolina offered to those courageous enough, or foolhardy enough, to cast their lot with her. Nine-year-old Rawlins Lowndes, the youngest son, was destined for fame and fortune. His potential for material success and political leadership was great enough to thrust the name of Lowndes into the front rank of colonial South Carolina's leading families. His achievements become all the more remarkable when viewed in the light of his father's career in the colony. For the career of Charles Lowndes was to be a maddening succession of frustration and failure that would drive him relent-

1. George B. Chase, *Lowndes of South Carolina, An Historical and Genealogical Memoir* (Boston, Mass., 1876), p. 12.
2. Implementing his Township plan of settlement, Johnson wrote to the Board of Trade on December 16, 1731, that several "Gentlemen of Great Fortune" had come "from Barbados and elsewhere to see how they like the Country"; to encourage their permanent settlement in the colony he issued to them special land warrants in five-hundred-acre units. Transcripts of Records Relating to South Carolina in the British Public Record Office, XVII, 275, South Carolina Department of Archives and History, Columbia, S.C. (Hereafter these records, compiled and transcribed by W. Noel Sainsbury, are cited SCPRO.)
3. Chase, *Lowndes*, p. 12.

lessly to utter and tragic ruin. To see in the father's failure the primary motivation behind the son's success is tempting; certainly the boy was profoundly affected by it. But for an explanation of the failure itself, the father's career must be examined.

The ultimate failure of Charles Lowndes stands out in sharp relief when set against the background of advantage and opportunity which characterized his early years. Actually few Carolinians of his day could have presented more impressive credentials. The Lowndeses were an old and numerous family of English landed gentry with a coat of arms and family seal, tracing their generations back to *"the anciente familye of Loundes of Legh Hall."*[4] In the seventeenth century members of this family held seats in Parliament, with William Lowndes of Westminster being by far the most distinguished among them. William Lowndes had been appointed secretary to the treasury in 1695, and "His intercourse with the leading statesmen was thenceforth very close."[5] For almost twenty years afterwards, serving simultaneously in Parliament and the treasury office in Whitehall, he was the most influential officer in the government's fiscal affairs, operating by his favorite maxim "Take care of the pence and the pounds will take care of themselves."[6] More recently, Thomas Lowndes of Overton, through close association with the Lords Proprietors of Carolina and influence with members of the Board and Trade, had been instrumental in arranging the Crown's purchase of proprietary rights in Carolina. For these services he was named South Carolina's first provost marshal under the Crown and was granted 12,000 acres of land in the colony.[7]

Charles Lowndes had descended from a younger son of the Lowndes family of Smallwood, which was itself a branch of the Lowndes family of Legh Hall.[8] By 1590 this junior branch was represented by Richard Lowndes, Gentleman, Squire of Bostock

4. Ibid., p. 7.

5. James Adam Cramb, "William Lowndes," *Dictionary of National Biography*, eds. Sir Leslie Stephen and Sir Sidney Lee (Oxford, England, since 1917 [edition of 1963–1964]), XII, 210–11.

6. Ibid., p. 211.

7. SCPRO, XV, 280–81, 298–99, 309.

8. Unless otherwise noted, all the following genealogical data on the Lowndes family may be found in Chase, *Lowndes*, pp. 10–13, 55–57.

House and Hassal Hall, Cheshire, England. The remains of Hassal Hall, a spacious stone manor house flanked by formal gardens and surrounded by a moat, bear mute testimony to the social standing and affluence of this branch of the family. John, the son and heir of Richard Lowndes, transferred the family seat from Hassal Hall to Middlewich before his death in 1667. The son and heir of John Lowndes was identified in the family records as Charles the Elder to distinguish him from his own son who was called Charles the Younger. It is this Charles Lowndes the Younger who founded the Lowndes family of South Carolina.

George B. Chase, the Lowndes family genealogist who had access to the old family records, found them extremely fragmentary for this period. They were sufficient nevertheless to show that Charles the Younger left England rather early in life—shortly after the War of Spanish Succession ended in 1713—and migrated to the Leeward Island of St. Kitts. Here, probably in 1717, he married Ruth Rawlins, daughter of Henry Rawlins, a prominent St. Kitts sugar planter. Chase's research further revealed that a connection between the Lowndes and Rawlins families had been established in England three generations earlier with the marriage of Richard Lowndes of Bostock House, Charles the Younger's great-grandfather, to an Elizabeth Rawlins in 1611.[9] This fact suggests that Charles Lowndes and Ruth Rawlins even before their marriage were probably related, though distantly, and that their marriage was anticipated if not actually arranged by their families.

At the same time, it should be noted that there were reasons other than the hospitality of the St. Kitts planters and the attractiveness of their daughters that lured more than one ambitious if somewhat romantic young Englishman to the island. St. Kitts, more so than any other island in the West Indies, offered to Englishmen unusual opportunities in the years immediately following the War of Spanish Succession. Since the 1620s half the island had belonged to France, but during the war the French colonials were driven out completely, and notwithstanding a severely destructive invasion by the French fleet in 1705–06, the entire island was

9. Ibid., p. 10.

handed over to the English in the Treaty of Utrecht in 1713.[10]
This acquisition opened to Englishmen thousands of acres of the
most fertile sugar-producing lands in the entire West Indies at
the very time that Charles Lowndes was leaving England for the
colony.[11] Henry Rawlins, and eventually his son-in-law, came into
possession of lands formerly belonging to the French, for Rawlins
gave to his daughter Ruth an estate in Basseterre, an area formerly
under French control.[12]

On this island of extraordinary beauty, marvelous fertility and
remarkably stable climate,[13] Charles and Ruth Lowndes spent the
most idyllic years of their marriage. In her dowry Ruth brought
to her husband a considerable amount of property, both real and
personal, probably including the estate in St. Peter's Parish in
Basseterre. Here they appear to have settled, with Charles entering
upon the career of sugar planter. Within four years Ruth bore her
husband three sons, named William, Charles, and the last born in
1721, Rawlins, in honor of her father. Being the son-in-law of
Henry Rawlins, Charles Lowndes assumed an appropriate position
among the island gentry and was eventually elevated to a position
on the provincial council as representative of his parish.[14]

All was not well with the affairs of the young planter, however.
His son Rawlins decades later would explain to his own inquisi-
tive children that their grandfather simply "embarrassed his property by free living and an unrestrained expenditure. . . ."[15] Such

10. Charles M. Andrews, *The Colonial Period of American History,* 4 vols.,
(New Haven, Conn. 1934–38), II, 250–61.
11. Gordon C. Merrill, *The Historical Geography of St. Kitts and Nevis, The
West Indies* (Mexico City, 1958), pp. 44, 75.
12. Chase, *Lowndes,* p. 12; see also Merrill, *St. Kitts and Nevis,* map opposite page 61. The sale of former French lands was until 1726 confined to the
Basseterre area, John Anderson to Edmund Gibson, August 15, 1726, Fulham
Papers, XIX, Lambeth Palace Library, American Colonial Section, microfilm
in the Library of the University of Georgia, Athens, Ga. (Hereafter cited Fulham Papers.)
13. The average annual extremes of temperature on St. Kitts vary less than
fifteen degrees, ranging from 65.5 to 89.8 degrees Fahrenheit; its rare beauty is
marred only by the dark coloring of its beaches, revealing their volcanic origin.
Merrill, *St. Kitts and Nevis,* pp. 18–21, 25.
14. Chase, *Lowndes,* p. 12.
15. Ibid., Lowndes might also have suffered from the effects of consolidation

improvidence was encouraged by growing ostentation among West Indian planters generally. Magnificent mansions began to appear in the islands in the 1720s along with other displays of the wealth to be gained from sugar.[16] Successful planters in increasing numbers, preferring a home in England to such splendor as plantation life afforded, chose to become absentee landlords and departed the islands. Certainly within the limited society of the St. Kitts gentry the Rawlins family, more provident than most of their contemporaries,[17] could hardly have escaped some embarrassment over the behavior of an irresponsible in-law. And a woman with the spirit and courage of Ruth Lowndes would have been humiliated if not indeed mortified at the prospect of becoming an object of pity and the subject of whispered conversations among the ladies of St. Kitts.

With thorny personal problems thus springing up about him, Charles Lowndes turned his gaze out over the northwestern waters and saw in the continental colony of South Carolina a greener pasture. His family and close friends were probably not surprised when he decided on emigration, resigned his council position and began to wind up his affairs in St. Kitts. Finally on the appointed day, he and his wife and sons were rowed out to a ship anchored off Basseterre and took passage for Carolina.[18]

The move to Carolina was potentially the most fortuitous that Charles Lowndes could have made in his circumstances. The

---

of many estates. Charles M. Andrews states that the population of the islands increased rapidly in the eighteenth century, crowding out the smaller planters who emigrated to other West Indian islands and continental colonies, and that St. Christopher, even to a greater extent than Barbados or Antigua, "became the land of large plantations" controlled by absentee landlords. Andrews, *Colonial Period*, II, 260.

16. Merrill, *St. Kitts and Nevis*, p. 79.

17. That the Rawlins family retained their position and affluence is attested by "A Stranger" to Bishop Howley, July 1818, Fulham Papers, XX, who mentioned two members of the family who owned "several hundred slaves" in 1818. That the St. Kitts society was quite limited is shown in a list of inhabitants made in 1729 which included 1,117 "Christian" men, 994 women, 1,586 children and 14,663 slaves. Cecil Headlam, ed., *Calendar of State Papers, Colonial Series, America and the West Indies* (London, 1973), 1730, p. 126.

18. Chase, *Lowndes*, p. 12. St. Kitts had no harbor deep enough to accommodate ocean going vessels, so cargo and passengers were carried out to them in smaller boats.

colony at this time was virtually a promised land of opportunity to men like Lowndes, possessed of proper connections and some wealth. A stormy decade of revolution and economic depression, punctuated by savage political upheavals and exhausting religious quarrels, was just then giving way to a prevailing mood of remarkable calm.[19] The succeeding decade would witness a surge of vigorous growth, accompanied by booming prosperity which would continue unchecked until the outbreak of war with Spain in 1739.

Two actions taken by the English Parliament contributed to this resurgence in Carolina during the 1730s. The first took place in 1729 when Parliament bought out all but one of the Lords Proprietors, thereby clearing the way for more stable government under the direct authority of the Crown. The second occurred in 1730 when Parliament threw open the European rice market south of Cape Finisterre to the direct Carolina trade. The resultant boom in the rice industry saw acreage and production double during the 1730s while slave ships in monotonous succession brought in more than fifteen thousand Negroes to meet the constantly increasing demand for slave labor.[20] Rapid expansion and opportunities for quick fortunes in land opened in 1731 with the doors of the land office, which had been closed since the provincial revolution of 1719. This last act set in motion a frenzy of fraud, speculation and feverish land-grabbing unparalleled in the history of the colony. Almost a million acres were added to the tax books between 1731 and 1738 alone.[21] Spreading out from Charles Town, a rapidly expanding economy was arising from the application of rice culture and slave labor to the rich lowcountry swamplands.

19. M. Eugene Sirmans, *Colonial South Carolina, A Political History, 1663–1763* (Chapel Hill, N.C., 1966), pp. 164–65.

20. David D. Wallace, *South Carolina, A Short History, 1520–1948* (Columbia, S.C., 1961), pp. 141–42, 145.

21. Sirmans, *Colonial South Carolina*, p. 174, estimated the number of acres granted to be 900,000, whereas Wallace, *South Carolina, A Short History*, pp. 145–46, set the amount in excess of a million acres. According to an enclosure in a letter dated June 25, 1745, from Benjamin Whitaker to the Lords of Trade, 1,453,875 acres were listed on the quitrent rolls in November 1731 when the land office opened, compared to 2,349,129 acres on the rolls in 1742, an increase of 895,254 acres. The enclosure errs by 990,000 acres in reporting the increase to be 1,885,254, a fact that might account for Wallace's higher estimate for the period from 1731 to 1738. See SCPRO, XXI, 347–48.

Such conditions were made to order for a generation of seasoned colonials, boldly adventurous and creative, individualistic, intensely competitive, jostling one another for advantage and heedless of the disorder they created as they went briskly about the serious business of building family fortunes in this exciting decade. Into this bustling society entered Charles Lowndes with more confidence than business acumen, and a lack of discretion in financial affairs bordering on recklessness. Those familiar with his career in St. Kitts might have guessed what the future held for him here; but the very nature of the society itself made it difficult if not impossible for anyone to predict his fate with certainty.

Despite the extravagant handling of his affairs on St. Kitts, Lowndes was still able to bring to South Carolina a respectable amount of property, paying something over seventy-nine pounds duty on his slaves and other personal effects.[22] Shortly after his arrival he purchased one thousand acres of land in Berkeley County.[23] This lay in two tracts of five hundred acres each, located twenty-two miles north of Charles Town on Goose Creek, a tributary of the Cooper River noted for the richness of its rice lands and the predominance of former West Indian planters among its settlers. Here he settled his family in a plantation home described as a "good dwelling house, 5 fireplaces in it" with a "good kitchin. . . ."[24] Arrangements for putting in a crop were made, and after his slaves arrived from St. Kitts, improvements included "new boarded Negro houses to hold 50 Negroes, a large new cypress barn 60 feet long, and many other good conveniences. . . ."[25] He was named to the rank of major in the colonial militia and soon claimed friendship with several members of the governor's Council. Of his new friends, none would be more valuable than John Colleton of Fairlawn Barony, a neighboring planter and justice of the peace for Berkeley County.[26]

22. Chase, *Lowndes*, p. 12.
23. Charleston County Deeds, K, p. 272, S.C. Archives.
24. *South Carolina Gazette*, January 18, 1735.
25. Ibid.
26. Lowndes counted among his friends such prominent Carolinians as Arthur Middleton, Ralph Izard, Robert Blake, Jr., and Nathaniel Broughton. John Colleton was the cousin of Sir John Colleton, Baronet, one of the original Lords Proprietors. Chase, *Lowndes*, p. 42.

This beginning in a new colony would have been more promising if Lowndes had been more frugal. But old habits are not easily broken, and the extent of his operations and his style of living soon put a strain on his financial resources. By the middle of February 1731, he owed James Crokatt, a Charles Town merchant, more than two thousand pounds current money.[27] When Crokatt demanded payment Lowndes was embarrassed for lack of ready capital and went to Benjamin Godin and Benjamin De la Conseillere, Charles Town merchants who also engaged in moneylending. Here on February 18, he drew "four setts of Bills of Exchange" on Papillon Ball, London merchant, in the amount of 350 pounds sterling, payable "at thirty days Sight" to Godin.[28] At the "special Instance and Request" of Lowndes, Godin endorsed the bills over to Crokatt and became thereby liable for their payment if they happened to be protested by Ball. To protect himself from loss, therefore, Godin required of Lowndes, according to the custom of such merchants, a mortgage to the thousand acres of his land in Berkeley County and ten of his slaves.[29]

Lowndes probably expected the bills to be honored by Ball, with whom he appears to have earlier established an account, but the bills came back protested, provoking the first serious crisis in Lowndes' affairs. By the terms of the mortgage, it would be foreclosed unless Lowndes could otherwise arrange for the payment of his debt to Crokatt within a year. In these difficult circumstances he was able to prevail upon John Colleton to assume responsibility for payment of the debt to Crokatt. The price of another year's grace appears high, nonetheless, for Lowndes mortgaged to Colleton on February 1, 1732, his Goose Creek plantation together with its rice and corn crops then planted as well as twelve slaves, most of his plantation stock, and household goods.[30]

27. The value of current money, or currency of South Carolina, in relation to sterling, was in 1731 about seven to one. By 1736 the relative value of the former had declined slightly, 750 to 760 pounds currency being worth 100 pounds sterling. Wallace, *South Carolina, A Short History*, p. 136. The particulars of Lowndes' debt to Crokatt are found in Charleston County Deeds, K, pp. 127–35, S.C. Archives.
28. Ibid.
29. Ibid. The mortgage to Godin was dated March 7, 1731.
30. Miscellaneous Records, BB, pp. 44–45, S.C. Archives.

The mortgage to Colleton was not an unmixed blessing. While it secured his release from obligation to Godin and gave him more time, at least, to put his affairs in order, the attachment of his crops reduced his capacity for speculative enterprise which seems to have been the avenue of most rapid accumulation of wealth. Of greater importance, perhaps, is the fact that it also meant the control over his destiny was shifting in the direction of more impersonal forces. And an unsettling sense of increasing urgency pressed upon him when he considered that a foreclosure by Colleton could all but wipe him out.

With his business activities thus circumscribed and his time limited, Lowndes turned his attention to the rapid acquisition of land. As a recent immigrant he was qualified by Carolina law to receive a grant of 2200 acres based in part on the size of his household at the rate of fifty acres per head.[31] He secured a warrant for the land in Colleton County and arranged for its survey. He also engaged in the common practice of securing temporary title to slaves in order to qualify for additional acreage.[32] On April 15, 1732, for example, he paid Henry Gibbes three hundred pounds for a mortgage to five slaves, and six days later received from "James Kinlogh [sic], one of the members of his majestys council," six hundred pounds for a mortgage to seven other slaves.[33] The device was only one of a multitude of abuses of the land distribution system, for the careless administration of the land office saw warrants for grants with vague boundaries issued by the hundreds, soon resulting in a chaos of overlapping boundaries and confused titles. Such laxity gave Lowndes good reason to hope that he might stabilize his declining fortunes with a few choice warrants.

At this critical juncture, his fortunes received a stunning blow.

31. By Governor Johnson's instructions, which stated that "no man should own more than fifty acres of land for each member of his family" including slaves, and which he applied only to new grants ignoring the amount of land a man already owned, Lowndes qualified for 2,200 acres. If this constituted the sole basis of his qualification (see above, note 2), his household would have totaled forty-four members. The quotation is from Sirmans, *Colonial South Carolina*, pp. 174–75.

32. This practice became notorious over the next few years. South Carolina, Council Journal, June 28, 1734–December 17, 1737 (hereafter cited SCCJ), PRO Photostats, I, pp. 438–40, S.C. Archives.

33. Charleston County Wills, IV (1731–1733), 353–54, 456–57, S.C. Archives.

On November 24, 1732, Landgrave Edmund Bellinger entered a "Caveat" against Charles Lowndes and Daniel Green concerning a tract of 3500 acres, which they were having surveyed and to part of which Bellinger claimed title.[34] This legal action could not deprive Lowndes of his qualification, but it blocked for an indefinite time his anxious efforts to secure title to the tract of 2200 acres. It appears obvious that he had been counting heavily upon securing the grant before the mortgage fell due, but a new survey was ordered, and until the dispute could be resolved, he would have to find other means of meeting the demands of his creditors.

Charles Lowndes' situation had now become so serious that he decided on a voyage to St. Kitts to secure assistance from friends and relatives there.[35] His departure was delayed through December, affording him an opportunity to witness the excitement generated by the arrival of James Oglethorpe and the Georgia settlers. Then on January 18, 1733, he sold at public auction "a choice parcel of Negroes, 4 Rhode Island Padds, and a chaise and Horse,"[36] and sailed shortly afterwards. During his absence John Colleton protected his interests by renewing the mortgage and putting off Crokatt, with satisfactory guarantees of payment, for another year.[37] By the end of April, Lowndes had returned, but the records fail to indicate that his trip resulted in any substantial improvement of his circumstances.

His mission to St. Kitts represented Lowndes' best if not his only real hope for recovery, and its failure left him in circumstances even more critical. His subsequent efforts to counteract

34. SCCJ, November 24, 1732, V, Part 1, 231. Bellinger was one of the most powerful men in the colony, Sirmans, *Colonial South Carolina*, p. 80. Because of confusion concerning overlapping claims, James St. John, the surveyor general, had been directed by the governor and Council on January 26, 1733, to "sett down the buttings and boundings of each platt," but the order came too late to help Lowndes. SCCJ, January 26, 1732, V, Part 2, 266.

35. The purpose of Lowndes' voyage is stated in an indenture dated February 1, 1733, made by Lowndes to John Colleton, and though the document is in poor condition the essential facts are clear: "And whereas the said Charles Lowndes is now . . . of this province . . . voyage to the Islands . . . Christophers . . . Antigua . . . of them by means . . . he will be rendered . . . of performing the conditions of the Obligation . . . ." Charleston County Deeds, P, p. 203, S.C. Archives.

36. *South Carolina Gazette*, Jan. 13, 1732 [1733].

37. Charleston County Deeds, P, pp. 201–206, S.C. Archives.

the relentless decline of his fortunes became more visionary, reflecting his increasing desperation. The booming rice industry offered a glimmer of hope by accentuating the need for a practical machine to prepare the product for the market. Grasping at this straw, Lowndes constructed an instrument designed for this purpose and in April 1733 petitioned the legislature, "praying that no act do pass to erect the Engine or Instrument Invented by the Petitioner for the better and more speedy way of Beating and pounding of Rice, and that all Persons who shall apply for the said Engine shall pay to the said Lowndes Sixty Pounds. . . ."[38]

Actually the idea was a popular one, and two other persons, Peter Villepontoux and Francis Garcia, were also petitioning the legislature for exclusive patents on their machines. With becoming impartiality the legislature passed resolutions encouraging all three to construct their new machines and to appropriate the benefit thereof to themselves.[39] Only one of the machines was of sufficient practicality to raise the hopes of its inventor,[40] but that of Charles Lowndes failed to check his waning fortunes. Even his petition to the Council in December 1733, praying that Landgrave Bellinger "be obliged to withdraw his Caveat," resulted only in another survey of the land in dispute.[41]

Considering the state of his affairs, it seems remarkable that Lowndes was able to stave off impending ruin for yet another year. This was due in no small part to his faithful friend John Colleton who agreed once more to renew the mortgage. He gained additional time in April 1734 when Papillon Ball moved to salvage what he could of the debt Lowndes owed him, accepting a bond for the debt, plus interest, payable in 1737.[42] In May we find Lowndes

38. SCCJ, April 26, 1733, V, Part 1, 434.
39. SCCJ, Dec. 15, 1732, V, Part 1, 246-47; ibid., Feb. 1, April 28, May 12, June 7-9, 1733, V, Part 1, 361, 440-41, 448, 467, 469.
40. Peter Villepontoux announced in May 1734 that his machine was in operation on his James Island plantation. In September he pronounced his invention a complete success, claiming that it would clean 1,000 pounds of rice per hour, and offering to furnish testimonies of six local planters to convince the skeptical. See the South Carolina Gazette, May 18, September 14, 1734.
41. SCCJ, Dec. 14, 1733, V, Part 2, 667. A few months later Bellinger received a grant of 2,000 acres in Colleton County, SCCJ, May 21, 1734, V, Part 2, 707.
42. Miscellaneous Records, AB, pp. 128-31, S.C. Archives. The debt to Ball on April 15, 1734, amounted to 665 pounds, 14 shillings 3 pence sterling, to be

acting as attorney for a group attempting to secure a land grant. After the Council postponed action on this petition, the records for the remainder of 1734 contain no reference to his affairs.[43] The months slipped by, and with the arrival of the new year, his time had run out.

Early in February 1735 the mortgage to Colleton again fell due, and this time there would be no renewal. Apparently with his friend's cooperation, he made a final offer of his Goose Greek plantation for public sale in January, "either with or without stock, provisions and plantation utensiles" for "one third of the payment down, the other 2 thirds in January next if required." He added a revealing postscript to his notice: "Necessity, not choice makes him settle, therefore [he] hopes the generous Purchaser will not take the Advantage."[44] When no generous purchaser came forward, the mortgage was foreclosed. Shortly afterwards a lease transferring the plantation from Colleton to Robert Hume identified it as the place "whereon Mr. Charles Lowndes lately dwelt."[45]

Lowndes was never able to recover from this staggering loss.[46] Still, he was not without some capital, and with his land claims pending he refused to give up hope until late 1735. Then on November 5, in a mood of deep despair, he loaded and cocked both his pistols, placed them ready at his side, and addressed a note to Arthur Middleton, Nathaniel Broughton, Ralph Izard, and Joseph Blake, Jr. Giving a full account of the misfortunes he had endured

---

discharged on April 15, 1737, by paying the debt "with lawfull Interest," or be sued for the penal sum of 1,300 pounds sterling.

43. SCCJ, May 18, 1734, V, Part 2, 705 *ff.*

44. *South Carolina Gazette,* Jan. 18, 1735.

45. Charleston County Deeds, P, pp. 115–16, S.C. Archives.

46. By the original provisions of the mortgage Lowndes lost at its foreclosure in addition to the thousand acres of land, twelve slaves, four horses, ten oxen, thirty head of cattle, "two large looking Glasses and Sconces four feather beads and furniture One Dozen of Large Silver Spoons, one Dozen of Silver Tea Spoons, One Horse Cart Six Pairs of Sheets One Dozen of Table Cloths one Silver Hilted Sword one Silver Watch One Dozen of Pewter Dishes four Dozen of Pewter Plates together with all the Produce or Crop of Rice & Corn now planted and that shall Grow & be Produced of from the land . . . unto the said John Colleton . . . for Ever more . . . ." Miscellaneous Records, BB, pp. 44–45, S.C. Archives.

"by law-suits and otherwise" since his arrival in the colony, he attempted to justify "the Crime of Self Murder" which he then premeditated, and recommended to them the care of his children after his death. He was at the point of concluding the note when John Colleton rode up to his house unexpectedly, distracting the brooding Lowndes, thereby preventing him from taking his own life.[47]

Hope may spring eternal in the human breast, but whatever remained in that of Charles Lowndes was shaken a few weeks later. The Council took up another of his petitions for a land warrant on November 29, and their disposal of its reads now like a pronouncement of doom: "And the said Petition was Rejected."[48] During the next three months unusually bad weather and steadily rising prices did nothing to improve his outlook.[49] Then on February 14, 1736, he announced his intention to dispose of his remaining property including four slaves, "One new English Cart . . . and several horse goods," with a request that his creditors send in their accounts, "that they may be paid, his time being very short."[50] Not all his creditors were satisfied with his efforts, and the suits against him continued. With his desperation becoming each day more acute he wrote again to John Colleton on March 7, 1736, exclaiming against several persons who he claimed were, by their "unjust Proceedings" against him, the cause of all his difficulties and his "Violent Design of laying Hands on Himself." Now he was "fully determined to clear himself or die, by cutting an Arterie or shooting himself through the Head," and "very much

---

47. *South Carolina Gazette*, May 29, 1736. In this note Lowndes mentions the number of children as four, although Chase's genealogical study of the family lists only the three sons. An item in the *South Carolina Gazette*, Feb. 13, 1775, states that "On Wednesday last died Mrs. Penelope Brown, Sister to the Hon. Rawlins Lowndes, Speaker of the present Hon. Commons House of Assembly of this Province who lately arrived here on a visit to her Brother," indicating that a daughter was born to Charles and Ruth Lowndes after their arrival in Carolina.

Concerning "Law-suits" against Lowndes, a search through the Judgement Rolls in the S.C. Archives revealed no record of any case to which Charles Lowndes was a party. No other common pleas records for this period (1730–1736) have survived.

48. SCCJ, November 29, 1735, PRO Photostats, I, CO5/437, p. 23.

49. *South Carolina Gazette*, March 13, 1736.

50. Ibid., February 14, 1736.

tempted to kill all his children, in order to be buried all in one Grave."[51]

Six days later on March 13 a letter appeared in the *Gazette* over the signature of "Philander" discoursing as if from personal experience on the miseries of bankruptcy. Its authorship now seems impossible to determine with certainty, but if it was not actually written by Charles Lowndes, its timing and subject matter were amazingly coincidental with his situation. Philander railed at the merchant for cruel and heartless treatment of the debtor, "how inexorable he was to all the entreaties and Tears of his miserable Neighbor and his distressed Family, who begg'd his Compassion with the lowest Submission, who employ'd Friends to sollicit and entreat for them, laying forth their misery in the most lively Expressions, and using all the Arguments, which the most moving Distress could dictate, but in vain." Then turning to the effects of bankruptcy, Philander described almost the very circumstances of Charles Lowndes:

> Nothing indeed can be more unhappy than the condition of Bankruptcy. The Calamity which happens to us by ill Fortune, or by injury of others, has in it some Consolation; but what arises from our Misbehavior or Error, is the State of the most exquisite Sorrow. When a Man considers not only an ample fortune, but even the very Necessaries of Life, his Pretense to food itself at the mercy of his Creditors, he cannot but look on himself in the State of the Dead, with his Case thus much worse, that the last Office is perform'd by his Adversaries, instead of his Friends. . . .

The essay provoked a response in defense of the merchant class, and the exchange continued to April 17 when it was abruptly terminated two days after Charles Lowndes went to prison.[52]

The increasingly brooding cast of her husband's mind caused Ruth Lowndes to become extremely alarmed for the safety of her children and herself. Besides the three boys, she now had a daughter, born since their arrival in Carolina. Finally she took the children and left him, and on March 26, 1736, petitioned the governor praying for separate maintenance from her husband and asking that he be required to give security for his good be-

51. Ibid., May 29, 1736.
52. Ibid., March 13, March 27, April 3, April 10, April 17, 1736.

havior towards her. The necessary writ was promptly issued. Three weeks later on April 15, the case was brought before the governor and Council, sitting as the Court of Chancery. Both parties appeared before the court, the petition of Ruth Lowndes was read, and Charles Lowndes made an unreported statement in response. The court then ordered Lowndes to make satisfactory provision for his wife's separate maintenance and to furnish her with a variety of articles sufficient for setting up a separate household, in addition to "Fifty Pounds in Current money, A Negro Woman and Two Children."[53] Lowndes refused. Thereupon the court ordered him committed to the custody of the provost marshal until he should give sufficient security that he would obey and fulfill the court order.[54] But Lowndes refused even to post bond and thus became the prisoner of Provost Marshal Robert Hall.

It is quite possible, indeed it is more than likely, that the imprisonment of Charles Lowndes during the next few weeks was accomplished through a gentleman's agreement between himself and Provost Marshal Hall, for such arrangements were not at all uncommon. Lowndes was certainly accorded various special privileges, and even kept his pistols with him in his modified confinement. But if the provost marshal considered his gentleman prisoner entirely harmless, he was tragically mistaken. About nine-thirty on Saturday morning, May 22, 1736, Charles Lowndes arranged on a nearby table certain of his papers including a letter inviting his friend John Colleton to come to his funeral, "and after having shav'd and dress'd himself, he laid down on the Ground, with a loaden Pistol in each Hand, he put one close to his Temple and blew out his Brains, which were found at a little distance all in one heap, his Scull being split in two."[55]

The violent death of Charles Lowndes by his own hand and the disintegration of his family which followed marks the nadir of the Lowndes family of South Carolina. Whatever fortune he left to his wife and children, it was surely not great. His most valuable legacy to them was the friendship of leading citizens in

53. Anne King Gregorie, ed., *Records of the Court of Chancery of South Carolina, 1671–1779* (Washington, D.C., 1950), pp. 381–82.
54. Ibid.; *South Carolina Gazette*, May 29, 1736.
55. Ibid., May 29, 1736.

the colony and important Lowndes family connections, however distant, in England. Because of these friends and relatives, his family not only was spared further humiliation, but provisions were made for their care and for the education of his sons in preparation for respectable careers.

Ruth Lowndes decided to return home with her daughter to St. Kitts after the death of her husband, and Wiiliam, her eldest son, accompanied his mother and sister back to the beautiful island of his birth. For reasons which the surviving records do not reveal, the two younger sons, Charles and Rawlins, were left behind in South Carolina as wards of Provost Marshal Hall.[56] If anyone suspected that the youngest son, fourteen-year-old Rawlins, was to play the most significant role in rebuilding the family fortune and restoring honor to the name of Lowndes in South Carolina, few indeed could have anticipated the ultimate measure of his success or the singularly ironic importance of the office of provost marshal in achieving it.

56. Chase, *Lowndes*, pp. 12–13.

CHAPTER II

The Marshalship

DURING THE FIRST HALF of the eighteenth century the name of Lowndes came to be synonymous with the office of provost marshal in South Carolina. The chief law enforcement agency in the colony, the office corresponded to that of high sheriff in England and found its counterpart in some colonies of the British West Indies. But in title as in the nature and extent of its powers, it was an institution unique among the mainland colonies. Moreover, it remains the key to a clear understanding of South Carolina regulator sentiment in the 1760s.

The forces at work shaping this office grew out of South Carolina's unique circumstances. Exerting their pressures over the first forty years of the century, these forces occupied the interests and employed the talents of several men. Three of these men, each in his time, bore a particular relationship to Rawlins Lowndes: the patentee, Thomas Lowndes, his distant kinsman; the deputy, Robert Hall, his guardian; and the assignee, George Morley, in whose service Rawlins found his first great opportunity. Because of its importance to the sectional history of South Carolina no less than to the rise of Rawlins Lowndes, the office merits examination.

Originally in the gift of the Crown, the office of provost marshal was customarily granted to favored individuals by letters patent under the Great Seal. The usual procedure saw a royal sign manual sent to the attorney general and the solicitor general ordering that letters patent be drawn containing a grant of the office. After the document had been prepared and submitted for the royal signature, it passed under the Great Seal and went into effect under terms stated in the patent itself.[1] The patentee invariably looked upon his office rather as a property acquired for its income than as a position of employment. Like other properties, it might be rented, leased, sold, or otherwise disposed of, depending upon the advantage such disposition offered its owner, the patentee. Before a colony could replace the marshal with the more efficient system of county sheriffs, the colony would have to buy the office from the patentee. In any case the actual execution of the office was left to a deputy, who assumed its duties in return for a stipulated share of its income.[2]

Except for an allowance for mileage traveled in the performance of duty, fees provided the sole basis of income for the marshal's office during the proprietary period. Among the extant statutes dealing with fees of this office, the earliest is an act of 1695 which indicates the provost marshal then functioned primarily if not exclusively under the authority of the Court of Vice-Admiralty.[3] The Court of Common Pleas was served by another officer, the "Under Sheriff," who also kept the provincial prison, until 1714 when the two offices were combined under the provost marshal.[4]

Under certain terms of their charter the Lords Proprietors of Carolina functioned in the stead of the Crown, issuing grants for offices as well as lands. The marshal's office was among those disposed of in this manner until 1714 when the proprietors vested in Chief Justice Nicholas Trott "the sole Nomination and Appointment of a Provost Marshal" to serve the region south of the Cape

1. *See* Charles M. Andrews and Francis G. Davenport, *Guide to the Manuscript Materials for the History of the United States to 1783, In the British Museum, in Minor London Archives, and in the Libraries of Oxford and Cambridge* (Washington, D.C., 1908), pp. 234–35.
2. Virginia, South Carolina, and the West Indies were the areas of English colonization most subject to deputations, ibid. Continental colonies that utilized the provost marshal system temporarily were Connecticut, North Carolina (to 1738), New Jersey, and Quebec. See Charles Garth to the Earl of Shelburne, July 11, 1767, SCPRO, XXXI, 397–400.
3. *The Statutes at Large of South Carolina*, eds. Thomas Cooper and David J. McCord, 10 vols. (Columbia, S.C., 1836–1841), II, 89.
4. Ibid., pp. 88–89. By proclamation of the Lords Proprietors dated September 8, 1714, the marshal was thenceforth to "Execute all process issuing out of our Said Courts," and to have charge, care and keeping of the provincial gaol and prisoners. SCPRO, VI, 67–68.

Fear River.[5] Since Trott was sole judge of the courts of common pleas, king's bench, and vice-admiralty, and since the marshal's primary duty was to carry out the orders of the courts, the logic of this grant was obvious enough. But the chief justice already occupied numerous salaried offices besides his monopoly of the provincial judiciary, all of which he administered in such a thoroughly partisan manner that he rendered himself an object of popular hatred and helped to bring about the overthrow of proprietary rule in 1719.[6]

The revolution of 1719 resulted in the transfer of governmental power from the proprietors to the Crown, although the lords retained for another decade their property rights in lands and offices. At the same time the chief justice lost much of his power, including control of the marshal's place, to the new royal governor, Francis Nicholson.[7] Nicholson departed the province in 1725 leaving affairs in the cheerfully corrupt hands of Arthur Middleton, president of the Council, whose sale of public offices provoked a controversy within six months. When censured for his conduct by the Commons House of Assembly, Middleton denied any wrongdoing, asserting that the offices of provost marshal, clerk of the crown, and vendue master "have bin alwayes loot upon as perquisets of the Govern[men]t and something has bin always given for them. . . ."[8] The traffic in offices contributed to a general deterioration of orderly government in the colony. Then in 1727 the judicial process broke down completely for want of a jury law; and for the next three years—lean ones indeed for the provost marshal—no courts of justice could be held.[9]

In the meantime, wheels had begun to turn in the mother country that would effect great changes in the colony. One of the prime movers in these developments was Thomas Lowndes of

5. Ibid.
6. W. Roy Smith, *South Carolina as a Royal Province, 1719–1776* (New York, 1903), pp. 12–13.
7. Joseph Boone and John Barnwell to Lords of Trade, received August 23, 1720, SCPRO, VIII, 77.
8. Arthur Middleton to Governor Nicholson, February 4, 1726, ibid., XII, 7–10.
9. Governor Robert Johnson to the Lords of Trade, November 14, 1731, ibid., XV, 33–40.

St. Margaret's, Westminster, a wealthy, enterprising, and somewhat arrogant member of Parliament whose fortune dated from the discovery that the family estate in the county of Cheshire rested on a solid and seemingly bottomless foundation of salt.[10] Thomas Lowndes had developed an interest in Carolina at least as early as the 1680s, probably because of the opportunities it offered for speculation in land. Sometime after 1686—the precise date is not a matter of record—he bought from the heirs of Thomas Price four baronies of land in the colony, 48,000 acres, along with the accompanying title of Landgrave.[11] This initial interest led him over the years, particularly after the revolution of 1719, to become more directly involved in the affairs of South Carolina where his lands were situated. By the middle of the 1720s, when a movement to have the Crown purchase the Lords Proprietors' remaining property rights in the Carolinas began to gather momentum, Thomas Lowndes was working very closely with the proprietors and representing their interests in Parliament. According to his account of it, Lowndes assumed an important role in bringing this movement to fruition in the agreement concluded in March 1728, wherein the claims of all but one proprietor were conveyed to the Crown. He said he was "Chiefly Instrumental" in the transaction, "privy to every Step that was taken," and personally drew up all but one of the documents used by the proprietors in the negotiations.[12]

Lowndes doubtless exaggerated his importance to these transactions, for he was never the sort to keep silence while his honest labors went unnoticed or unrewarded. Nevertheless, it is abundantly clear that he did perform valuable services for the proprietors. It was in recognition of his services in their behalf that he

10. An excellent brief summary of Thomas Lowndes' career is found in James Adam Cramb, "Thomas Lowndes," *Dictionary of National Biography,* XII, 208–10; *see also* Chase, *Lowndes,* p. 11, note, for information on the extensive salt deposits underlying the Lowndes estate in Cheshire.
11. A memorandum dated July 1, 1726, records Thomas Lowndes' surrender of the four baronies to the Lords Proprietors, receiving in exchange five baronies the next day, for which he was required to pay a quitrent of one penny sterling annually "at the Royal Exchange of London on the Feast of St. Michael the Archangel forever . . ." SCPRO, XII, pp. 73–76.
12. Thomas Lowndes to Lords of Trade, February 22, 1734, ibid., XVI, 287–89.

received from them a payment of £100 sterling, an additional barony of land, and a patent conferring upon him the offices of provost marshal, clerk of the peace, and clerk of the crown.[13]

The patent for the offices was dated September 27, 1725, and the most interesting clause in it related to its duration. It was to continue in force during "the several and respective lives of the said Lowndes and Hugh Watson of the Middle Temple, Gent[leman] to execute the same by the said Thomas Lowndes, his heirs and assigns, or by their sufficient Deputy or Deputies."[14] This meant, of course, that the patent should obtain so long as either Lowndes or Watson lived, although Watson had no other connection with the offices. It proved to be a significant clause, as events turned out, for Thomas Lowndes died in 1748 but the patent remained in effect until Watson's death in 1759. The patent further stipulated that during these years, Thomas Lowndes, his heirs and assigns were to "receive take and enjoy all Salaries, Wages, Fees, Allowances, Benefits, Immunities, Privileges, Advantages and Emoluments" incidental to the offices.

Lowndes appears to have taken the view of the typical patentee and looked upon his offices as a species of property to be valued for its income and disposed of at a profit. The marshal's place held more potential value than the clerk's, but there is nothing in the records to suggest that Lowndes ever intended to assume the duties of either office. In fact he paid little attention to them until 1729 when passage of an act confirming patentees in the possession of their offices quickened his interest.[15] He surrendered his proprietary patent, as required by law, and set about the business of learning what his property was actually worth, concentrating his attention on the more valuable marshalship.[16] By November 30, 1730, when he received the royal patent bearing the impress of the Great Seal and the signature of Holles New-

13. Ibid., pp. 287–97 and enclosure, p. 298; ibid., XV, 298–303.
14. The patent is reproduced in Chase, *Lowndes*, p. 13, note.
15. Cooper and McCord, *Statutes*, I, 60–71.
16. John Drummond to Lords of Trade, April 14, 1733, states that Thomas Lowndes sold the offices of clerk of the crown and clerk of the peace to Drummond for James Wedderburn who afterwards executed these offices in the colony. The price was not stated. SCPRO, XVI, 85.

castle, he had learned much about the marshalship. He had also discovered that the office could be less a valuable than a troublesome property.

Available for Lowndes' examination in 1729 were provincial statutes and related documents which revealed the most salient features of the marshal's office at that time. Its powers, responsibilities and fees were essentially the same as those of sheriff, under sheriff, and gaol-keeper in South Britain.[17] Although the position carried no salary, the schedule of fees established in 1695 had doubled in 1714 when the office absorbed that of under sheriff. After 1714 the marshal was responsible for the execution of all processes issuing out of the provincial courts. In addition to other duties usually associated with the office, such as summoning juries, attending the quarterly sessions of the Court of Common Pleas and the semi-annual sittings of the Court of General Sessions, the marshal was required to provide the colony a gaol or prison. This unique responsibility, which the provincial government had no desire to assume, was complemented by another. The authority of the provost marshal, unlike that of the usual colonial sheriff whose powers were confined within the limits of his county, extended throughout the colony.

The advantages inherent in such wide-ranging authority as the marshal enjoyed, at least in terms of income, were obviously great and would continue to grow as the colony expanded. Its equally obvious disadvantages were increased but not seriously by the passage of a law in 1721 establishing five county and precinct courts. The administration of government in the colony still remained highly centralized with the great bulk of judicial processes issuing out of the courts of Charles Town.[18] Another provision of

17. A provincial statute of 1721 defined the responsibilities of the office as follows: "And the provost marshal shall be answerable for all escapes of prisoners out of the said prison, or out of the hands of his deputies, or other malfeazances and neglect of his said deputies, and shall be subject to such action or actions, penalties and fines, as any sheriff or sub-sheriff in South Britain are subject unto . . . ." Cooper and McCord, *Statutes*, VII, 175.

18. The county courts, two in Berkeley and one each in Craven, Colleton and Granville counties, each presided over by five justices of the peace with three required to constitute a quorum and their quarterly sessions limited to three days, could hear no plea of any criminal matter extending to life or limb

this law allowed the first process issued by the courts to be either a summons or a capias.

A writ of capias was the same as a summons except that a capias had to be served on the body of the defendant personally by the marshal or his deputy, while a summons carried the same force if merely left at the defendant's "most notorious" place of residence.[19] The marshal quite naturally came to prefer the summons, and he was usually indulged in his preference by the courts. This pleased the creditor merchants of Charles Town who had advocated the summons initially as it made easier the securing of judgment against defaulting debtors.[20] Over the years, however, abuses crept into the system until 1726 when popular agitation against the summons, stimulated by economic decline, forced the passage of an act which outlawed the summons and restored the capias.[21] The "capias act" as it came to be called, delighted the debtor interests for it made the marshal's work so much more difficult that afterwards "not One Writt in five [was] executed."[22] In addition the capias act required the marshal to post bond for the due performance of his office. To make matters even worse, the provincial government stopped paying an allowance for the maintenance of prisoners.[23] Such were the circumstances of the marshal's office when Thomas Lowndes surveyed it in 1729.

Lowndes possessed influence with the Board of Trade and proceeded directly to press for repeal of the capias act. On April 17, 1730, he laid a petition before the board urging repeal on the ground that the act damaged commerce since planters could not be made to pay their debts unless served personally by the marshal or his deputy. He called attention to the lack of a subsistence allowance for prisoners and argued the unreasonableness of requiring the provost marshal to provide it. One week later Thomas

---

nor any civil cause "if the matter in difference do exceed the value of one hundred pounds sterling." Such cases and all appeals from the county courts were to be heard in Charles Town. Ibid., VII, 166–67.

19. Ibid., p. 169.
20. See ibid., II, 611–13.
21. Lords of Trade to Governor Robert Johnson, April 2, 1731, SCPRO, XV, 24–26.
22. William Bull to Thomas Lowndes, December 24, 1729, ibid., XIV, 111.
23. Ibid.

Lowndes was granted an audience before the board to deliver his arguments in person. On this occasion he was supported by Francis Fane, the board's legal counsel, who agreed that the act made the execution of civil law in the colony too difficult. Fane promised to consult Governor Johnson "personally on this subject" before South Carolina's new chief executive left London.[24] Whatever the result of their consultation, it was not made public and produced no immediate effect on the Lords of Trade. Lowndes would have to wait.

Governor Johnson arrived in Carolina later that year and immersed himself in the enormous task of bringing some order out of the chaotic conditions in the province. He succeeded remarkably during his first year, while in London Thomas Lowndes noted with increasing annoyance that Johnson was taking no action to secure repeal of the capias act. Finally on March 24, 1731, Lowndes again approached the Lords of Trade, this time backed by a powerful interest group. He petitioned for the act's repeal, "and the Merchants of London trading to that Province did likewise. . . ."[25] Eight days later the Lords directed Governor Johnson to recommend two changes in the law: to restore the summons and to require the deputy marshal resident in the colony rather than the patentee to post the performance bond.

The governor was obliged to follow the board's instructions, but he had now been in the colony long enough to be influenced by popular opinion; and popular opinion strongly supported the capias act. Writing to the board in August 1731, Johnson expressed doubt that the Assembly could be persuaded to restore the summons because of past abuses,

> many people having had judgement obtained against them without knowing they had ever been summoned, and consequently in no capacity of making their defence, for opportunities were taken when the people were abroad (perhaps at the Cherakee Mountains) to thrust a summons under a persons door, and the Marshal swearing he left the summons at the partys dwelling house was sufficient to

24. Thomas Lowndes to Lords of Trade, April 17, 1730, ibid., pp. 86–87; Journal of the Board of Trade, entries dated April 21, 24, 1730, ibid., pp. 7–8.
25. Lords of Trade to the Crown, March 7, 1732, P.R.O. Photocopy, CO5/381, p. 181, S.C. Archives.

proceed against the Defend[an]t Ex Parte so judgement went against him. . . .[26]

Johnson failed to mention the security clause, but did report the recent passage of a law regulating juries which gave the plaintiff in civil cases the right to decide where his case was to be tried. This so-called jury law spelled the doom of the precinct courts as it brought virtually all the legal business back to Charles Town, pleasing the merchants and greatly simplifying the work of the resident provost marshal. Three months later the governor reported the passage of a tax bill, the first in four years, which restored the subsistence allowance for prisoners, "a very beneficial article to the Marshall's place."[27]

Thomas Lowndes was doubtless pleased by these laws, but he was still not satisfied, for the Assembly had refused to restore the summons. He had additional reason to be annoyed. Every effort he had made over the past two years to establish a satisfactory arrangement with George Bampfield, then the resident provost marshal, had failed. In fact, Bampfield had not even acknowledged the patentee's authority or his property rights in the office. The upshot was that for two years Lowndes had been laboring to improve his property and had not yet received a farthing for his pains. In these circumstances the governor's sympathetic report of provincial opinion on the capias act proved sufficient to goad Lowndes into recriminations against Johnson. Lowndes memorialized the board accusing the governor of violating his instructions in order to control the marshal's place for his own profit.[28]

When Johnson received a copy of Lowndes' memorial from Peregrine Fury, the colonial agent, he had just buried one son and three servants, victims of an epidemic of violent malignant fever. In no mood to tolerate the accusations of a self-seeking patentee, he wrote a long letter to the board denying the charges, explaining the circumstances of the marshal's office, and giving

26. Governor Johnson to Allured Popple, Secretary to the Board of Trade, August 13, 1731, SCPRO, XV, 29–31.
27. Governor Johnson to Lords of Trade, November 14, 1731, ibid., pp. 33–40.
28. Governor Johnson to Lords of Trade, September 28, 1732, ibid., pp. 229–34.

his personal opinion of the patentee in language cauculated to raise blisters:

> I found Mr. Brampfield Marshall I continued him till at his own request as is notorious to all the Province. I appointed a person of his recommending, he telling me he desired to be dismist because his affairs required him going to England and about six months after he told me he had altered his mind, and he desired to be restored which I granted him. . . . I defy Lowndes to prove that I had any profit by this but did it only to serve a man I thought was worthy of the place and one Mr. Popple [secretary to the Lords of Trade] had a friendship for. Mr. Lowndes has sent no Exemplification of his patent nor appointed any Deputy in the meantime the office must be supplied, so how have I wronged him above £200 as he has told my friends. I can't find out nor he neither.

Johnson then turned his wrath on the patentee, charging that Lowndes had "cunningly made this Province his property by the late Lords Proprs neglect to the amount of £4000 or £5000 sterling nobody knows for what other merit than a consumate assurance pretending he knows everything, betraying everybody and altering his opinion as often as he finds it for his interest." Finally, according to Johnson, Lowndes was only interested in the matter because he was afraid "he won't have so good an opportunity of getting £1500 Sterling which is his price for the [patent] not intrinsically worth £700."[29]

At this juncture a solution to the problem was suggested to Lowndes by provincial Chief Justice Robert Wright. As neither the summons law of 1721 nor the capias law of 1726 has yet received royal approval, Wright pointed out that the capias law could be negated and the summons law restored by simply disallowing the one and approving the other.[30] Lowndes presented Wright's suggestion to the Lords of Trade who adopted it and passed their recommendation of disallowance on to the Crown. The controversy over the capias act finally ended with its disallowance by proclamation on July 21, 1732.[31]

The governor thus lost the contest to the patentee, but Johnson

29. Ibid.
30. Chief Justice Robert Wright to Thomas Lowndes, August 6, 1731, ibid., pp. 31–32.
31. Royal Proclamation dated July 21, 1732, ibid., pp. 139–40.

had an opportunity to take satisfaction two years later when he signed into law an act requiring the marshal to post security of £1000 pounds sterling for the due performance of his office.[32] By that time, however, Thomas Lowndes was no longer responsible for the office. He had repeatedly spoken to Allured Popple about the secretary's part in keeping George Bampfield in Lowndes' office without paying him anything for it. But he had been put off with one evasion after another until he lost his temper, denounced Popple, and subsequently lost all influence with the Lords of Trade.[33] The quarrel had little effect on the value of the marshalship, for Lowndes, his property substantially improved, assigned it to George Morley, a London merchant trading to Carolina, on February 11, 1732, for £1000 sterling.[34] As the assignment was the same as a transfer of title, Morley assumed all responsibility for the office.

In the meantime George Bampfield had begun to reap the much improved benefits of the office. In 1731 on four accounts submitted to the Assembly for the maintenance of prisoners he received payment of almost fourteen hundred pounds, current money, the equivalent of £200 sterling.[35] Prospects for 1732 appeared equally promising until suddenly the hazards of office descended upon him. While attempting to serve a writ early in March, he was assaulted and beaten "in so barbarous a manner, that his life is

32. Cooper and McCord, Statutes, VII, 184–88. Actually the performance bond was to be posted only when a gaol was built at public expense, which was not done until 1772.

33. For documents relating to Lowndes' quarrel with Popple, see SCPRO, XVI, 228–29, 239–41, 300.

34. The assignment is dated February 11, 1731, by the Julian Calendar, according to which the new year began on March 25. According to the Gregorian Calendar, which went into effect by act of parliament on January 1, 1752, the date of the assignment would have been 1732. See the South Carolina Gazette, Jan 1, 1752, for details on the calendar change. For the assignment, see SCPRO, XV, 309–13; ibid., XVII, 448–49. Morley was listed among London merchants trading to Carolina in ibid., XVIII, 194. For the price Morley paid, see January 30, 1748, The Journal of the Commons House of Assembly, 1736–1750, ed. J. H. Easterby, 9 vols. (Columbia, 1951–1962), vol. 1748, pp. 46–47. (The published volumes of this journal are hereafter cited Easterby, ed., Commons Journal, with appropriate dates which designate each volume.)

35. Cooper and McCord, Statutes, III, 337–39.

despair'd of."[36] The badly battered Mr. Bampfield did recover sufficiently to return to work, but he did not long survive the incident. In the oppressive heat of July he set out on a similar errand into the wilds of Craven County only to drown when his canoe overset in a nameless creek near Cape Romain. But there were those who took careful note of his passing. Thomas Whitmarsh recorded it in his recently established *South Carolina Gazette,* with an announcement that a Mr. Neal had replaced Bampfield as provost marshal.[37] Elizabeth Bampfield made application to the General Assembly for the £727 15s. due her late husband.[38] And in London, assignee George Morley resolved on a voyage to Carolina to put his office in order.

When Morley arrived in Charles Town early in 1733,[39] his office, despite recent improvements, lacked two highly desirable features: a salary and a prison built and maintained at public expense. He hoped to persuade provincial officials to remedy at least one of the defects, but his hopes were disappointed. The Commons House quietly ignored his petition for the building of a prison with public funds, forcing him to hire a house and have it fitted out as a prison at his own expense.[40] His only success, and the most important result of his visit here, was the private arrangement he made to insure the smooth functioning of his office and to facilitate the transfer of authority from one deputy to the next. He secured the services of attorney Charles Pinckney to act as his agent in the colony and to cooperate with the governor in appointing new deputies when necessary.[41] With Governor Johnson's approval, and probably at the suggestion of Pinckney, he appointed as his first deputy Robert Hall, a Charles Town attorney whose promise at the provincial bar was hereupon permanently diverted into law enforcement.

36. *South Carolina Gazette,* March 18, 1732.
37. Ibid., August 5, 1732.
38. Cooper and McCord., Statutes, III, 361–62.
39. *South Carolina Gazette,* February 3, 1732[3].
40. Journal of the Board of Trade, entry dated November 6, 1735, SCPRO, XVII, 275. Morley informed the Board that "the charge of the prison is about £50 per annum."
41. *South Carolina Gazette,* October 11, 1735.

Evidence for a later period shows that Morley received for his office a fixed annual rent paid by the deputy, an arrangement probably initiated in 1733 with his appointment of Robert Hall.[42] In return for the annual rent, the deputy was allowed to keep all fees and other income incidental to the office with the single exception of the marshal's salary, a royal grant of £40 sterling which Morley received annually after 1739 to compensate the marshal for having to furnish the colony with a prison.[43] Morley pocketed the salary, leaving his deputy to provide a prison out of his own pocket.

Robert Hall proved an excellent choice as resident provost marshal. A man with good judgment, strength of character, and personal dignity, Hall served the colony and the patent-holder faithfully for eight years, from 1733 to 1741. Perhaps the most important contribution Hall made to the marshalship was that through his conscientious public service and sheer force of character the office began to take on a new dignity and a vastly improved image. During his tenure three incidents occurred which reveal the hazards of this office and something of Robert Hall himself. He had no sooner taken office than he was thrust into the center of a quarrel between the Commons House and the king's officer, Surveyor General James St. John.[44]

St. John had earlier clashed with the provincial government over charges of gross malfeasance in office and exorbitant fees. Formally confronted with the evidence, the surveyor general exploded, insulting both governor and Council, provoking Johnson to seek his dismissal. St. John retaliated by organizing a powerful campaign to overturn the quit rent act of 1731, a key feature of Johnson's township program. He very nearly succeeded, and in anticipation of victory the surveyor general, his deputy Benjamin Whitaker, and Dr. Thomas Cooper began illegal surveys in Craven County, whereupon the Commons House ordered their arrest. St.

42. See John Guerard to George Morley, June 8, 1754, The John Guerard Letterbook, South Carolina Historical Society, Charleston, S.C., (the repository cited hereafter SCHS).

43. Morley's salary was paid out of the quitrents. See "An Account of the Quit Rents" dated February 23, 1741, SCPRO, XX, 352.

44. For a detailed account of this controversy, see Sirmans, Colonial South Carolina, pp. 177–84.

John and Dr. Cooper were accordingly taken into custody by John Brown, messenger of the Commons House, and turned over to Provost Marshal Hall for safe keeping. Cooper's lawyers met the same fate when the House interpreted their writ of habeas corpus as an attempt to abridge its rights and privileges.

At this point, with counsel and client locked up in his gaol, the marshal was presented with a problem when Dr. Cooper initiated a suit against the House messenger with the help of Chief Justice Robert Wright, who sent the provost marshal a writ for Brown's arrest. Though technically required to serve the writ, Hall demonstrated shrewd judgment when he laid it instead before the Commons House for their consideration. This prudent move violated law and the judge's orders, but it spared Hall the indignity of being himself arrested and locked up in his own prison, and earned him the gratitude and confidence of the Commons House. Both House and Council subsequently vindicated the marshal and condemned the judge, pronouncing the writ "not according to Law or the Rules and Practice of any Court in this Province." [45]

Provost Marshal Hall emerged from this episode with increased prestige, but he was not so fortunate the following year when a routine order from the Court of Vice Admiralty almost got him killed. In late October 1734, a warrant was issued out of the Court of Vice Admiralty for the arrest of a Captain Gordon on suit for a debt of fifty-six pounds. With warrant in hand, the marshal boarded a small boat and headed down to Gordon's ship in Rebellion Road, but Gordon drove him off with cannon fire. The judge of Vice-Admiralty and Governor Johnson then sent Mr. Bernard, Master of His Majesty's Ship *Squirrel*, to assist Hall. Thus reinforced the marshal dropped down the bay, but when the party approached Gordon's ship the captain warned them to keep off and again opened fire:

> Mr. Bernard told his men to give way and got into the Wake of the Ship under her Stern so that they could not bring the Carriage-Guns to bear on her, and rode up to the Ship, the Captain and the Ship's Crew all the time firing upon the Boat. When the Boat got to the side of the Ship, the Captain endeavored to fire a Carriage-Gun into

45. *South Carolina Gazette*, April 28, May 12, June 2, 1733.

her, but the Boat coming too close to the Ship's side, the shot could do her no damage, then the Boat fired into the Ship, and the Captain was shot through the Body, whereof he instantly died.[46]

Charges were brought against the boarding party, but when the case was finally heard in April 1735, all defendants were aquitted.[47]

The most severe criticism directed against Provost Marshal Hall during his entire eight years in office was precipitated by the escape in September 1735 of two notorious offenders, Thomas Mellichamp and Joshua Morgan, who had been caught redhanded counterfeiting South Carolina currency in a James Island barn. Afterwards rumors circulated through the city alleging that Hall had been grossly negligent in failing to take adequate precautions to secure such notorious criminals. The pressure of public opinion might have forced his resignation had not Charles Pinckney come to his defense. Pinckney took testimony and published the affidavits of several key witnesses which completely exonerated the provost marshal.[48] No other incident connected with his administration would generate as much public excitement as the Mellichamp gaolbreak, although the Charles Lowndes' suicide in May 1736 probably excited more curiosity and spawned more gossip.

Just how or why Robert Hall happened to become guardian of young Charles and Rawlins Lowndes after the death of their father is something of a mystery and probably will remain so, at least until more positive information on the subject is uncovered. The most obvious conjecture, if not the only logical explanation, is that Thomas Lowndes of Westminster exercised through George Morley some influence on developments which resulted in Morley's deputy serving as guardian of the two boys. Nothing in the materials examined, however, can confirm this probability. Hall may very likely have suggested the arrangement himself, since he appears to have lost a teenaged son by drowning not quite a month before the Lowndes children lost their father.[49]

46. Ibid., November 2, 1734.
47. Ibid., November 2, 1734; April 26, 1735.
48. Ibid., August 23, September 27, October 11, 1735. The issue of October 11, containing the depositions of witnesses, is the best evidence on Hall's dignity and conscientious service.
49. *South Carolina Gazette*, May 1, 1736.

As wards of the resident provost marshal, Charles and Rawlins Lowndes could hardly have been more advantageously placed to prepare them for the legal profession or the marshalship. One suspects that their general education had been neglected during the worst of the family crisis and afterwards was along lines more practical than formal, judging from certain grammatical weaknesses and the complete absence of allusions to classical literature in Rawlins' extant writings and speeches. Their new circumstances brought them into daily contact with various aspects of the marshal's office, the provincial gaol, and the workings of the judicial system. There can be little doubt that the boys lent assistance in performing chores in connection with the marshal's routine duties, receiving training that both would find quite useful in later years. Moreover, their guardian possessed a large library which he utilized in directing his charges in the study of law over the next four years.[50] In time Rawlins developed a particular talent for the legal profession, but such were their circumstances and Robert Hall's example that both Charles and Rawlins eventually decided to follow in their guardian's steps.

Attending the courts as fledgling law students were wont to do, they became familiar with a seamier side of colonial life. How many sessions they attended to hear the pleas entered, the arguments presented, the verdicts rendered and the sentences pronounced is anybody's guess. They certainly discovered colonial justice to be harsh at best and brutal at worst, with punishment meted out to a motley procession of offenders passing through the prison. Provincial law demanded that all punishment except imprisonment be carried out in full and open view of the people, so that this part of the marshal's work took on the nature of public spectacles, varying in magnitude according to the type of punishment to be inflicted.

The Lowndes brothers became accustomed to seeing petty criminals like the habitual thief Alexander Forbes whipped at the cart's tail through the town; or Timothy Randall and Elizabeth Davis at the gaol door stripped to the waist and lashed on their bare backs for stealing a tea kettle and two silver spoons; or

50. Chase, *Lowndes*, p. 13.

James Young, convicted of forgery, standing in the pillory exposed to public ridicule from ten o'clock to twelve noon on market day, but considering himself more fortunate than the common horse thief whose ear was nailed to the pillory and sliced off when his time was up.[51] Branding, a punishment usually inflicted in lieu of the death penalty on a person convicted of a capital offense but admitted to the benefit of clergy, was carried out in open court according to law with the gaoler wielding the hot irons.[52] A more dramatic fate, public execution by hanging, awaited the less fortunate capital offender such as Sarah Chamberlain, hanged in 1738 "for the Murder of her Bastard Child." Likewise the murderer Blakely died on the gallows in 1737 while his accomplice, "in consideration of his acting as Executioner, was reprieved."[53] The most barbaric punishment was reserved for slaves like Boatswain, convicted of arson in August 1741 and burned at the stake in Charles Town.[54] Such spectacles invariably attracted throngs of curious spectators, and we can easily believe that the Lowndes brothers were as curious as their contemporaries.

As Charles and Rawlins became more familiar with the operation of the provincial gaol, they came to understand why its inmates might consider imprisonment a punishment more to be dreaded than the lash. Prison conditions were universally bad and those in South Carolina appear to have been worse than most. Law required the separation of felons from prisoners accused of lesser crimes, but overcrowded conditions frequently prohibited a strict adherence to the letter of the law. Consequently felons, petty criminals, debtors, runaway slaves, men and sometimes women were all confined together in the same crowded, makeshift quarters.[55]

Grand juries repeatedly calling these conditions to the attention of provincial authorities led to the establishment of a "Workhouse" in Charles Town in 1737. The Workhouse relieved some of the pressure by providing facilities for run away indentured ser-

51. *South Carolina Gazette*, March 27, 1737; March 23, 1738; March 29, 1740.
52. Cooper and McCord, *Statutes*, II, p. 455.
53. *South Carolina Gazette*, April 2, 1737; March 23, 1738.
54. Ibid., August 15, 1741.
55. Ibid., March 30, 1734.

vants and slaves, vagrants and deserting seamen.[56] Even so, the prison remained inadequate for its purpose, as another grand jury pointed out in November 1737 reiterating the want of a public prison, "which is highly necessary, not only for the more effectual securing of Criminals, but also for the better accomodating poor and unfortunate Debtors, whose misery is often greatly increased, by being confined in stifling Rooms . . . with Felons."[57]

This interest in better prisons and concern for the welfare of unfortunate debtors were not, of course, unique in South Carolina, but they stimulated the South Carolina Commons House in 1739 to emulate Parliament in appointing a committee to investigate prison conditions. On the appointed day Marshal Hall conducted the legislators through the provincial gaol where they inquired into every aspect of its operation. The committee report delivered in February 1740 was damaging to Hall.[58] Both medical care and subsistence were reported inadequate. One prisoner was seriously ill with an infected foot and another claimed they were fed less than the daily pound of bread and pound of beef required by law, the beef more often than not beeves' heads. On the committee's recommendation the House cut the subsistence allowance in half and struck £500 from the marshal's annual account, more than one fourth the total.[59]

If the House was trying to impress upon Marshal Hall their displeasure with him, they could hardly have chosen a more effective method than to strike out one fourth of his annual account. But to cut in half the per diem allowance for prisoners was quite another thing, a decision better calculated to worsen rather than improve prison conditions. Previous grand jury recommendations that a new gaol be built were completely ignored; nor could the House be persuaded to take any other step in the direction of

56. November 21, 1766, manuscript Journal of the Commons House of Assembly, 1765–1768, XXXVII, Part I, 213, S.C. Archives, hereafter cited Commons Journal. Microfilmed copies of these volumes are identified by the appropriate colonial office number designations. The law establishing the workhouse was dated May 29, 1736.

57. *South Carolina Gazette*, November 5, 1737.

58. February 7, 1740, Easterby, ed., *Commons Journal, 1739–1741*, pp. 184–85.

59. Ibid., pp. 284–86, 321.

prison reform than to instruct the marshal to feed his prisoners the full amount required by law. The well-intentioned inquiry thus reached a conclusion more than a little inconsistent with the humanitarian spirit that had initiated it. The reasons for this result go beyond the Commons' traditional conservatism in fiscal matters which touched upon the interests of patent officers. The Stono insurrection of September 1739 and the outbreak of war with Spain six weeks later are other factors which exerted a powerful influence.

Any number of black prisoners could have told how the electrifying insurrection and its fearful aftermath had blunted, even brutalized, official concern for their welfare. The immediate effect was a stringent new slave code passed in 1740. Afterwards runaways attempting to escape to Spanish Florida were no longer merely flogged and sent back to their masters, but were executed "and afterwards hung in Chains at *Hang-Man's Point* opposite this Town, in sight of all Negroes passing and repassing by Water." [60] At the same time, the outbreak of war with Spain heralded the end of a prosperous decade and the onset of lean times in the colony when strict economy in government would become not merely desirable but a matter of hard necessity. Already the belligerents were engaged in an undeclared naval war, with the first Spanish prize brought into Charles Town harbor on October 13, 1739. As prizes one after another were brought in, the gaol filled with prisoners of war and spilled over into the Workhouse, into Granville's Bastion, and upon occasion into almost any other facility that would serve the purpose. [61] These rapidly changing circumstances crushed the impulse toward prison reform in South Carolina, and the provost marshal, like everybody else, had to start counting the pence.

In the year 1740, his last as provost marshal, Hall crowned his record of public service by participating prominently in a colorful spectacle. On April 28 virtually all important provincial officials, military units, and leading citizens turned out in full ceremonial regalia to march in solemn procession from the Council chamber

60. *South Carolina Gazette*, April 12, 1739; January 10, 1743.
61. Ibid., May 3, 1740.

to the four corners of the town to hear "His Majesty's Declaration of War against the King of Spain" proclaimed, to the accompaniment of booming cannon, volleys of small arms fire, and "loud Huzzas."[62] The provost marshal led the procession, marching immediately in front of Lieutenant Governor William Bull and carrying the great Sword of State, symbol of the king's authority, which he flourished in traditional fashion at the end of each declaration.

Few colonials could resist the pomp and ceremony of such impressive and infrequent state occasions as this one, certainly not Rawlins Lowndes who seems to have taken delight in such spectacles. But most found it easy enough to resist the exhortations of Georgians then trying to raise two regiments of South Carolina volunteers to accompany General James Oglethorpe on an expedition against St. Augustine. Neither of the Lowndes brothers enlisted in this campaign and were thereby available to join in the thirty frantic hours of desperate fire-fighting required to stop a terrible holocaust that burned out the heart of Charles Town from Broad and Church streets down to Granville's Bastion on November 18 and 19, 1740.[63]

Fire of a different sort, though no less consuming, flared up about the same time when the "famous *Son of Thunder*, the Rev. Mr. GEORGE WHITEFIELD" arrived in town.[64] Speaking twice a day to overflow crowds, this remarkable evangelist not only ignited a spiritual revival in the burnt out city, but also sparked the anger and resentment of Commissary Alexander Garden, upon whose charges Whitefield was arrested in January 1741. The provost marshal brought him before the chief justice to post bond for a later appearance when, it was hoped, the matter would be settled.[65]

If Robert Hall himself arrested George Whitefield, which is doubtful, it was his last official act of consequence. One week later, on January 23, 1741, Lieutenant Governor Bull wrote to the

62. Ibid.
63. Ibid., November 20, 1740.
64. Ibid., January 15, 1741.
65. Ibid.

Lords of Trade that Hall was dead, without a word of explanation as to how or when or the cause of death.[66] The *Gazette* carried no mention whatever of the event. Such scant public notice marked the passing of the kindly marshal who had taken two orphaned boys into his home five years earlier, brought them up as his own sons, and left them in 1741 trained in the law and ready to embark on their separate careers.

66. Journal of the Board of Trade, April 16, 1741, SCPRO, XX, 333–34.

CHAPTER III

Provost Marshal

W HETHER CHARLES AND RAWLINS LOWNDES still remained in the household of Robert Hall at the time of his death— for Charles had reached his majority by 1741 and could himself have assumed legal responsibility for nineteen-year-old Rawlins— the death of their guardian was shortly afterwards followed by a reunion of the Lowndes family in South Carolina. William, the eldest son, after accompanying his mother and sister back to St. Kitts, had married there in 1739 and was returned to Carolina by 1741.[1] Ruth Lowndes probably came back to Carolina at the same time; by 1743 she was operating a school for girls at her residence on King Street.[2]

What employment Charles and Rawlins found between 1741 and 1745 now seems impossible to say with any degree of certainty. Although both were trained in the law, the extant court records contain no evidence to show that either became a practicing attorney during these years, or, for that matter, at any time thereafter.[3] They might have considered planting rice, but unlike most

1. The *South Carolina Gazette*, January 2, 1742, lists William Lowndes as a steward in a ceremony held by the Order of Masons in Charles Town on December 28, 1741.

2. The following advertisement appeared in ibid., August 15, 22, 29, 1743: "RUTH LOWNDES gives Notice, that she intends to set up a school where she now lives, in King Street, almost opposite to Doct. *Tailfer's* where any person that will favour her with their Children, may have them taught with the greatest Care and Diligence, Reading and all sorts of plain and Sampler Work."

3. Neither the Judgement Dockets, Court of Common Pleas, Book No. 1 (1739-1755) and Book No. 2 (1755-1773), S.C. Archives, nor the Minutes of the Court of Common Pleas, (1754-1763), Typescript in S.C. Archives, con-

young men of their age then entering the profitable business, the Lowndes brothers possessed neither lands nor slaves nor capital sufficient for the purpose. When the price of rice rose to sixty shillings per hundredweight in May 1741—the highest since before the war and double that of 1740—they could do little more than curse their fate and sigh wistfully of missed opportunities.[4] But the high price did not hold, and with each passing year the crops diminished in value as the hazards of wartime commerce increased, demonstrating all too plainly the vulnerability of the Carolina rice planter. In 1742 the price eased down to fifty shillings per hundredweight; within another year it had dropped to forty; it hovered above thirty through 1743 until the French entered the war in 1744, then plunged downward. It finally hit bottom in May 1745, when one hundredweight of prime Carolina rice could bring only ten shillings in the Charles Town market.[5] The collapse of the rice market dislocated the entire provincial economy, reversing the flow of credit and driving debtor planters to the wall. Hard times settled over the colony, and everybody knew relief would come only when a diminution of hostilities made the sealanes safe for merchantmen.[6]

---

tains a record of any case in which either party was represented by Rawlins or Charles Lowndes as legal counsel. The Judgement Dockets, beginning with the February term of 1747, list the names of practicing attorneys beside the titles of cases in which they participated. The names which appear most frequently in these records, by last name only, are Wright, Pinckney, Grindlay, Michie, Burrows, Rutledge, Rattray, and Williams; but the name of Lowndes, other than as a litigant, appears nowhere among them. Rawlins did exercise an occasional power of attorney in executing wills and arranging property transfers, but there is no evidence in the extant court records of South Carolina to show that he ever practiced law. See Charleston County Deeds, A–6, pp. 133–36; ibid., C–6, pp. 5–7; ibid., F–6, pp. 525–27; ibid., S–6, pp. 290–93, S.C. Archives; Judgement Rolls, S.C. Archives, *passim*; "Abstracts from the Records of Court of Ordinary, 1764–1771," compiled by Mabel L. Webber, *South Carolina Historical and Genealogical Magazine*, XXXII (October, 1931), 292 (hereafter cited *SCHGM*); ibid., XXXV (January, 1934), 26.

4. *South Carolina Gazette*, May 3, 1740; May 7, 1741.

5. Ibid., February 6, May 3, 1742; February 7, November 7, 1743; February 6, August 6, November 5, 1744; May 6, 1745.

6. A House committee reported that the "Causes of the Decay of the RICE Trade" were owing chiefly to "the great Freights, high Insurance, Scarcity of Shipping, other extraordinary Charges on Trade, occasioned by the present War, which had reduced the Price of Rice so low that it will not pay the Ex-

In these circumstances it was perhaps both necessity and wisdom that led the Lowndes brothers to seek employment in public service. Charles made arrangements with the widow of Edmund Bellinger to rent the potentially profitable Ashley Ferry northwest of the city. He took over the business in March 1747, converted the basis of its operation from credit to cash, and announced plans to enlarge the enterprise by opening a "Public House" for the accommodation of travelers.[7] In the meantime Rawlins secured the office of deputy provost marshal.

After Robert Hall died in January 1741, attorney Charles Pinckney had secured a William Williamson to fill the vacancy. Almost nothing is known of this "victualer" and sometime constable of Charles Town beyond the fact that he proved unequal to the opportunity and lasted less than eighteen months in the post. He took over its duties in February 1741, was presented by the grand jury a year later "for setting at Liberty a Spanish Prisoner after he had been legally committed by Three Magistrates, without taking Bail or being lawfully discharged," and was replaced by Samuel Hurst six months later.[8] Hurst, a member of a Charles Town mercantile firm, successfully combined the careers of merchant and marshal without serious public criticism until the summer of 1745. Then a major gaolbreak produced reverberations which resulted in his resignation.[9]

At this point Rawlins Lowndes succeeded to the marshalship. That influence was applied in his behalf seems more likely than not, although evidence to confirm this probability has not yet come to light; neither the materials in the British Public Record Office relating to South Carolina nor any other source consulted

pense of raising and manufacturing it; and consequently, in a very short Time, must unavoidably reduce the Planter to extreme Poverty," *South Carolina Gazette*, December 10, 1744.

7. Ibid., March 9, 1747. Charles Lowndes appears to have operated the ferry for no more than two years, for an advertisement in ibid., April 24, 1749 stated that John Gordon was then keeping the ferry. On May 2, 1749, Charles Lowndes assumed the duties of Keeper of the Common Gaol in Charles Town. See March 14, 1750, Easterby, ed., *Commons Journal, 1749–1750*, p. 459.

8. February 17, February 18, March 20, 1741, ibid., *1739–1741*, pp. 488, 489, 551; November 27, 1742, ibid., *1742–1744*, pp. 72, 115; *South Carolina Gazette*, March 27, 1742. Hurst became deputy provost marshal on August 9, 1742.

9. January 18, 1746, Easterby, ed., *Commons Journal, 1745–1746*, p. 64.

contains any reference to the circumstances of his appointment. James Glen, the new governor who approved it, was well acquainted with George Morley[10] and surely consulted the assignee and his attorney on Lowndes' appointment; but no record of such consultation appears to have survived. In view of his legal training and familiarity with the office, Rawlins was as well qualified for the post as anyone in the colony, and might well have been selected simply on his own merits. He was quite mature for his twenty-four years, serious-minded with habits of diligence, industry, and careful attention to detail. In any case, the wisdom of selecting him to be the chief law enforcement officer in South Carolina would have to be proved, and he set about proving it.

From the very beginning of his tenure Rawlins Lowndes addressed himself to the duties of his office in a more businesslike manner than did his predecessors. On November 11, 1745, he published his first notice in the *Gazette*, warning "that none of his deputies are authorized by him to receive (on any Pretence whatsoever) any Money or Debts on any Execution or otherwise . . . unless they have his Instructions in Writing, under his Hand." From then on, Lowndes kept the public informed through frequent advertisements of the latest activity concerning his office. A constant stream of legal notices placed in the *Gazette* by Marshal Lowndes over the next three years reflected the condition of the provincial economy, as each downward turn stimulated the business of his office and multiplied his fees, while each recovery slackened the pace.

Creditor merchants crowded the Common Pleas docket with suits for debt, implementing an Act of Parliament of 1731 "for the more easy Recovery of Debts in this Majesty's plantations and Collonies in America." This law provided that houses, lands, slaves, "and other Hereditaments and Real Estates" could thenceforth be seized and sold to satisfy lawful debts.[11] Seizures and sales

10. Morley had conferred with Governor Glen before the latter left England for the colony and it was he who recommended to Glen the house of Charles Pinckney on East Bay Street as a suitable residence for the governor. See June 7, 1746, ibid., *1745–1746*, p. 207. For several years George Morley served as Charles Pinckney's business manager in England, see Harriott Horry Ravenel, *Eliza Pinckney* (New York, 1896), p. 172.

11. Charleston County Deeds, DD, pp. 6–10, S.C. Archives.

in execution occurred with astonishing frequency during these
years, greatly increasing the marshal's income though contributing
to the general gloom. Fortunes in slaves, houses, household and
mercantile goods, plate, plantation stock, ships (including "an
unfinished SCHOONER on the Stocks . . . with Timbers and
Plank enough to compleat her"), town lots and buildings (among
them the "Playhouse" on Queen Street), and several thousand
acres of land passed under the hammer of the provost marshal,
or the vendue master at the marshal's order. All were "taken in
execution by *Rawlins Lowndes, Provost Marshal*" and sold at
public outcry, "fairly and Openly . . . Knocked to . . . the Highest
Bidder. . . ."[12]

Lowndes' income from these transactions was considerable. According to the fee laws of 1736 and 1743, which then determined
fees for patent officers,[13] he was allowed "For each execution on
the body of goods, if not above one hundred pounds proclamation
money, twelve pence per pound, if above one hundred pounds
proclamation money, six pence."[14] The extant records show that
choice town lots alone regularly brought more than £1000 currency, with one sale of two lots on Meeting Street bringing £7000.[15] In
addition to his percentage on such sales, the marshal was allowed
other legal fees: two shillings sixpence for serving every warrant on
land and eight shillings for each warrant served "on the water,"

12. Notices of seizures and sales in execution occurred with a frequency
much too great for each to be cited separately here. *See* the *South Carolina
Gazette*, 1746 through 1750. The above quotations were taken from ibid.,
November 24, 1746; July 10, 1749; Charleston County Deeds, MM, pp. 163–64,
S.C. Archives.

13. Although the fee law of 1736 was disallowed and that of 1743 was never
confirmed, patent officers adhered to the terms of these acts fearing retribution by the Assembly if they did not. See Jack P. Greene, *The Quest for Power,
The Lower Houses of Assembly in the Southern Royal Colonies, 1689–1776*
(Chapel Hill, 1963), pp. 158–59; SCPRO, XXXI, pp. 217–22.

14. Cooper and McCord, *Statutes*, II, 709, explains the relative value of proclamation money as follows: "Proclamation Money . . . acquired that denomina-
tion from a proclamation of Queen Ann in the sixth year of her reign. . . .
The standard fixed by the proclamation was one hundred and thirty-three
pounds, six shillings and eight pence paper currency, for one hundred pounds
sterling. The nominal value of proclamation currency was established at one
fourth below the value of sterling."

15. Charleston County Deeds, HH, pp. 53–54.

one shilling three pence for serving each citation, three pence per mile for travel one way, six shillings for summoning a special jury, two shillings for each person presented and prosecuted, and one shilling for each person acquitted by proclamation.[16] The extraordinary volume of legal business brought on by the depression was turning the marshal's place into one of the most profitable posts in the province.

All this, of course, was not directly related to his operation of the provincial prison, which was supported by a different set of fees. The marshal was legally entitled to two shillings for each commitment, a like fee for drawing a bail bond, as well as a per diem allowance of one shilling three pence for maintenance of each prisoner.[17] These were to be paid by the prisoners themselves, except in the case of of indigent criminals and prisoners of war whose fees were paid by the provincial government. Debtor cases presented a special problem. All too frequently suits for debt revealed that the debtor's property sold in execution was insufficient to discharge his obligations, and the unfortunate man was committed to the marshal's care. The debtor remained in gaol until his debt was paid, unless he could plead benefit of the "Act of South Carolina for the Relief of Poor Debtors." This law provided for his release "from the perpetual imprisonment to which he would be otherwise subject" upon proving that his total estate amounted to less than forty shillings sterling.[18]

Owing to the twin circumstances of war and a depressed economy, the provincial gaol did a land-office business that soon presented the provost marshal a serious problem of overstrained facilities. The gaol became so overcrowded with defaulting debtors and prisoners of war that to accommodate the latter the Workhouse, Granville's Bastion, "the Vault in Broad Street" and the

16. Cooper and McCord, *Statutes*, III, 417–19.
17. Ibid., pp. 417–18. The provost marshal's accounts paid by the provincial government for the maintenance of prisoners averaged about £700 annually. See February 13, 1746, Easterby, ed., *Commons Journal, 1745–1746*, pp. 89–90; December 4, February 9, June 11, 1747, ibid., *1746–1747*, pp. 81, 164, 369; March 11, June 28, 1748; ibid., *1748*, pp. 159, 387; May 5, 1749; March 14, 1750; ibid., *1749–1750*, pp. 51, 459.
18. *South Carolina Gazette*, October 18, 1735.

house of Joseph Tobias, the colony's interpreter in the Spanish language, had been pressed into service by January 1746.[19]

Concern for imprisoned debtors was expressed by Governor Glen in a message of January 18 to the Commons House of Assembly. Glen's former experience as a sheriff in Scotland gave him a fair appreciation of the difficulties faced by Marshal Lowndes, and the governor suggested that the old powder magazine might be converted into a debtor's prison to be maintained at public charge:

> When you consider, Gentlemen, the unhappy Situation of those unfortunate Persons that may be confined in Gaol for Debt, and what an Addition it must be to their Miseries to be under the same Confinement and often in the same Room with the most notorious Criminals, I doubt not but your Humanity will induce you to provide for an Expence to relieve such of your fellow Subjects as may be imprisoned for Debt from that additional Evil.[20]

The humanity of the legislators was not evident in their response; they merely tabled the message, leaving Marshal Lowndes to rely on his own resources in finding adequate security for his prisoners.[21]

The Assembly was primarily concerned with efforts to solve the colony's profound economic problems. Several expedients were proposed. As early as May 1745 the governor, Council, and Commons House had petitioned the Crown to remove rice from the enumerated list and allow it to be transported "directly to Places where it may be disposed of to some advantage" in order to "prevent the utter Ruin of our Rice Trade."[22] Peregrine Fury, the colonial agent, duly presented their memorial to the Board of Trade in February 1746, but to no avail.[23] Numerous letters to the *Gazette* suggested diversification of crops such as wheat, olives, hemp, flax, indigo, and silk as an alternative to planting rice.[24] Others warned planters against buying slaves on a speculative

19. January 17, 1746, Easterby, ed., *Commons Journal, 1745–1746*, pp. 50–51.
20. January 18, 1746, ibid., pp. 64–66.
21. Ibid.
22. May 8, 1745, ibid., *1744–1745*, pp. 476–78.
23. Journal of the Board of Trade, entry dated February 5, 1746, SCPRO, XII, 124–25.
24. *South Carolina Gazette*, October 1, 1744 *ff*.

basis, but none offered a satisfactory solution to current problems.[25]

As the depression deepened in 1746, a groundswell of popular agitation moved through the lowcountry parishes demanding that some action be taken to relieve the indebted planters, "distressed by creditors hard pressed to meet their own obligations."[26] The movement was organized by groups of planters who "assembled themselves together and rode about the Southern parts of the Province to secure Petitions of a most extraordinary nature. . . ."[27] So effective were their efforts that the General Assembly which gathered in Charles Town in the late summer of 1746 was presented with virtually identical petitions from several parishes in Granville, Colleton and Craven counties.[28] The petitions offered four suggestions to relieve "the general Calamities and Misfortunes of this province": (1) that more currency be issued to relieve the scarcity of money; (2) that staple commodities of the province be made legal tender; (3) that the sale of slaves to the Spanish provinces (by merchants seizing them for debt in Carolina) be prohibited; and (4) that cases involving sums between £20 and £100 currency be determined "by a sufficient Number of Justices and Freeholders."

The Assembly debated each of these proposals before rejecting all but the last, finally producing a bill which was signed into law by Governor Glen on June 13, 1747. The statute represented a serious invasion of the jurisdiction of the Court of Common Pleas. Called the "Justices Act," the measure empowered any two justices of the peace and three freeholders to constitute a court with authority to determine actions of debt where the amount in dispute was between £20 and £75 currency.[29] Lacking a suspending clause, the law went into effect immediately, to the "very great prejudice of the King's Patent Officers."[30]

25. Ibid., August 23, November 24, 1746.

26. Easterby, ed., *Commons Journal, 1746–1747*, viii.

27. George Morley and James Wedderburn to the Lords of Trade, October 20, 1747, SCPRO, XXII, 248–49, 316–19.

28. November 29, 1746, Easterby, ed., *Commons Journal, 1746–1747*, pp. 63–67.

29. June 13, 1747, ibid., p. 395.

30. George Morley to Lords of Trade, February 5, 1748, SCPRO, XXIII, 83.

The interests of all officers who derived income from the operation of the Court of Common Pleas were seriously injured by the new law, although such legislation was not without precedent in the colony. Since 1692 justices of the peace had been authorized to determine actions not exceeding forty shillings currency, an amount which had been raised to £10 in 1721 and to £20 in 1726; all other cases of debt were tried by jury in common pleas.[31] But when the new law increased the jurisdiction of these inferior courts to actions involving £75 currency (equal to £12 sterling) it took from the Court of Common Pleas most of its business and from its officers most of their fees. Marshal Lowndes' income was reportedly reduced by 75 percent when the law went into effect.[32]

It is small wonder then that protests and petitions against the Justices Act reached the Board of Trade before a copy of the law itself. George Morley, who had lobbied successfully against the fee law of 1736, moved to protect the interests of the marshal's place. He and James Wedderburn, the Clerk of the Court of Common Pleas, laid before the Lords of Trade on October 20, 1747, a petition claiming that the Justices Act not only contained no suspending clause but deprived the king's officers of their rights and threatened to destroy the Court of Common Pleas as well as trial by jury in the colony.[33]

When the Lords of Trade asked Governor Glen for an explanation, he defended the measure, giving an account of conditions in the colony at the time the bill was passed. He stated that the circumstances of many of the planters was "unspeakably bad, no words can heighten their distress . . . and as some had already taken Sanctuary in other Provinces, and others were preparing for flight," he had approved the bill "as the only expedient that occur'd to me to save this Province from sinking in impending Ruin. . . ."[34] The Assembly stoutly supported the governor's

31. Ibid., pp. 84–87.

32. January 30, 1748, Easterby, ed., *Commons House Journal, 1748*, pp. 46–47.

33. George Morley and James Wedderburn to the Lords of Trade, October 20, 1747, SCPRO, XXII, 248–49, 316–21. For Morley's success against the fee law of 1736, *see* "Report to the Lords of the Committee of Council upon the Petition of Mr. Morley &c. against the Act for Regulating Fees," March 15, 1737, P.R.O. Photocopy, CO5/381/Part 2, pp. 473–83, S.C. Archives.

34. Glen to the Lords of Trade, October 10, 1748, SCPRO, XXIII, 220–21.

position and directed agent Fury to press for allowance, "recommending to him the supporting of the said Act against all Opposition, with the most powerful Means. . . ."[35]

Fury did what he could, but the Lords of Trade eventually recommended disallowance. In stating their principal objections in a message to the Crown on March 4, 1748, the lords pointed out the weaknesses of the law and the superiority of the old system;

> . . . the Execution of all Process upon Actions above the sum of Twenty Pounds has hitherto been in the Provost Marshal or his Deputy who gives Security, whereas by this act that Power is vested in the Constable who is to levy all Money on Execution and to pay it over to one of the Justices, who is to pay it to the Plaintiff, which Provision we humbly apprehend will not answer the Intention of the said Act in as much as neither the Justice or Constable give any security or are under any Penalty in case they shall detain any Money levied upon such Executions. . . .
>
> That there is no Oath prescribed by this Act to be taken by the Plaintiff in order to prove his Debt, or by the Witnesses to be examined in any Action brought before the said Court, and that the Execution of this Act may likewise be attended by Difficulties for want of Persons in all parts of the said Province properly qualified for that purpose. . . .[36]

Notwithstanding the combined efforts of governor, Assembly, and colonial agent, and doubtless to the great relief of patent officers, the Justices Act came back disallowed in August 1748.[37]

No one could have been more pleased with the disallowance than Marshal Lowndes, for he had in the meantime suffered another setback. Having to function under the disadvantages of the

35. May 19, 1749, Easterby, ed., *Commons Journal, 1749–1750*, pp. 138–39.
36. Board of Trade to the Crown, March 4, 1748, SCPRO, XXIII, 84–87.
37. The disallowance of the Justices Act resulted in Fury's dismissal. The Assembly had already lost its trust in Fury over his part in suppressing their criticism of General James Oglethorpe following the failure of the St. Augustine expedition in 1741. *See* Sirmans, *Colonial South Carolina*, pp. 211–12. Fury was retained as the colony's agent, however, until he informed them on December 9, 1748, of the disallowance of the Justices Act, "acquainting them, from the Disappointment that attended his utmost efforts in defence of that Law, he could not flatter himself with better Success in maintaining hereafter any other act of the like Nature." Upon reading this letter, the House voted to replace Fury with James Crokatt. May 19, 1749, Easterby, ed., *Commons Journal 1749–1750*, p. 142.

Justices Act since June 1747, he had of necessity come to rely more heavily on the profitable operation of the gaol. Then on the morning of December 16, 1747, a fire of mysterious origin broke out in the roof of the gaol, "which burnt with such Fury that the whole Building was consumed in a few Hours."[38] Lowndes was able to save all his prisoners, with only one man "committed on Suspicion of Murder" escaping during the confusion. The marshal made temporary arrangements with John Hutchins, warden of the Workhouse, to secure most of his prisoners, took the remainder into his own home, and applied to the provincial government for emergency assistance.

Lowndes' petition was brief and to the point. The recent burning of the gaol had made it impossible for him to execute the most essential duties of his office, he said, and asked "that something may be speedily done" to provide secure housing for his prisoners, for a publicly supported gaol was long overdue:

> That a Public Gaol is so necessary to the Well-being and Suport of Society that few under any Government are without one. And the Petitioner is persuaded and informed that this Province is the only one of Great Britain that never had erected or established such a Place of Security. The evil Consequences that have arisen from such a Want are apparent and obvious. Public justice has been rendered fruitless and ineffectual by the frequent Escape of Prisoners both before and after Sentence. And at this Time the Petitioner has no better Pledges for the Security of Debtors, Felons, or other Criminals than their own Promises not to depart his Dwelling.[39]

Governor Glen strongly endorsed the petition, expressing his astonishment that the colonial government had neglected to provide a public gaol for so long a time. It was a public responsibility which the marshal in his present circumstances could hardly be expected to bear:

38. *South Carolina Gazette*, December 21, 1747. Only later did Marshal Lowndes learn that the fire had been deliberately set by John Collings, a prisoner of war, who was subsequently discharged from prison, went to Spanish Florida, and there boasted "that he was the person who burnt the Prison in Charles Town, For which purpose he Kept a Match two Days, waiting on an Opportunity, and intended to have reduced the Town to Ashes." Ibid., April 4, 1748.

39. January 30, 1748, Easterby, ed., *Commons Journal, 1748*, pp. 47–48.

However Gentlemen may have formerly thought that the Profits of the Provost Marshal's Office were so great as to enable him to hire a convenient House for keeping his Prisoners in, they cannot surely now entertain any such Notion, since the Profits from that Office from various Causes have within a few Years past been reduced from two hundred and twenty Pounds to one hundred and thirty Pounds Sterling per Annum, and within this last Year, by Means of the Operation of a Law passed in the last General Assembly, they have been again reduced from one hundred and thirty to thirty Pounds Sterling per Annum. . . .[40]

Glen saw here an opportunity to "purchase out the Office of Provost Marshal intirely and bring in the use of Sheriffs in the several Counties in his Stead." He felt that if a proposal were made for that purpose, George Morley, "the present Patentee,"[41] might be willing to sell.

If Glen was correct in his belief that Morley could be bought out, the Assembly missed a fine opportunity indeed. The House did appoint a committee to look into the matter but no report of their deliberations was ever heard.[42] Apparently they quietly dropped the issue when disallowance of the Justices Act restored to the marshal's office its previous jurisdiction. Over the next two decades the basic cause of growing discontent in the backsettlements was the antiquated and increasingly inefficient judicial and law enforcement systems. Not till this discontent turned to rage and erupted in the violence of regulator activity would the Assembly make the change Governor Glen had recommended twenty years earlier.

On the marshal's petition for a public supported jail the Commons took no action whatever. Lowndes would only ask once. He made arrangements for a gaol himself, and during the six remaining years of his tenure in the office, he never brought the subject up again.

The year 1748 proved to be a memorable one for the whole colony. King George's War had for some time been drifting toward a truce, and the lessening of hostilities brought renewed energy to commercial activities. Since February 1747, when rice was sell-

40. Ibid., pp. 46–47.
41. Ibid.
42. Ibid., p. 48.

ing locally at fifteen shillings per hundredweight, the price had been steadily rising. It was up to thirty-two shillings in April 1747, to thirty-five in May, to forty in June, to forty-five in August where it reached a plateau. It diminished slightly in the early months of 1748, then with rumors of peace it hit fifty shillings in June, mounted to fifty-five in July, and held that figure after the cessation of arms was proclaimed on August 15, 1748.[43]

To the advantages provided by the recovery of the rice market, the colony learned that the Crown had added another this year by awarding a bounty of six pence per pound for the production of indigo.[44] As the seasons for rice and indigo production complemented each other perfectly, Governor Glen accurately predicted that these staples must become the "two Pillars" of the provincial economy. Successful planters soon discovered that, by augmenting rice with indigo, they could double their capital every four years.[45]

Peace, prosperity, and high promise returned to Carolina in 1748, but the year was especially significant to Rawlins Lowndes for more personal reasons. On August 15, the same day that the cessation of hostilities was proclaimed, he was married in St. Philip's Church to nineteen-year-old Amarinthia Elliott of Stono in St. Paul's Parish west of Charles Town.[46]

Amarinthia proved an affectionate wife and was "much beloved" by her husband,[47] but the marriage was even more important in terms of Lowndes' career. Amarinthia's dowry included a plantation at Stono, and it was characteristic of her husband's meticulous attention to detail that he should promptly order the property surveyed and walk its boundaries with the surveyor.[48] By this acquisition Lowndes moved into the select circle of landed gentry of the South Carolina lowcountry, and incidentally met the property

43. *South Carolina Gazette*, February 16, April 27, May 18, June 8, August 17, 1747; June 1, 1748; July and August, 1748, *passim*.
44. March 31, 1749, Easterby, ed., *Commons Journal, 1749–1750*, pp. 18–19.
45. Ibid., pp. 18–19, 99, 102–3; Ravenel, *Eliza Pinckney*, p. 106.
46. *Register of St. Philip's Parish, Charles Town South Carolina, 1720–1758*, ed. A. S. Salley, Jr. (Charleston, S.C., 1904), p. 189; Charleston County Deeds, R-6, pp. 253–54, S.C. Archives.
47. Henry A. M. Smith, contributor, "The Gravestones in the Church Yard of Old St. Paul's, Stono," *SCHGM*, XI (January, 1910), 73.
48. Charleston County Deeds, R–6, pp. 253–54. The land, in two tracts, amounted to 463 acres.

qualification for a seat in the provincial legislature as a representative of St. Paul's Parish. Moreover, he was now allied with the venerable, numerous, and socially prominent Elliott family of South Carolina, a matter of much importance to his future political career.

For the purpose of launching his political career, Lowndes' marriage could hardly have been better timed. The booming rice and indigo markets were claiming first attention with the planter interests, causing increasing numbers of them to absent themselves from service in the House or to refuse election altogether, opening opportunities for rising young men with political ambitions such as Lowndes. Then another obstacle was removed. The election act of 1745, which had excluded from membership in the House all Crown officers including the provost marshal, came back disallowed in 1748.[49] Governor Glen had no choice but to dissolve the Assembly and call for new elections. When this was done so many of the newly elected members refused election, or simply failed to appear, that a new House could not be mustered.[50] The pervasive political apathy forced Governor Glen again to dissolve the Assembly on February 15, 1749, and call another election for mid-March. In this election the Parish of St. Paul returned three members: Frederick Grimkee, William Elliott, and Thomas Sacheverell. Now Grimkee and Elliott refused to qualify, necessitating a by-election to fill the two vacancies. Finally on April 25 and 26, the voters of St. Paul's elected David Crawford and Provost Marshal Rawlins Lowndes, who agreed to serve.[51] Thus began Lowndes' thirty-year career in the Commons House of Assembly.

Lowndes had not yet taken his seat when circumstances presented an opportunity to demonstrate his support for the prerogatives of the House. For some months the provost marshal had employed as keeper of the common gaol William Mouatt, who also served as a messenger of the House when the Assembly was in session. On the last day of the previous Assembly the House had drawn a message critical of Governor Glen's conduct, but before

---

49. Easterby, ed., *Commons Journal, 1749–1750*, x.
50. Ibid., x, xi.
51. February 16, March 28, April 1, May 4, 1749, ibid., pp. 3, 7, 21–22, 37–38; *South Carolina Gazette*, February 25, 1749.

the message could be delivered, someone informed Glen of its critical tenor, whereupon the governor abruptly prorogued the Assembly and subsequently dissolved it.

Mouatt was suspected to be the person who informed the governor in violation of the oath required of House messengers. Well aware of the suspicion, he petitioned the House protesting his innocence, but a majority of its members was convinced of his guilt and dismissed him on April 3.[52] When Lowndes was elected three weeks later, he persuaded his brother Charles to take over the duties of gaoler, and fired Mouatt on May 1.[53] Charles Lowndes assumed his new duties the next day, and Rawlins took his seat in the Commons House on May 4, 1749.

The first session of Lowndes' service in the House lasted less than one month, from May 4 to June 1, 1749. Governor Glen had only good news in his speech to the Assembly. He announced that a definitive treaty of peace had been signed "in October last," and informed the legislators officially of the parliamentary grant of the bounty on indigo. He expected Indian relations to be improved through another parliamentary grant of £3000 sterling for Indian presents as well as provision for a fort to be built in the Cherokee territory at the expense of the Crown.

In this brief session, the House took steps to prevent frauds in the making and packing of indigo and to name James Crokatt the next agent for the colony in recognition of the former Charles Town merchant's successful efforts to secure the bounty. The members also passed a new tax bill and devoted considerable time to the manner of disbursing Indian presents and to Governor Glen's answers to several queries from the Lords of Trade.[54] Rawlins Lowndes dutifully attended the meetings of the House throughout the session, sitting in the back of the hall with other freshmen legislators; but having received no committee assignments, he was left relatively free to attend to the duties of the marshal's office.

Shortly after the session ended, Lowndes enjoyed his first oppor-

52. March 31, April 3, 1749, Easterby, ed., *Commons Journal, 1749–1750*, pp. 20–21, 26.

53. May 12, 1749, March 14, 1750, ibid., pp. 87, 459.

54. May 5, June 1, 1749, ibid., pp. 52–55, 276–77, 280. James Crokatt was the same merchant of Charles Town who had figured in the career of Rawlins' father, Charles Lowndes, in the late 1730s.

tunity to participate in an important state occasion. On June 12, "with great Solemnity and universal Joy," the king's proclamation of peace was published officially in Charles Town. People from all over the lowcountry flocked into the city to witness the impressive spectacle. The high point of the celebration was the traditional procession from the council chamber to the four corners of the town, with the former orphan boy now the king's officer, dressed in ceremonial robe and carrying the great Sword of State "immediately before the Governor, and all the Gentlemen of the Council followed him two and two. . . ."[55] Lowndes developed a fondness for such pomp and ceremony. Tall and erect, he carried himself with much dignity, a characteristic which marked all his public deportment and would one day evoke from his critics scornful comment.

Through the summer months Lowndes devoted most of his attention to the patent office. Almost every issue of the *Gazette* carried announcements of jailed debtors petitioning for release under an act for the relief of insolvent debtors. Their periodic release only made room for others as seizures and sales in execution for debts contracted during the lean years of war continued apace. The marshal conducted an impressive property sale in July and another in August before attending the regular sitting of the Court of Common Pleas later that month and the Court of General Sessions in October.[56]

During the brief intervals of relative freedom from such official responsibilities, the marshal applied his considerable energies to the operation of his Stono River plantation and the harvesting of his rice crop. The latter task was made more difficult by the continued absence of Jack, his Negro driver, who had run away in May shortly after Lowndes had purchased him.[57] With rice selling at sixty-five shillings per hundredweight in the Charles Town market, no one needed to remind Lowndes of the importance of bringing in a good harvest.[58] But his hopes were probably not realized that year. Climatic conditions had not been favorable and rice production throughout the province was down nearly thirty percent from previous years.[59] Nothing of this sort could have dampened his spirits, however, for Amarinthia was becoming great with child, expecting their first-born in January.

When the third session of this General Assembly opened on November 21, 1749, the back row seat of the freshman legislator was empty. It remained vacant day after day over the next three weeks as the House elected a new speaker, Andrew Rutledge, to replace William Bull who had been appointed to the Council, and deliberated the points in the governor's message. Attendance in general was so poor that the House accomplished little more than to set in motion the machinery to purchase the freedom of Caesar, a slave who had perfected a "cure for poison," before it adjourned for the holidays on December 14.[60]

Rawlins Lowndes was too ambitious to absent himself from the House through mere neglect of duty. Subsequent events suggested that a matter infinitely more serious could have been the cause, for something was going terribly wrong with Amarinthia's pregnancy. On January 14, 1750, both she and her first born died in childbirth, bringing to a sudden and tragic end the scant fifteen months of her life as Mrs. Rawlins Lowndes. The funeral service was held in Old St. Paul's Church, Stono. Afterwards her bereaved husband and the procession of mourners moved out to the graveyard. There on a bluff commanding a vast and dismal expanse of salt marsh and crowned by ancient live oaks, Amarinthia was buried, babe in arms, "at her own particular Desire near her deceased Parents."[61]

This second visitation of personal tragedy to Rawlins Lowndes proved more profound than the first. Amarinthia was the great love of his life, and her sudden death left him a changed man. He

59. Exports of rice from November 1, 1749, to October 16, 1750, totaled 47,593 barrels, ibid., October 16, 1750. The crops usually ran near 75,000 barrels.

60. November 24, 1749, Easterby, ed., *Commons Journal, 1749–1750*, p. 293 ff.

61. Smith, "The Gravestones in the Church Yard in Old St. Paul's, Stono" op. cit., p. 73.

would marry twice again, but neither of her successors could ever replace the beloved Amarinthia in his heart nor claim the affection he felt for her as long as he lived.[62] Something of his own youth and gentleness remained buried at Old St. Paul's when the twenty-nine-year-old marshal returned to his duties in Charles Town.

62. Mrs. St. Julien Ravenel, *Life and Times of William Lowndes of South Carolina, 1782–1822* (Boston and New York, 1901), p. 2.

CHAPTER IV

Representative

RAWLINS LOWNDES resumed his duties in the Commons House on January 24, 1750, the second day of the session that followed the tragic death of his wife and child. As a member of the House he participated in the several controversies with the governor through 1753 and in another with the Council beginning in 1754. While Governor Glen stood at the peak of his political career in 1749, within a year he began to experience mounting difficulty in his dealings with the provincial legislature and the home government as well. Pressed by a hostile Board of Trade, Glen became increasingly solicitous of the king's prerogative, which, in turn, aroused the anger of the Assembly and resulted in attacks on his constitutional position.[1] The issues revolved around Indian relations, fortifications, expansion, and paper money.[2]

Since the primary responsibility of Rawlins Lowndes continued throughout the period to be the marshal's office, he could be expected to concern himself more directly with issues affecting law enforcement and the courts. The position taken on any given issue by an individual legislator cannot always be readily discovered in the legislative record where debates and individual ballots were never recorded. Committee appointments provide a useful index of Lowndes' activities, and committee reports and resolutions are often helpful in suggesting his position on a specific question. Of one thing, though, we may be certain: He could not have risen

1. Sirmans, *Colonial South Carolina*, pp. 278–79.
2. For an excellent treatment of the larger issues of the Glen administration after 1749, *see* ibid., p. 278 *ff*.

to the second rank of leadership in the House by 1752[3] without the support and approval of its most influential members. And such confidence and approbation was extended only to those who could be depended on to defend the rights, privileges, and powers of the Commons House.

Rawlins Lowndes received no major committee appointments in the session which lasted from January through the middle of March 1750. The House itself was largely occupied with routine matters through this session, except for the administrative problems caused by the colony's rapid expansion. A sprinkling of petitions from the burgeoning backsettlements calling for representation in the Assembly were passed over, but others demanded attention. Since the disallowance of the "Justices Act" in 1748, the larger and older coastal settlements of Georgetown and Beaufort viewed with mounting impatience and resentment the judicial system which required of both plaintiff and defendant a long, expensive and often dangerous journey to Charles Town in pursuit of justice.[4] And the growth of the provincial capital, pushing its limits steadily up the peninsula, stimulated grand juries to call repeatedly for a division of St. Philip's Parish in two. Separate bills to establish courts in Georgetown and Beaufort and to create St. Michael's Parish out of the southern half of St. Philip's were introduced in March 1750.[5] Lowndes had reason enough, as Provost Marshal, to vote against the court bill and none to oppose the parish measure, but neither received majority approval in 1750. Even so, both questions remained very much alive and would be revived.

While the main concern of the Glen administration in this decade was Indian affairs, the governor's acute sensitivity to criticism from the Board of Trade got him into major disputes with the Commons House over several issues essentially local in nature. One of these was the Jury Bill. The jury lists were periodically revised and brought up to date by all members of the Commons House working from tax lists furnished by the Public Treasurer.

3. Greene, *Quest for Power*, p. 482.
4. March 3, 1750, Easterby, ed., *Commons Journal, 1749–1750*, p. 433.
5. March 6, 13, 1750, ibid., pp. 436, 454–55.

Pursuant to an order of November 1750 the tax lists were laid before the House on January 18, 1751. According to custom, members from the several parishes examined the lists with instructions to "take out the Names of such Persons from the said Lists as they shall be of opinion are fit to be appointed to serve as Jury men at the Courts of Law in this Province."[6] The names were accordingly selected and given in by the various members. When the new lists were fashioned in the form of a bill, it was placed in the charge of Rawlins Lowndes. Securing House approval of the measure, Lowndes carried the bill to the Council for their assent; then, with Chief Justice James Graeme, he found the bill truly engrossed, saw it through its final passage by the Assembly on February 26, and carried it to Governor Glen for his signature.[7]

Almost two months passed before the Governor responded, and his response, when it came on April 18, was sufficiently solicitous of the prerogative to provoke the House. Glen instructed the Commons that "By the Laws of some other of His Majesty's Colonies no person is capable to be of a Jury for the Tryal of any Treason, Felony, Breach of the Penal Law, or any other Pleas of the Crown, or of any Estate or Freehold . . . unless such person to be a Freeholder, and be possessed of a visible Estate, real and personal, of the value of one hundred Pounds Sterling at the lease." For all other cases, he said, the juror must be worth fifty pounds sterling. He claimed that South Carolina's practice of selecting jurors by the ballot system was not in accord with practice in Great Britain or any other colony, and suggested that a law be passed setting the value of men's estates below which they should not be capable of serving as jurors.[8] So Glen withheld his approval of the bill.

A House committee including Lowndes immediately took up the Governor's message, and their report the following day expressed the controlled anger of its members.

In answer to your Message of Yesterday we assure your Excellency that we are not only sensible of the value of that part of the English Constitution of having Tryals by Juries but also of our great privi-

6. January 18, 1751, Commons Journal, XXVI, part 1, 44.
7. February 26, 1751, ibid., pp. 127, 129, 130.
8. April 18, 1751, ibid., p. 271.

lege of having Juries drawn by Ballot. It is our ancient and approved
Method established by Law, and we are firmly of Opinion that any
Person who shall endeavor to deprive us of so glorious a Privilege
is an utter Enemy of this Province.[9]

The basic cause of their annoyance was a very practical consideration. If the governor's recommendations were adopted, it "would
not leave a sufficient number to share in the Jury service, but would
be an intolerable Burden upon a few." The House agreed with the
committee but tempered their language and sent the message on
to Glen, adding further that a recent act of Parliament had incorporated into British law the practice of drawing juries by
ballot.

Nevertheless Glen stood by his guns, quoting his instructions
thus: "You are, for the better administration of Justice, to en-
deavour to get a Law passed (if not already done) wherein shall be
set the value of Men's Estates, either in Goods or Lands, under
which they shall not be capable of serving as Jurors."[10] The House
remained firm but employed a softer tone in explaining their position. Their only concession was to disqualify insolvent debtors
from jury service. Glen was satisfied and approved the bill on May
4, 1751, but not without again lecturing the Assembly on the "Vanity and Weakness in British Colonies" trying to improve on the
British Constitution, which he thought hardly possible.[11]

The governor compounded this first offense with several more.
Although he personally approved of a bill to incorporate the
Charleston Library Society, he saw a violation of the king's prerogative and vetoed it on a technicality.[12] Public reaction to this
veto was nothing compared to the public wrath generated by his
refusal to sign the highly popular bill for dividing St. Philip's
Parish. Its advocates pointed to the rapid growth of the parish
embracing the capital city that made its administration unwieldy
and its representation in the Assembly insufficient. Glen admitted
their case, but found the bill another violation of the prerogative

9. April 19, 1751, ibid., pp. 279–80, 282–83.
10. April 24, 1751, ibid., pp. 306–7.
11. May 8, 1751, ibid., XXVI, part 2, 398–401.
12. May 4, 1751, ibid., p. 401.

and his instructions as well. In rejecting it he said he had heard threats that complaints would be made to the Crown; so be it, he must follow his instructions.[13] The House sent a blistering reply, ordered all documents pertaining to the subject printed in the *Gazette* and joined the Council in petitioning the Crown directly for approval of the measure.[14]

But the veto which exhausted the patience of the Assembly was Glen's rejection of the Renewal Bill, a routine measure designed to continue in force several necessary laws, including the General Duty Law, near expiration. Immediately following this veto the House asked leave to adjourn to October, even though the vital appropriations bill had not yet been drawn, protesting that they saw no prospect "of having any success to their best Endeavours for the Public Service."[15] Glen explained his reasons for the veto, stating his principal objection that no part of the funds raised from the General Duty Law were to be applied to retiring paper money in circulation, a subject "very much complained of by the Lords of Trade."

Thoroughly disgusted with the governor's nervous concern for ministerial opinion, the House resorted to the power of the purse. Deleting the word "Salaries" from the category in the appropriations bill headed "Salaries to Public Officials," they struck out the provision of £700 for the governor's house rent.[16] Lowndes carried the amended appropriations bill up to the Council, and the House voted to send to the Crown articles of complaint against the governor.[17]

Glen could get along well enough without the rent money, but the prospect of a formal complaint to a board already so critical of his administration left him thoroughly alarmed. He let it be known that he would reconsider the vetoes, and through the intercession of friends a compromise was arranged. On May 31 he prorogued the Assembly to June 4, so that the vetoed bills could

13. April 24, 1751, ibid., XXVI, part 1, 310–15.
14. April 24, 1751, ibid., pp. 315, 317; May 9, 1751, ibid., XXVI, part 2, 417–18.
15. May 4, 7, 1751, ibid., pp. 402–5, 407–9.
16. May 9, 1751, ibid., pp. 420–24.
17. May 9, 10, ibid., pp. 431–32, 457–58, 462–63.

be redrawn. Slightly amended, though still not meeting his main objections, they received his approval on June 14.[18] The compromise restored a degree of amity between the governor and the Assembly, and in this spirit the session adjourned to November.

Quite in contrast to the decline in prestige of Governor Glen and not unrelated to it, the stature of Rawlins Lowndes was clearly on the rise. The serious-minded young representative of St. Paul's Parish gave his support to the policies of the House and earned the confidence of its leadership. Throughout the controversy he was repeatedly assigned the modest but not insignificant honor of conveying important messages and bills to the governor and Council, such as the Jury bill, the House's stinging message to the governor on the St. Philip's veto, the appropriations bill with Glen's house rent struck out, and the opening message from the House following the brief prorogation.[19] Through significant committee appointments he helped frame the Jury bill, revise the Negro laws and write the law providing for a new State House to be built in Charles Town, all approved by the governor this session.[20]

But Lowndes had a right to be more pleased with his success in solving one of the serious problems attending operation of the prison. The problem was explained in a petition submitted by Charles Lowndes, now Keeper of the Common Gaol, and read in the House on February 8, 1751. The gaoler was

> at daily and continual Expense in maintaining and keeping insolvent Debtors, who, after they have spent and wasted all they have, are arrested and thrown into Goal; where the Petitioner is obliged to find them with Lodging, Bread, Meat and all other Necessaries and Attendance; and very seldom or never is reimbursed one Shilling.
> ... the Laws in force concerning insolvent Debtors do not oblige the Creditor either to maintain the Debtor himself, or to pay the Goaler his lawful Fees. By means whereof Suits are very often commenced against Persons not worth one Shilling whom the Petitioner is obliged to keep at his own Expence until they are discharged by the Acts for the relief of insolvent Debtors. And the Petitioner often represented this to the Creditor; who to indulge his own capri-

18. May 31, June 6, 14, ibid., pp. 523, 525–26, 612–13.
19. February 8, 1751, ibid., XXVI, part 1, 103; May 9.
20. February 26, 27, 1751, ibid., XXVI, part 1, 127–29, 150–51; June 6, 1751, ibid., XXVI, part 2, 526.

cious Temper keeps the Person of his Debtor in Goal, without any regard to the Hardship which it lays on the Petitioner.

The bulk of his prisoners were insolvent debtors, the great majority of them admitted to the benefit of the existing laws and released. Most could pay only a small fraction of their fees, he claimed, and many "not one Farthing."[21]

When a House committee soon after introduced a bill to give further relief to debtors, Rawlins Lowndes offered an amendment "for obliging the Plaintiff to pay the Provost Marshal the Fees for insolvent Debtors committed to his Custody."[22] Lowndes doubtless anticipated objections from creditor merchants, but the amendment was approved and the bill shortly afterwards became law. The change proved greatly beneficial to the patent office but soon after, whether out of envy or anger, an attempt would be made to replace the marshal.

Meanwhile an outbreak of violence on the Cherokee frontier which took the lives of four South Carolina traders prompted Governor Glen to call the Assembly into emergency session on August 27, two months earlier than scheduled. Alarmed at the news, the planter members interrupted their preparations for the rice harvest and hurried to Charles Town where the governor calmly informed the Assembly that the crisis had passed. The Cherokees had yielded to demands and agreed to deliver up the parties guilty of the outrage. He hoped, though, that the Assembly would take this opportunity to adopt two proposals he considered necessary for improved relations with the Cherokees. First, pass a new Indian trade law to replace the one recently expired, and second, build a fort among the lower Cherokee towns to protect them from incursions of their enemies thus bringing them into closer alliance with the British.

Not a planter in the House considered the state of Indian relations critical enough to justify further neglect of the rice harvest, so they promptly asked leave to adjourn. Glen, supported by the Council, denied their request and lectured the impatient members on their duty. The House responded with a temporary ordinance to regulate the Indian trade for six months but would do no

21. February 8, 1751, ibid., XXVI, part 1, 100–2.
22. May 2, 1751, ibid., XXVI, part 2, 378, 380–81, 384, 386.

more. Glen let them go on August 31, and a month later routinely dissolved the Assembly for new elections.

Following the dissolution of this General Assembly, Rawlins Lowndes shifted his political base from St. Paul's farther westward to the Parish of St. Bartholomew, a change that would be permanent. Amarinthia having died a minor, Lowndes was by law required to return her dowry including the Stono plantation to the surviving Elliott heirs.[23] This left him without the required property qualification in the parish. But by this time he had acquired the "Horseshoe" plantation in St. Bartholomew's Parish, Colleton County. After the Assembly was dissolved by proclamation on October 4, 1751, his new neighbors two weeks later returned him as one of their representatives.[24] They continued to do so at each new election throughout his legislative career, although they seldom saw him. The nature of his duties as provost marshal and perennial member of the House required that he always maintain as his principal residence his home in the city.

Another significant change in his life occurred in December. In the two years since the death of Amarinthia, he had steadily risen in political stature and personal wealth to become one of the colony's most eligible young widowers, now regularly referred to as "Rawlins Lowndes, Esquire." And one suspects that there were more than a few young ladies of Charles Town who felt a pang of disappointment on reading the following announcement in the *Gazette* of January 1, 1752: "*Charles Town*, December 24: Last Night RAWLINS LOWNDES, Esq; was married to Miss MARY CARTWRIGHT, a young Lady of great Beauty, and bless'd with the most valuable Accomplishments." The second Mrs. Rawlins Lowndes was also blessed with many children in her marriage; the first one, a daughter, would be named Amarinthia in honor of the wife her husband had lost but evidently had not forgotten.[25] As if to underscore these changes in his political career and personal life, the same issue of the *Gazette* which announced his mar-

23. Charleston County Deeds, R6, pp. 253–54, S.C. Archives.

24. October 4, 1751, Commons Journal, XXVI, part 2, 662; November 14, 1751, ibid., XXVII, part 1, 21–22, 26; *South Carolina Gazette*, October 30, 1751.

25. Salley, *Register of St. Philip's Parish, Charles Town, South Carolina, 1720–1758*, p. 102.

riage also proclaimed a historic calendar change from Julian to Gregorian, effective January 1, 1752.[26]

Little had changed concerning outstanding issues between the governor and the Assembly when the new House met on January 7. Governor Glen reiterated his proposal for a fort on the "Keewohee River" in the Cherokee nation. The House again balked, now claiming that the location proposed might be in North Carolina and refusing to act on the proposal until the colonial boundary could be fixed. They could be coaxed to no further action on the matter beyond naming Lowndes and several others to confer with a similar committee from the Council to consider the best means of ascertaining the boundary, and adjourned to March 4. The joint committee met twice during the recess but accomplished nothing. The Council members would not discuss the boundary question without also discussing the fort, a procedure which Lowndes and his colleagues had been enjoined to avoid.[27]

When the Assembly met again on March 4, the fort issue settled down to an open struggle for power between the Commons House and the governor. To eliminate the boundary question the House authorized Glen to purchase a strip of Indian territory lying between Long Canes and Keowee where the fort was to be situated. But then they challenged the governor directly, by demanding to see the originals of all documents relative to Indian affairs, "of every kind, and not copies but originals, without any exception or reserve whatever. . . ."[28] This was to be a condition of their cooperation in establishing the proposed fort. To yield would violate his instructions, so Glen rejected the demand, adding that it was "neither so decent as might have been expected . . . or consistent with the British Constitution."[29] His own position was altogether consistent with the intentions of the Lords of Trade, who wanted Indian relations controlled by the governor rather than by the Assembly. A few days later when he sent down copies of several

26. This issue also suggests the extent of his activities as provost marshal, for approximately one-fourth of the entire issue is taken up with advertisements and notices inserted by Lowndes.

27. January 25, March 4, 1752, Commons Journal, XXVII, part 1, 182–89, 194–95.

28. March 11, 1752, ibid., p. 234.

29. March 13, 1752, ibid., p. 274.

documents, the House refused to read them, "it being the Opinion of this House that the Originals ought to have been sent. . . ."[30] From this point on the House refused to consider any message relating to Indian affairs until their demand had been met. Glen proved equally stubborn, and in the resulting deadlock the Assembly was adjourned to April 14.

In April the House met in a mood somewhat more cooperative. It passed the long-desired Indian Trade Law and also granted the governor his back rent, but the members continued adamant in their demand to see the original documents on Indian affairs. The necessity for settling the dispute was rendered more urgent by growing restlessness among the Cherokees over the government's failure to do anything about a recent Creek raid into the territory. Glen warned of an all-out Indian war unless something were done promptly, but the House seemed totally unconcerned. By unanimous resolution they took no action, claiming to be "kept much in the Dark, relating to Indian Affairs; and cannot help observing that they seldom have any Accounts of them unless money is wanted to carry into Execution some matter recommended by his Excellency."[31]

Facing a united and determined House, Glen realized that to accomplish anything he would have to yield, regardless of instructions. On May 5, he surrendered, sending down two letters from the Cherokee nation and excusing his capitulation thus: "I have therefore to save the time of copying sent the Originals which I desire you will return as soon as that Business is over."[32] Fully satisfied with its victory, the House promptly appropriated £3000 to build the fort. Before adjourning for the summer, however, they rejected another proposal from Glen, calling for a systematic survey of all the colony's fortifications.

Throughout the quarrel, the last important controversy between Governor Glen and the Commons House, Rawlins Lowndes was learning valuable lessons in how to resist Crown authority. At the same time he took careful note of another controversy which affected his interests more directly but commanded less attention

30. March 14, 1752, ibid., p. 255.
31. April 24, 29, May 1, 1752, ibid., XXVII, part 2, 370–71, 401–5, 417.
32. May 5, 1752, ibid., p. 444.

and evolved much more slowly. This was the growing demand for courts outside the capital. Within little more than a decade, the highly-centralized judicial and law enforcement systems would be joined with the issue of inadequate backcountry representation to create an intense sectional controversy. But during the early 1750s, the issue was not so much inadequate representation for the backsettlements as the lack of courts and law-enforcement machinery outside the capital. Lowcountry indifference to the growing needs of the backsettlements was becoming notorious. Repeated petitions had failed to liberalize the judicial system and attendant law enforcement. Finally on January 21, 1752, a House committee recommended that the House consider establishing county courts in the counties of Granville and Craven.[33] The lawyers and merchants in the House, as well as the provost marshal, were certainly not anxious to be put to the inconvenience of traveling to Georgetown or Beaufort for the trial of cases when the present system kept all such business in Charles Town, so nothing was done until April. Even then the House would only sanction a stop-gap measure, requesting the governor "to appoint Justices of the Peace in the distant Parts of this Province."[34] Speaker Andrew Rutledge went further, naming a committee of seven to bring in a bill establishing courts at Georgetown and Beaufort. A majority of the committee—the provost marshal, two lawyers and a Charles Town merchant—had nothing to gain and in fact stood to be greatly inconvenienced by a change in the system. Thus composed the committee failed to bring in a bill.[35] The district court movement was effectively blocked, but continuing agitation meant it was far from dead.

Before adjournment, Lowndes was accorded the highest honor he had yet received in the House. Along with Thomas Smith, Robert Pringle and George Saxby, he was named a commissioner "to stamp and sign the Sum of Twenty Thousand pounds in paper Bills of Credit" to be exchanged for old bills. Completion of the task would require two years, when in March 1754, with the old

33. January 21, 1752, ibid., XXVII, part 1, 125.
34. April 22, 1752, ibid., p. 344.
35. The committee included Lowndes, merchant John Dart and lawyers James Michie and James Parsons, April 22, 1752, ibid., pp. 343-44.

bills burnt and the new plates destroyed, he would stand with the other commissioners "in their places" and receive the thanks of the House.[36]

Through the summer of 1752 prospects for the rice harvest appeared quite promising until September when disaster hit the colony. On the night of September 14, the "most violent and terrible Hurricane that ever was felt in this province" struck South Carolina. With its center passing directly over Charles Town, the storm left in its wake a broad swath of death and incredible destruction throughout the lowcountry.[37] Provost Marshal Lowndes was responsible for co-ordinating efforts in the stricken capital to prevent wholesale looting following the storm; and a proclamation by Governor Glen enjoined the militia, the town watch, and all constables and magistrates to assist the marshal in maintaining order.[38] In addition to widespread destruction of homes, buildings, ships, and other property, more than half the rice harvest was destroyed along with much of the corn and other subsistence crops. The major effort of the legislators over the next six months would be directed toward securing enough food for the survival not only of the population but of the livestock as well.[39] During the same period numerous daily advertisements concerning attachments and sales by the provost marshal suggest the manner in which this disaster, like others before it, quickened the business of his office by bringing so many of his less fortunate friends and neighbors to economic ruin.[40]

The destruction wrought by the storm also provided the rationale for two proposals sent to the House when it was summoned into special session on September 27. By thoroughly wrecking the fortifications around Charles Town, the hurricane had furnished Governor Glen with the best possible argument for his proposed survey of fortifications and an integrated general plan for their reconstruction under the direction of John William Gerard De

36. February 27, 1754, ibid., XXIX, 148–49.
37. *South Carolina Gazette*, September 19, 1752.
38. Ibid.
39. *See* November 24, 1752; February 24, March 1, 2, 1753, Commons Journal, XXVIII, part 1, 13, 216–19, 265–66, 283–84.
40. *See South Carolina Gazette*, March 5, 26, April 2, May 7, 28, June 25, July 2, August 6, September 3, 1753.

Brahm, a skilled military engineer recently arrived in South Carolina. At the same time, Jacob Motte, possibly the most inept treasurer in the history of the colony, found in the general ruin left by the storm a convenient excuse for the near bankruptcy of his office and for calling on the House to assist him in maintaining the public credit. Besides the problem of finding enough food for the colony, the Assembly would be principally concerned with these two issues through the next few months. Among its members, Rawlins Lowndes had now moved up to the second rank of leadership and would assume a prominent role in handling these questions.

Governor Glen offered his recommendation for the fortifications survey on October 5, but the House had not had time to take it up when on the same day a petition from the provincial treasurer was read. Motte expressed gratitude for his appointment as Treasurer in 1743 and for the cooperation of the Assembly with his office since that time. Then he dropped the bombshell:

> And thinks himself obliged . . . to acquaint his Excellency and their Hon^rs. that the great loss which he sustained by the dreadful Hurricane, and some other unfortunate Incidents which happened before, have greatly reduced and impoverished the Memorialist, in so much that he thinks it absolutely necessary that his Accompts with the Public should be examined and settled, that a true state of the same may be known.[41]

The news, while alarming enough, could not have been entirely unexpected by members of the government acquainted with Motte's slipshod methods.[42] Both House and Council immediately appointed committees to devise means of meeting the fiscal emergency revealed by the treasurer. The next day Motte commenced refusing to honor tax certificates, seriously threatening the public credit. Both governor and Council urged the House to take immediate action "to prevent the Credit of these Certificates from sinking," only to be met by a request for adjournment. The House, its planter members obviously more concerned with salvaging what they could of the rice crop than the state of the public credit, complained of being "too bare" to come to any resolution so impor-

41. October 5, 1752, Commons Journal, XXVII, part 2, 609, 611–12.
42. On Motte's accounts, *see* ibid., XXVIII, part 1, 95 *ff.*

tant to their constituents. Their attitude so infuriated Glen that
he "washed his Hands of it," and adjourned the session to November.[43]

With the rice harvest in, less than half the usual amount and
selling at seventy shillings the hundredweight,[44] the Assembly reconvened on November 21, ready for business. The House promptly resolved to pay all tax certificates in case of a deficiency in
Motte's accounts and within three days had set up a trustee system
to settle the "Treasurer's Affair." Eight trustees, three from the
Council and five from the House, were authorized to take into
their possession all "Lands Tennements Goods and Chattels,
Rights and Credits whatsoever" belonging to Motte, and to sell
the same in order to reimburse the treasury in the full amount of
the shortage, £90,000; the surplus, if any, was to be returned to
Motte. The Council approved the plan and appointed as trustees
Charles Pinckney, Hector Berenger De Beaufain and William
Bull, Jr.; the House selected Gabriel Manigault, Thomas Smith,
John Savage, David Caw and Rawlins Lowndes. When Motte
signed all his possessions over to them on December 31, 1752, the
trustees declared themselves "ready and willing as well out of
Friendship to him . . . as out of their Zeal for the Publick Service to
take upon themselves [the trust] without any Reward or Compensation whatsoever for their trouble."[45]

This was not the only kindness extended by Lowndes and his
colleagues to the errant provincial treasurer. His appointment
and tenure were controlled by the House, but the members took
no thought of seeking his removal. On the contrary, they sympa-
thized with him and joined forces to help him keep his office.
Gabriel Manigault, upon resigning the office in 1743, had posted
a surety bond in the amount of £7000 sterling for the faithful execution of the office by his successor. When Motte revealed the true
condition of his affairs in 1752 and threw himself on the mercy
of the House, Manigault stood to lose a fortune if investigation
should reveal the treasurer to be bankrupt. Manigault now informed the treasurer that the risk was too great for one man to

43. October 7, 1752, ibid., XXVII, part 2, pp. 640–44.
44. *South Carolina Gazette*, November 20, 1752.
45. Charleston County Deeds NN, pp. 70–86, S.C. Archives.

stand alone and suggested he find others to assume the bond. Motte had surprisingly little difficulty in finding other backers. Twenty-six gentlemen came forward to assume the risk collectively. Rawlins Lowndes was the tenth to subscribe, bonding himself in the amount of £270 sterling.[46] By this act, Lowndes demonstrated that, although scrupulously honest himself and meticulous in keeping the records of his own office, he did not feel that the treasurer's conduct warranted his removal. Such lax standards of conduct were condoned by the Assembly as well. Thus Motte continued in office while the trustees labored over the next six years to settle his accounts.

While the treasurer was experiencing little difficulty in rallying friends to his support, Governor Glen found few in the House who could be persuaded to rally behind his grand plan for fortifications. Rawlins Lowndes served on two separate committees that dealt with the proposal. Both reported against it. Chairing one of the committees, Lowndes expressed their main objection to the governor's plan when he pointed out that the subject was the proper business of the Commissioners on Fortifications in whose hands he recommended it be placed according to the usual procedure.[47] The House agreed and rejected the governor's plan. The question was eventually disposed of when the Assembly voted to petition the Crown for funds to rebuild the colony's defenses.

The year 1753 witnessed a return of better relations between governor and Assembly. Glen did veto the annual tax bill when he found fault with its provision accepting Spanish coin in the payment of taxes, but the House struck out the offending clause without protest. In the House itself, Rawlins Lowndes continued his move toward the front rank of leadership. He was rarely absent from its daily sessions, and his conscientious and dependable service brought upon him an increasingly heavy burden of responsibility. Committee assignments in particular came to him with greater frequency. On four successive days in April, for example, he was named to a committee to encourage shipbuilding, to another on a proposed canal from Ashepoo Creek to Pon Pon in Colleton

46. November 25, 29, December 14, 1752; March 1, 2, 1753, Commons Journal, XXVIII, part 1, 34, 37, 52, 134, 275, 288–89.
47. December 7, 13, 1752, ibid., pp. 85–92, 93, 110–17, 124.

County, to a third to audit the account of the Commissary General, and to the standing committee on Indian Relations.[48] Nor were his responsibilities suspended when the assembly adjourned, for his work with the trustees of the public treasurer's estate and the commisioners for stamping and signing the new issue of currency was carried on between sessions throughout the year. But such were his talents and energy that Lowndes could discharge these various tasks to the complete satisfaction of the House leadership, carry on the booming business of the marshal's office and meet the demands of his Horseshoe plantation. The ambitious marshal was all too human, however, and in time his extensive activities began to take its toll on his health.

Lowndes was by no means unique in the extent of his activities or the variety of his interests. His example illustrates the rule rather than the exception. James Glen was probably the only man in the provincial government without other business interests. While others returned to their personal affairs, the governor utilized the intervals between sessions in 1753 to make two trips into the interior to cement relations with the Cherokees and build Fort Prince George on the Keowee River. In December Glen returned to Charles Town proud to announce the fort completed and garrisoned by twenty men.[49] The achievement had the desired effect, and quiet returned to the Cherokee frontier. Afterwards the governor's handling of Indian relations ceased to be a subject of controversy, and during the two remaining years of his administration he got along quite amicably with the provincial legislature.

As if to fill a need for continuous disputation the legislative session which opened on January 8, 1754, marked the beginning of an entirely new controversy between the House and the Council when they fell to quarreling among themselves over the office of the colonial agent. The dispute was touched off by a request from James Crokatt, the agent in London, to be relieved of his position.[50] The House urged him to continue in his post, but the Council accepted his resignation and moved to replace him. The

48. April 3, 4, 5, 6, 1753, ibid., XXVIII, part 2, 342, 348, 353, 358, 376–77.
49. *South Carolina Gazette*, December 17, 1753.
50. January 15, 1754, Commons Journal, XXIX, 12 ff.

House saw in the Council's action an invasion of the Assembly's power over the office, and a long and bitter dispute was under way.

Rawlins Lowndes attended the sessions with his usual regularity and consistently supported the prerogatives of the House, which achieved the expected unanimity in its contest with the Council. But as provost marshal, Lowndes was more directly concerned with the revival of the district court movement. He was again named to a committee to consider the subject. A recommendation from this committee on January 30 proposed "That Courts of Justice, to handle all Causes, Civil and Criminal, be established in Amelia Township, in George Town, and in some convenient place in Granville County."[51] In consultation with a committee from the Council details were worked out.

The results of these deliberations, reported to the House on February 26, 1754, were twenty-two proposals[52] whose adoption might have forestalled the Regulator Movement of the next decade. The first would establish three courts outside the Charles Town district: one at Georgetown, another at Beaufort and a third at "the Congarees" to serve the interior townships of Amelia and Orangeburg. The remainder spelled out the courts' jurisdictions and other details of operation similar to the Precinct Court Law of 1721. Certainly Lowndes took careful note of the sixth proposal which would oblige the provost marshal "to serve all process by himself or Deputy in the several Districts." This additional responsibility was not to go entirely uncompensated, as the sixteenth proposed "That Court Houses or Prisons be built at the public charge." Moreover, most cases and all appeals would still be heard in Charles Town: Number seven provided "That all processes be issued from the Court of Common Pleas in Charles Town and returnable before the Judges of that Court where the Defendant resides or the Judges of the Courts of Charles Town as the Plaintiff shall think fit." Without this provision, the bill's advocates knew it would have no chance of passage, since the merchants, who were the plaintiffs in most cases tried, could combine with the lawyers to defeat it.

Even with this compromise, opposition to the plan proved too

51. January 30, 1754, ibid., pp. 52–54.
52. February 26, 1754, ibid., pp. 137–38.

great to overcome. Introduced toward the close of the session, the District Court Bill passed its first two readings; but on its third reading on May 7, the House "Ordered that the further consideration of the said Bill be adjourned."[53] Lowndes may well have voted against the bill, since he and George Morley, the patentee, consistently acted to protect each other's interests in their respective spheres.

In the course of this session an unusual charge, one that could have been politically damaging, was brought against Lowndes in his capacity as provost marshal. During a brief recess in mid-February, attorney David Graeme brought suit against Thomas Wright, a member of the Commons House, and got one of Lowndes' deputy marshals to serve the writ. Service of the writ violated the immunity of members while the House was in session, and Wright brought complaint against both Graeme and Lowndes claiming a "Breach of Privilege." The charge was a serious one, for the Commons House was extremely jealous of its rights and privileges and zealous in the protection of its members. The matter was referred to the Committee on Privileges and Elections for their disposition. Despite Graeme's profuse apology and withdrawal of the suit, he was found guilty and given an official reprimand.[54]

Lowndes, on the other hand, stood his ground. At this stage of his promising political career he could ill afford to be reprimanded by his own colleagues for a violation of their rights. His testimony before the committee was not reported, but the breach was contrary to the scrupulous regard for procedure that he consistently observed. On March 2, the committee reported that "Mr. Wright and Mr. Lowndes differing in relating the Facts, and Mr. Lynch who was present being out of Town, Your Committee could not come to any Resolution on the Complaint against Mr. Lowndes."[55] The facts of the matter appear to have been in Lowndes' favor, for the missing witness shortly returned and nothing further was ever reported on the matter.

53. May 7, 1754, ibid., p. 337.
54. March 2, 1754, ibid., pp. 162, 164.
55. Ibid.

Lowndes was actually on the verge of giving up the office of provost marshal and his seat in the House as well, but for a more serious reason than the threat of censure. For some time now his health had been in decline, and he had decided on a voyage to England for its recovery. In addition, George Morley was trying to raise the rent above the £130 sterling paid annually for the office by his deputy. In correspondence with Morley, Lowndes informed him that the office would not support a higher rent and warned that if he insisted on having more he would have to find a new deputy.[56] John Guerard, a Charles Town merchant who had recently succeeded Charles Pinckney as Morley's agent in the colony, wrote Morley that if Lowndes resigned,

> . . . I should been at a Loss about Letting it to any other. I wish the Gentleman that wrote You of the Considerable advantage that accrued of Late to the Office had at the same time pointed out a Proper Person to farm it at a Larger Rent in Mr. Lowndes Stead that You would be Equally as Satis[fied with.] But Unless Such a One could be found beforehand it would have been attempted takeing it out of said Gentlemans hands, however, I was very glad to find You was willing to Lett it rest with him on the Terms he has Lately had it.[57]

Lowndes apparently intended to farm the office out to his brother Charles and resume its duties on returning from England. But when he learned that the office could not be executed by a deputy under him, he resigned.[58] Through an agreement with Guerard, Charles Lowndes became the new provost marshal of South Carolina on June 5, 1754.[59] A few days later Lowndes made his farewells, and accompanied only by his manservant Cato, boarded the London packet, the *Charming Nancy*, and set sail for England.[60] Considering the tragic fate of his first wife four

---

56. John Guerard to George Morley, June 8, 1754, The John Guerard Letterbook, SCHS.
57. Ibid.
58. Ibid.
59. Miscellaneous Records, KK, p. 22, S.C. Archives.
60. Ibid. Guerard wrote, "This goes per Capt. White in whom said Mr. Lowdens [*sic*, elsewhere clearly identified as "Rawlins Lowndes"] imbargues for the Recovery of his Health . . . ." *The South Carolina Gazette*, June 11,

years earlier, of all the facts gleaned from the extant record of his life, the timing of his departure strikes the most discordant note, for Mary was seven months pregnant when her husband departed for England.

1754, states,"Sailed since our last . . . the Charming Nancy, [William] White, for London . . . ."

CHAPTER V

To the Front Rank

Hᴵˢ ˢᴏᴊᴏᴜʀɴ in England kept Rawlins Lowndes away from home for eighteen months, from June 1754 to December 1755. During most if not all of that period he kept a journal in which he made daily entries recording his activities and expenditures. Only a portion of the journal has survived, beginning with the entry of October 10, 1754, and ending on February 16, 1755.[1] Although incomplete and the daily entries quite brief, the journal nonetheless permits the tracing of his activities while in London and affords some insight into the man himself.

In the house of a Mr. Smith, within walking distance of Kensington Gardens and Hyde Park, Lowndes took "rooms" sufficient for himself, Cato and an occasional guest. For the improvement of his health he placed himself under the care of Doctor John Fothergill. His doctor prescribed rest, relaxation, mild exercise, and pills. Lowndes complained that the pills were ineffective, but his frequent walks in the park and surrounding neighborhood had a beneficial effect, and his health gradually improved. A Mr. Beresford, perhaps Richard Beresford of St. Thomas and St. Dennis Parish in Carolina, who had served in the Assembly with Lowndes in 1749, also lodged at Mr. Smith's. The two friends

---

1. This document in the William Lowndes Papers, Southern Historical Collection, University of North Carolina, Chapel Hill, N.C., is erroneously listed as the diary of Charles Lowndes, who, we now know, executed the office of provost marshal while his brother Rawlins went to England. There is nothing in the journal itself to identify the author positively as either Charles or Rawlins, but other evidence above and below proves that it was the latter. All information concerning his residence in London is taken from this journal, the pages of which are not numbered. (Hereafter cited Lowndes Journal.)

spent many a winter evening together playing cards or backgammon in Lowndes' quarters, sharing their joint stock of liquors with mutual friends from Carolina, who spent an occasional evening with them.

Their circle of friends was large enough, consisting mostly of fellow Carolinians then resident in London for one reason or another. Lowndes mentions in his journal the representatives of more than two dozen prominent Carolina families. These included the Charles Pinckneys, the William Middletons, John Drayton and his son William Henry, young Arthur Middleton, the George Bellingers, Samuel Brailsford, the John Watsones, the Jermyn Wrights, Edmund Atkin, the Thomas Corbetts and James Abercromby. Within this group, Lowndes established close friendships with John Watsone and Samuel Brailsford. Watsone was a former Charles Town merchant who had brought his family to London in 1750 to reside there while his children attended English schools. Lowndes saw the Watsones almost daily for dinner and the theatre followed by a round of cards, the chief entertainment of Carolinians in London. After his return to Carolina, Lowndes acted as Watsone's attorney in handling several of his business affairs.[2] Brailsford, the partner of Thomas Middleton in a mercantile firm, was, like Lowndes, without a wife in London, and the two were frequent companions at the various dinners, plays and card parties.

Conscious of the deficiencies of his provincial education, Lowndes took advantage of the opportunities for self-improvement that his temporary residence in London afforded. He visited Parliament from time to time to see the imperial government in operation and toured the usual points of interest in the metropolis. More ambitiously, he undertook the study of French, but soon found the effort too demanding. Securing the services of a French master, on October 15 he "Began to learn French and took the first Lesson, paid for instruction a Guinea, and a half a Guinea for Books. . . ." Daily thereafter, like a diligent student, he pursued his studies in the language of diplomacy. His provincial training never having exposed him to the subtleties of grammati-

2. See Charleston County Deeds, VV, pp. 411–25; Savannah, Georgia, *Georgia Gazette*, October 18, 1764.

cal construction,³ he found the going increasingly difficult: "[October] 22d. Another lesson in French, staid home all day studying." After two weeks of daily lessons, his determination began to flag, and he "desired the Master to come every other day only...."⁴ But even the slower pace could not be maintained. On November 14, citing the press of other business, he suspended the lessons briefly; then on December 4, he discharged the French master, "not intending for some time at least to employ him any more." The lessons were never resumed.

By this time Lowndes had established a fairly regular daily routine. He usually had breakfast in his rooms with Beresford or Cato (followed by his French lessons as long as they lasted) and then took a walk in the park. In the afternoon he went "into the city" on business or to read the papers and meet friends for dinner and cards at one of the Carolinians' favorite coffee houses. The Bedford was preferred for its fare, but to post mail for Carolina or to get news from home Lowndes always went to the Carolina Coffee House. Evenings usually found him with friends at Drury Lane or Covent Garden enjoying the works of Shakespeare, Sheridan, Beaumont and Fletcher, and lesser lights of the world of English drama as interpreted by David Garrick, "Mrs. Cibber" and a host of other London players. Afterwards one of the Carolinians would usually invite the others to his lodgings for supper and a round of cards.

By November Lowndes was well enough to enter fully into the social life of his friends in London. The following entries are typical of the record he left of their activities:

Nov. 3d. Dined by invitation of Mr. Brailsford at the Bedford ... no other company with us but his two Female Cousins, wore my New Bagg Wigg brot home to day, after Dinner went together and walked in Sommerset's Gardens. . . .

Nov. 13 . . . Dined by Agreemᵗ in Ordinary in Lancaster Court, Northumberland Coffee house mostly Beef & half pint of Wine, per 1/5 . . . Mr. Pinckney, Mʳ Drayton & his son, Mr. Middleton, Mr. Abercromby, Mr. Brailsford, Mr, Beresford Mr. Atkins & myself. . . . Mr. Pinckney insisted on our going to drink a bott[le] of

3. *See* below, Chapter VII, at footnotes 52 and 53.
4. Lowndes Journal, October 29, 1754.

Madiera which Mr. Drayton, Mr. [George] Morley, Mr. Beresford
& myself (being all the Company that was left) did and supped there,
the principal Conversation related to Mr Drayton's courtship, Mr
Morley and Drayton very mellow.

[Nov] 19th . . . Dined with Mr Watsone about 4 o Clock Mr & Mrs
Watsone, Miss Betsey and Myself went to the play at Drury Lane the
Chances; a very thronged house, his Majesty there, saw Mr Corbett
& his Wife, Mr Middleton & his wife and Mr Brailsford. . . .

Assuming that he continued to attend the theater throughout
his stay in London, Lowndes must have been quite well versed
in English drama by the time he returned to Carolina.

Lowndes' daily routine was sometimes interrupted by more
serious matters. On October 25 Beresford sent Lowndes word that
he had been arrested for debt by "Old Crips." Lowndes went immediately to "the Springing house" to arrange bail for his friend.
Evidently Beresford's neglect of financial affairs did not improve,
for less than two weeks later he was arrested again, at home, by
two men disguised as tradesmen, requiring Lowndes once more
to arrange his bail.[5] Much more serious were the interruptions
occasioned by illness, especially when one of the group contracted
the smallpox. Mrs. Whitehead came down with the dreaded disease
in November but survived the ordeal. A few days later Cato
alarmed his master, complaining of violent headache and stom-
ach sickness, "but it went off. . . ."[6] George Bellinger was not so
fortunate. He caught the infection in mid-October, lingered for
two weeks and died on October 29. During his illness his Carolina
friends did all they could to assist Mrs. Bellinger, and when he
died she depended on Watsone and Lowndes to handle the funeral
arrangements. On November 1 the funeral took place at St. Margaret's Church, Westminster, with Lowndes leading the melancholy procession "as Chief Mourner and the rest two and two into
the Church where [the body] was interred in the Middle Isle on
his Mother's Coffin. . . ."[7] For the widow Bellinger as well as
Lowndes and several others in the group, their Carolina friends
were the nearest thing to family that they had in London.

5. Ibid., November 8, 1754.
6. Ibid., November 18, 20, 1754.
7. Ibid., October 30, 31, November 1, 1754.

If Lowndes was deeply affected by the long and distant separation from his own family, his journal does not show it; nor does the record contain any suggestion that he ever met or attempted to contact any of his distant relatives then living in England. He rarely mentioned his family and never revealed his feelings toward them in the journal. The entries merely recorded the receipt of letters from his wife or his brother in Carolina and his correspondence to them and to his mother, who had since returned home to St. Kitts. He recorded in mid-December the purchase of several gifts for his wife, mostly fine linens and lace and a French prayer book.[8] Although Mrs. Lowndes had given birth to their first child, Amarinthia, less than two months after her husband sailed for England, the journal's only reference to his daughter was on December 20 when Lowndes wrote that Watsone had showed him a childs' dress that "he Intended for a present to my Child in Carolina."[9] It might be well to note here that the record was not intended to be a diary but a factual journal and account book in which expressions of sentiment would normally be considered out of place. Lowndes reserved virtually all matters concerning his family life to the privacy of family correspondence, none of which has survived.

The journal also offers some very rare clues to Lowndes' style of dress and physical appearance. He was a tall man, dignified and reserved in manner, but beyond that no reliable physical description of him has been found.[10] By affording a glimpse of his wardrobe, the London journal helps to correct this deficiency.[11] Preparing for a November trip to Bath with Brailsford, Lowndes secured a tailor in old Soho, was fitted for a new "Suit of Cloathes," and bought "6 yds $\frac{1}{4}$ of Gold Lace [ornamentation] for a Waistcoat a [for] 7/6 and carried it to my Taylor."[12] On November 26

8. Ibid., January 17, 1755.
9. Ibid., December 20, 1754.
10. Richard Barry, *Mr. Rutledge of South Carolina* (New York, 1942), p. 242, states on no apparent authority that Lowndes was a small man. Lowndes described himself simply as "a *tall white man*." See, *South Carolina Gazette and Country Journal*, March 23, 1769 (Supplement).
11. On the other hand, Barry's description of Lowndes in "bright yellow small clothes," Barry, *Rutledge*, p. 242, seems to be supported by the evidence below.
12. Lowndes Journal, November 15, 18, 1754.

he made a "Memorandum of Cloaths packed for Bath." The list included "a New Suit of Cloaths, a Brown Cloath Coat, 2 Laced Jackets, 12 Clean Shirts, 5 Clean Stocks [cravats], 4 foul New Shirts, 5 dirty Stocks, 2 pr of Clean Drawers, a Cloak, 5 Handkerchiefs, 9 pr. Stockings . . . a Bagg Wigg, a Sword and Belt. . . ." Somewhat later he bought more cloth and "Ruffles for Shirts," black worsted stockings and an overcoat.[13] Dressed in ruffled shirt, worsted stockings, London tailored suit and lace-trimmed small clothes, powdered wig, sword and belt, the tall and dignified Lowndes was a fine figure of an eighteenth-century gentleman.

The planned excursion to Bath never took place. It was canceled when William Middleton invited Lowndes and Brailsford to spend the Christmas holidays at Crowfield, Middleton's country estate in Suffolk. They accepted, but before leaving, Lowndes settled accounts with Beresford and "tossed up for the remainder of our stock of liquor." Beresford won it and they parted.[14] On December 22 Lowndes "set out with young Mr. Drayton . . . in a Post Chays" through the wintry English landscape, arriving at Crowfield the following night.[15] He left no record of the holiday festivities or his impressions of Crowfield, but to have a "Crowfield" of his own in Carolina became a fixed ambition of Rawlins Lowndes.

Following his return to London on January 5, 1755, Lowndes resumed the now familiar routine of dinners, plays, and card parties, but he also began to devote more attention to business affairs. He was especially interested in the London indigo market. Apparently encouraged by the interest shown in two small samples of Carolina indigo he had taken to a dyer in November, he had sent for a barrel of the dyestuff. When it arrived in late January, Lowndes carried samples to dyers in the city. Despite the outbreak of war with France the previous summer, Lowndes found them using French indigo "of a rich coppery color." They told him they had experimented with the Carolina product "about a year ago" but did not find it very good and had not used it "for sometime

13. Ibid., November 26, 27, 29, December 13, 1754.
14. Ibid., November 26, 28, 1754.
15. Ibid., December 22, 1754.

past."[16] He failed to record their opinion of his samples, but his knowledge of the London indigo market would prove quite valuable after his return to Carolina.

The record ends in February, although Lowndes continued in London through the summer of 1755, avoiding for another year the "sickly seasons" of Carolina. In October he and Cato took passage on the *Fair American* for home. The voyage was made apparently without incident despite the ever-present threat of French warships and privateers. On December 11 the *Gazette* announced the arrival of Rawlins Lowndes and his fellow passengers "all in good Health."[17]

Leaving Lowndes aboard the *Fair American* for the moment, it may be well to make one or two observations regarding his sojourn in England, for the bare facts have more to tell than he recorded in the pages of his journal. His stated purpose for going, for example, was simply the recovery of his health, but the length of his stay and his activities there suggest additional reasons for the lengthy excursion. His health does not seem to have seriously bothered him after a few weeks in London. His undertaking the study of French only to discover that languages require long and patient study in addition to mastery of his own is equally suggestive. The same might be said of his other activities: his constant attendance on the plays and, not at all incidentally, studying the commanding presence and impressive delivery of David Garrick; his visits to Parliament where he could study the great men of England in action;[18] his scuttling plans to take the waters at

16. Ibid., November 4, 5, 1754; January 22, 1755.

17. *South Carolina Gazette*, December 11, 1755. The date of arrival was December 7.

18. Carolinians studying law in England were advised to observe David Garrick and outstanding members of Parliament in order to improve their own elecution and oratory in preparation for political careers. *See* John Rutledge to Edward Rutledge, July 30, 1769; John B. O'Neall, *Biographical Sketches of the Bench and Bar of South Carolina*, 2 vols. (Charleston, S.C., 1859), II, pp. 120–27; Maurice A. Crouse, "The Manigault Family of South Carolina, 1685–1783" (Ph.D. dissertation, Northwestern University, 1966), pp. 121, 136; *see also* Marvin R. Zahniser, *Charles Cotesworth Pinckney* (Chapel Hill, N.C., 1967), pp. 11–20; George C. Rogers, Jr., *Evolution of a Federalist: William Loughton Smith of Charleston, 1758–1812* (Columbia, S.C., 1962), pp. 80, 82, 90–95. On the

Bath in favor of participating in the holiday festivities at an English country estate; the obvious pride with which he purchased clothing in the latest London fashion for Mrs. Lowndes and himself, "wore my new Bagg Wigg brot home to day."

The trip to England can be better understood when viewed in the perspective of South Carolina society of the 1750s. Up to the middle of the eighteenth century the most obvious characteristic of this society was its acquisitiveness. The previous generation respected men of talent, character, and industry, especially those who could acquire wealth and status, and elected them to positions of political leadership. The founders of the Rutledge family of South Carolina, Doctor John Rutledge and his brother Andrew, an outstanding lawyer, discovered this when they arrived shortly after 1730, married wealth (the Sarahs Hext, mother and daughter), and moved readily into lowcountry society and political prominence.[19] Lowndes had also profited from this general attitude and the opportunities available to him. By 1754 he had established a solid reputation for character and integrity, built a comfortable fortune and reached the second rank of leadership in the Commons House.

By mid-century, however, the society had begun to mature and the nature of its self-image to change. An essay on "the properest Method of absterging the Posteriors" would have been as much out of place among the founders of the Charleston Library Society, and among the gentlemen who voted to erect a new State House for the more appropriate housing of their dignified proceedings, as the anonymous author who penned the frivolous piece a generation earlier.[20] A new generation of Rutledges, Pinckneys, Middletons, Draytons, and Manigaults was emerging, for the most part born to wealth, educated in England, and taking on the pretentions of aristocratic status. Culture and polish were becom-

---

study of French as a mark of "polite accomplishment," *see* Frederick P. Bowes, *The Culture of Early Charleston* (Chapel Hill, 1942)), pp. 46–47.

19. Richard B. Clow, "Edward Rutledge of South Carolina, 1749–1800: Unproclaimed Statesman" (Ph.D. dissertation, University of Georgia, 1976), chapter I.

20. *South Carolina Gazette*, July 14, 1733; Sirmans, *Colonial South Carolina*, p. 182.

ing more important. These were characteristics conspicuously
lacking in Lowndes who had had little opportunity to acquire
them. Ambitious for higher status and recognition among his
peers, he utilized the opportunity afforded by a recuperative
voyage to England to correct the deficiency with some success.

That his closest friends in London were two merchants, Watsone and Brailsford, is another fact that should not be overlooked;
for after his return home he developed an otherwise implausibly
firm friendship with the classically educated and democratically
minded merchant, Christopher Gadsden. Henry Laurens also held
Lowndes in particular regard, judging from occasional remarks
scattered through the great Charles Town merchant's voluminous
correspondence of succeeding decades.[21] These were all essentially
self-made men, who knew the value of integrity and wasted much
of their income protecting themselves from men who could not be
trusted. Such considerations would have a distinct tendency to
effect political alliances in the years ahead.

War between England and France had broken out in the colonies during Lowndes' absence, but he found little evidence of it
on his arrival in Charles Town. It is true that the long-expected
arrival of a new governor, William Henry Lyttelton, had been
delayed again owing to his capture by a French squadron; and
four transports loaded with Acadians from Nova Scotia rode anchor in Rebellion Road.[22] Otherwise little had changed. James
Glen, still occupying the governor's office, was engaged more deeply
than ever in his fortification schemes, now promoting the construction of Fort Loudoun deep in the Cherokee country. The old
quarrel between the House and Council, far from being settled,
was still going on amid growing bitterness on both sides. In contrast to the colony's economic stagnation during King George's
War, the provincial economy was only slightly injured by the renewal of hostilities with France. Indigo production was actually
stimulated as the war continued to reduce the French supply.

21. *See* especially Henry Laurens to Rawlins Lowndes, August 5, 9, 1778,
Letterbook no. 11 (March 6–September 23, 1778), South Carolina Historical
Society, Charleston, S.C. (The microfilm edition of these letterbooks is cited
hereafter as Henry Laurens Papers, microfilm, SCHS.)

22. *South Carolina Gazette*, December 4, 11, 1755.

With business-as-usual in Charles Town and prices steady in the rice market, the war seemed far away indeed.

His health restored and his mind free from the pressure of public responsibilities for the first time in a decade, Lowndes could devote full attention to his private affairs. He certainly familiarized himself with the latest developments in provincial politics, but he did not reenter public life for another twenty months. The freedom from public cares offered Lowndes a rare opportunity to indulge himself with his family. We may be sure that Amarinthia soon became well acquainted with the father she had never before seen, and that the curiosity of Mrs. Lowndes concerning such things as her husband could tell her about London life and fashion was at least partially satisfied. His planting interests, of course, required most of Lowndes' attention during this period, especially the clearing of new lands for indigo. Rice continued to be his most important crop but, despite the failure of the indigo crop of 1756,[23] Lowndes continued to expand production each year until he was listed in 1762 among "the considerable planters of indico."[24] He was now operating two thriving plantations, the Horseshoe in Colleton County and another at Goose Creek, 3420 acres.[25]

As his affairs prospered into the 1760s Rawlins Lowndes came into his own, emerging as one of the colony's foremost citizens. He purchased in 1762 a suitable home, paying £7000 for a "Capital Mansion" located on a huge lot on the south side of West Tradd Street.[26] An active layman in the Anglican church, he was named in 1764 to the board of vestrymen for St. Michael's, the parish that was carved out of St. Philip's in 1751. The following year he was extended the same honor by the parishioners of St. Philip's.[27] In both cases Lowndes assumed the vestryman's responsibility

23. Henry Laurens to John Knight, May 28, 1756, Henry Laurens Papers, microfilm, SCHS.

24. *South Carolina Gazette*, September 25, 1762.

25. Ibid., December 9, 1756; Quit Rents, Receipts and Disbursements, 1760–1768, Part I, p. 104, S.C. Archives.

26. Charleston County Deeds, ZZ, pp. 574–78, S.C. Archives. For a sketch of this house made in 1796 see Alice R. Huger Smith, ed., *A Charleston Sketchbook 1796–1800 by Charles Fraser* (Rutland, Vermont, 1959), plate no. 2. The original high-hipped roof was altered in shape after fire damage.

27. *South Carolina Gazette*, October 8, 1764, April 13, 1765.

for local government in the capital city. In the meantime he was expanding his business activities to include investments in real estate and money loaned at interest. By the end of the decade he had added 3800 acres to his land holdings in the lowcountry parishes, held a warrant for 7300 acres in Georgia, and owned at least three houses and other property in the city as well as slaves in numbers sufficient to operate his Goose Creek and Horseshoe plantations.[28] His income at this time can be reasonably estimated as ranging between £15,000 and £20,000, current money, annually[29]

The success of Lowndes' private interests paralleled his move into the top echelon of political leadership in the colony. He was recommended for a position on the Council in 1760 but never sat on the board.[30] An incident back in 1756 had destroyed the Council's prestige. After Governor Lyttelton finally arrived he settled the long-standing dispute between House and Council, then summarily removed from the Council William Wragg, its most outspoken member. When Wragg's removal was upheld by the Lords of Trade the Council's prestige withered.[31] Afterwards several other members resigned, and native colonials such as Lowndes refused membership in the Upper House. The Council thus degenerated into a refuge of placemen from England, while the influence and prestige of the House increased markedly.

Lowndes' rise to preeminence in the House over the next few years was due first to his diligent service and later to his leadership

28. For his land holdings and investments of this decade *see*, in addition to the sources cited above, Charleston County Deeds, B3, pp. 49–55; South Carolina Colonial Plats, vol. 9, p. 61; Judgement Rolls, 1758, no. 6A; ibid., 1766, no. 194A, no. 273A; ibid., 1767, no. 493A; ibid., 1768, no. 21A, no. 327A; ibid., 1770, no. 78A, all in S.C. Archives. On April 5 and May 3, 1763, Governor Thomas Boone granted warrants for lands south of the Altamaha River totaling 513,600 acres, the largest of which was a warrant issued to Rawlins Lowndes for 7,300 acres. The further disposition of this warrant apparently is not a matter of record. *See* Shelburne Papers, vol. 49, p. 239, William L. Clements Library, Ann Arbor, Michigan; SCCJ, May 3, 1763, XXIV, p. 56; Leila Sellers, *Charleston Business on the Eve of the American Revolution* (Chapel Hill, N.C., 1934), p. 42.

29. See details quoted below in Chapter XI, at footnote 11.

30. Sirmans, *Colonial South Carolina*, pp. 310–13.

31. William Bull to Lords of Trade, July 2, 1760, SCPRO, XXVIII, 370–71; Rogers, *Evolution of a Federalist*, p. 38.

in disputes with the royal governors and the Council of placemen. He reentered the Commons as a representative of St. Bartholomew's parish in October 1757 and moved toward the front rank of House leadership, his three years sabbatical notwithstanding. A suggestion of the larger role Lowndes intended to play as well as the portent of a future rivalry with young Peter Manigault was evident on the first day of the session. When the House unanimously chose Benjamin Smith as Speaker, both Lowndes and Manigault rose from their seats and escorted Smith to the speaker's chair. Manigault was the only son of the enormously wealthy Gabriel Manigault. He had been educated in England before entering the House in 1755, and was a natural leader who would within a very few years rival Lowndes for the speakership.[32]

The special committees to which Lowndes was appointed in 1757 serve as an index to the special problems brought on by the war. One took up a petition from the church wardens of St. Philip's Parish, overburdened by the hundreds of transported Acadians in the city, who depended for survival on public charity.[33] Another committee sought to determine the best method of distributing Indian presents to maintain friendly relations with the Creeks and Cherokees now sending delegations to the provincial capital.[34] A third wrestled with the problem of how to encourage enlistments in the South Carolina Regiment.[35] His fourth assignment was to a committee charged with finding quarters for 1700 British regulars recently arrived in Charles Town.[36]

This session ran on for seven months without finding really satisfactory solutions to any of these problems. Virtually nothing was done to alleviate the problems posed by the concentration of Acadians in the city; and had it not been for the assistance provided by Gabriel Manigault and other charitable citizens many more of the refugees would have died.[37] The matter of Indian

32. October 7, 1757, Commons Journal, CO5/474, p. 4, microfilm, S.C. Archives; on Peter Manigault see Crouse, "Manigault Family," pp. 139–49.

33. November 18, 1757, Commons Journal, CO5/474, p. 32, microfilm, S.C. Archives.

34. November 16, 1757, ibid., p. 28.

35. May 3, 1758, ibid., p. 191.

36. October 12, 1757, ibid., p. 12.

37. July 16, 1760, ibid., CO5/473, pp. 337–38.

presents was postponed to a later session. To help fill the ranks of the South Carolina Regiment, Lowndes introduced and pushed through a bill "impowering Magistrates to inlist Vagrants" in the regiment, hardly a solution though an acceptable expedient.[38] His committee on the quartering problem recommended the construction of new barracks to accommodate one thousand men, but progress was so slow that the issue flared into an angry dispute between Col. Henry Bouquet and Governor Lyttelton. The barracks were finally completed in February, just in time for seven companies of troops to be withdrawn from the colony, relieving the housing problem.[39] The tax bill, with Lowndes serving on the committee that framed it, was this session's only important contribution to the war effort. Before adjourning in May 1758, the Assembly voted more than £166,000, most of it earmarked for military expenditures.[40]

Thus far the House had got on rather well with Governor Lyttelton, who had compiled an impressive record since his arrival in the colony. Besides settling the long-standing legislative dispute and reducing the Council to obedience, he completed the construction of Fort Loudoun. But while the House might grant unprecedented sums for the war effort, it would quarrel over small change where its rights were concerned. The first issue developed in the next session over a bill submitted by James Laurens and Co. for supplies furnished for the use of Georgia. The committee on the public debt was supported by the House in twice rejecting the bill, feeling that Georgia should pay it. When Lyttelton went ahead and paid the bill out of the contingency account, the House bristled. Rawlins Lowndes, speaking for his colleagues, insisted on "the Right and Authority of this House to judge of the Propriety and Legality of Demands against the Public. . . ."[41] The House agreed and forthwith cut from its appropriation for the contingency fund the amount of the bill, directing Lyttelton to seek compensation from Georgia. The governor let the matter stand, explaining that his action had been required by the urgent

38. May 9, 1758, ibid., CO5/474, p. 196.
39. October 13, 14, 21, 1757, ibid., pp. 14, 15, 25.
40. January 17, May 19, 1758, ibid., pp. 56, 225.
41. December 8, 1758, ibid., CO5/475, pp. 33-34.

necessity for the stores in question. He avoided another potential dispute in April 1759, when the House followed the recommendation of another committee headed by Lowndes and rejected Lyttelton's proposal for a new powder magazine.[42]

Two other actions touched on controversies, one about to close, another about to begin. In terms of future controversy, the most significant piece of legislation passed this session was a new election law which enlarged the qualifications of electors and their representatives.[43] Its significance, however, would not be realized for some time to come. On the old controversy, a few days before the session ended Lowndes reported that the "Treasurer's Affair" dating back to 1752 had been finally settled. He informed the House, "at the Desire of the said Trustees," that they had completed their task and balanced the treasurer's books. How little treasurer Motte had learned from the affair was revealed when he died in office in 1770 owing the colony some £124,000.[44]

In the summer of 1759, growing troubles on the Cherokee frontier reached a crisis when communications with Fort Loudoun were cut off. Governor Lyttelton hastily summoned the Assembly into emergency session in July to prepare for war. The assembled House thoroughly disappointed the bellicose governor by voting not only against a punitive campaign but also to disband the South Carolina Regiment. They would only consent to send two companies of rangers, forty-four men, to protect the frontier, while the Assembly adjourned for the summer. Still determined to lead an expedition against the Cherokees, Lyttelton called another emergency session in October when parties of hostile Cherokees began to press the garrisons of both forts in their nation. Now the House, with Lowndes and Manigault serving as usual on its most influential committees, agreed to supply funds for the expedition but cautioned Lyttelton against a declaration of war. The funds voted were a good deal less than the governor had asked for, provoking Lyttelton into a curt message of adjournment on October 13 before he set off into the interior.[45]

42. April 4, 1759, ibid., pp. 199, 214.
43. November 29, December 6, 1758; April 7, 1759, ibid., pp. 14, 27–28, 227.
44. April 4, 1759, ibid., pp. 225–26.
45. *See* July 5 to October 13, 1759; ibid., CO5/473, pp. 7–53, *passim.*

Three months later, in January 1760, Lyttelton returned to the capital proclaiming his expedition a success. Actually he had made a shambles of the delicate relations with the Cherokees, violating his word by holding hostage a delegation after having guaranteed them safe conduct, placing full blame on the Indian nation and demanding the eventual surrender of two dozen Cherokees for execution.[46] A full-scale Indian war erupted along the Cherokee frontier almost as soon as Lyttelton returned. He hurried off a request to General Jeffrey Amherst for military assistance and again called the General Assembly into emergency session on February 4.

The House convened on the sixth and proceeded immediately to select a committee of five—Rawlins Lowndes, Peter Manigault and three other members—not to deal with the crisis but to rebuke Lyttelton for his curt censure of the House at the late adjournment.[47] The committee charged Lyttelton with "a Violation of that most essential Privilege" belonging to the House, "free Liberty of Speech to propose and debate any Matter according to Order and Parliamentary Usage," and gave him fair warning that "we never shall implicitly or against our Judgment comply with any demand made upon the Public even though we were sure of incurring your Excellency's censure."[48]

Lowndes himself carried the message up to Lyttelton the next day, but once again the governor declined to quarrel. He merely reported on the expedition and urged support for the war effort but otherwise remained silent. Having had its say, the House turned its attention to the twin plagues of war and pestilence, for the smallpox was raging among the Acadians in Charles Town.[49] One week later Lyttelton received appointment to the governorship of Jamaica. Within seven weeks more he had sailed from Carolina, leaving affairs in the very capable hands of Lieutenant Governor William Bull, Jr.[50]

46. Sirmans, *Colonial South Carolina*, pp. 333–34.

47. February 6, 1760, Commons Journal. CO5/473, p. 56, microfilm, S.C. Archives.

48. February 6, 1760, ibid., p. 56.

49. February 7, 14, 1760, ibid., pp. 57–60, 85.

50. March 11, July 17, 1760, ibid., pp. 95, 340. In a message of July 17, 1760, Lieutenant Governor Bull stated that Lyttelton left on April 4, 1760.

After the Cherokee War was under way and Lyttelton had left the colony, the Commons House and the governor's office reversed positions on the Indian war. Bull was considerably less bellicose than his predecessor and favored a defensive war. By contrast, leaders of the House, once the war had begun, abandoned dilatory tactics and urged the "severest Chastisement" of the Cherokees. Even before Lyttelton departed, the House had agreed to send a thousand men to relieve Fort Prince George, offered a bounty for each Cherokee scalp taken, and threatened to sell captives into West Indian slavery.[51] Not a few members resigned to take up arms against the Indians. Even so, the war was not easily won. Two more years, each featuring a major military campaign into the Cherokee country, would be required to restore peace on the Carolina frontier.

Over these next two years Rawlins Lowndes was largely concerned with the problems of financing the war effort. It is doubtful if anyone in the Commons House played a more significant role than he did in providing ways and means during 1760 and 1761. He chaired a variety of committees which dealt with virtually every phase of the legislative process involved in colonial finance. In April 1760 he presided over the Committee of the Whole that made the decision to issue public orders in meeting the emergency.[52] In June he delivered the report of another committee which calculated the cost of "the late Expedition" and added it to the annual tax bill.[53] He served on another in July that voted nearly a third of a million pounds to defray the cost of prosecuting the war in 1760 and laid on real estate and personal property a tax to retire the bills in five years.[54] He headed the commission charged with stamping and signing the public orders, reported the task completed six months later and shared the responsibility for seeing the old bills burned as they were retired from circulation.[55] He also helped write a bill that would have armed 500 blacks for the war effort had the House not struck down the measure.[56] By the time the Cherokee

51. February 9, 1760, ibid., pp. 68–70.
52. April 28, 1760, ibid., pp. 155–57.
53. June 18, July 9, 10, 1760, ibid., pp. 297, 319–20.
54. July 15, 16, 1760, ibid., pp. 326–27.
55. April 25, May 23, June 16, 1761, ibid., CO5/479, pp. 98, 154.
56. May 20, 1761, ibid., p. 74.

leaders sued for peace in August 1761, the Commons House had voted well over £600,000 to meet the extraordinary expenses incurred by the war.

One item in the tax bill for 1761, not at all related to the war effort, reveals perhaps more about Lowndes' influence and recognized position of leadership than any other. Former governor James Glen had never been reimbursed for "considerable sums" he had advanced for the public service while in office. He drew up an account of these expenditures and prevailed upon Lowndes to introduce his petition for reimbursement in the House. The confidence was well-placed. Lowndes persuaded a House committee to recommend the full amount petitioned for, £1084 sterling. But since Glen had also petitioned the Crown for reimbursement, the House decided their grant should be limited to £500 sterling.[57] The decision was a fair one, giving Glen no cause to doubt the wisdom of having placed the matter in Lowndes' charge.

Quarrels between the House and Council, which seemed endemic to the legislative process in South Carolina, yielded to the spirit of cooperation through most of the war, then flared briefly in the spring of 1761. The dispute made little difference so far as the war was concerned, since Colonel James Grant's summer expedition broke the heart of Cherokee resistance, and peace negotiations were soon under way. Nor did Rawlins Lowndes take a very active part in the events of that spring and summer, possibly owing to a recent recurrence of his old illness.[58] He did not even appear at the brief September session where his colleagues reluctantly agreed to drop their demands for the execution of several chiefs as a condition of peace, thus paving the way for the final peace agreements of December.

A turning point in South Carolina history came in December 1761 with the arrival of the new royal governor, Thomas Boone. An arrogant ex-governor of New Jersey, Boone came to personify many of the worst features of royal government in the colonies. He was imperious in his behavior toward the colonials, con-

57. April 29, May 1, 8, 1761, ibid., pp. 52–53, 59, 69.
58. The House on June 13, 1761, "ordered that Mr. Lowndes have leave to [be] absent from the Service of this House for the Reestablishment of his Health," June 13, 1761, ibid., p. 152.

temptuous of the rights of their legislature, high-handed in his disregard of traditional courtesies extended to the Assembly, and stubbornly reckless of the consequences. A resounding clash with the Commons House, notoriously jealous of its powers and capable of displaying in their defense as much arrogance, stubbornness, and highhanded behavior as any royal governor, was inevitable. The clash, when it came, was touched off by a dispute over the election of Christopher Gadsden and developed into a monumental controversy involving the fundamental right of the House to control its own membership. But it did not come immediately.

Governor Boone was in South Carolina nine months before the famous Gadsden election controversy erupted. His first official act was to announce on December 26 the disallowance of the election act of 1759 and the dissolution of the Assembly which the disallowance made necessary. New elections held the following February under the old law of 1721 returned essentially the same membership to the House, with one notable exception: Charles Lowndes, the brother of Rawlins, was returned by St. Pauls' Parish but refused election, necessitating the issuance of new writs for a by-election to fill the seat.[59] In the meantime the new Assembly convened in March under the same leadership as the old one. Benjamin Smith was again chosen Speaker while Rawlins Lowndes and Peter Manigault each received a lion's share of committee appointments.[60] The House promptly offended the new governor by rejecting two of his first three proposals, one for a new election law and another to furnish manpower for the imperial war effort. Next they passed a bill placing the Indian trade under a public monopoly, naming Lowndes and several other members to a committee to supervise the distribution of Indian presents.[61]

At this point the tension began to mount. Governor Boone flatly declared that he would ignore the legislature's attempt to control the distribution of Indian presents, and proceeded to do so.[62] Then, instead of honoring the tradition which permitted

59. April 21, 1762, ibid., CO5/480, p. 72.
60. *See* February 11 to March 26, 1762, ibid., pp. 4-55.
61. March 26, 30, May 7, 20, 29, 1762, ibid., pp. 58, 92, 113, 135-36.
62. May 29, 1762, ibid., p. 137.

the House to name the date of adjournment as well as the time when the next session should begin, Boone initiated a series of monthly prorogations. Thus the Assembly was prorogued on May 29, reconvened one month later to deal briefly with a false alarm occasioned by rumors of a Creek uprising, then suffered another prorogation on July 9. The process was repeated a month later when the House met only to be told that there was no new business and were dismissed for another month.[63]

These irritating tactics were passed over in silence by the legislature, which once more convened as directed on September 9. This session promised to be as brief as the last until the House asked for time to pass a bill regulating lotteries. In the midst of their deliberations word came down from the Council concerning an irregularity in the by-election held recently in St. Paul's. Investigation revealed that the church wardens of St. Paul's had neglected to make a proper return on the writ. Called before the House, the wardens corrected the error, which the House accepted without requiring the wardens to be sworn on this particular return.[64] Christopher Gadsden, who had easily won the election over two opponents, was then called in and administered the usual oath required of new members. To complete the process, Gadsden was escorted by two members of the House to the governor's office to take the state oath. They soon returned to report that the governor commanded the House to attend him in the council chamber immediately.

In the council chamber Boone made a dramatic speech. He had examined the House journal, "having I confess some curiosity to know whether any thing new had occurred . . . And Gentlemen, if I was curious before, I am astonished now, I perceive you have endeavored, as far as in your power, to dispence with an Act of Assembly, to a rigid execution of which your body owes, or ought to owe, its existence." He reminded them that he had recommended a revision of the election law of 1721 but the House had refused to do it. Now he understood that the church wardens had not been sworn on Gadsden's election return, so "in order . . .

63. May 29, June 29, July 9, Aug. 9, 1762, ibid., pp. 145, 152, 153.
64. September 10, 13, 1762, ibid., pp. 154–56.

to Manifest in as public a Manner as I can, my disavowal of so undeniable an infraction of the Election Act, I do hereby dissolve this present General Assembly, and it is dissolved accordingly."[65]

Boone had wanted a quarrel with the House, but in selecting this incident as its basis he revealed a fatal flaw in judgment. The House had violated the letter of the law, but certainly not its spirit. Moreover, the infraction represented no serious violation of procedure or prerogative. Thus he could count on very little sympathy from his superiors. And everyone knew he could expect the House to offer the strongest possible resistance to such a challenge of its fundamental rights.

New elections were duly held and the Assembly convened on October 26. The new House had time only to organize and reelect Smith as their Speaker before Boone abruptly prorogued the Assembly to November 22. On that date, as if nothing at all had gone amiss, Boone delivered a routine speech on Indian affairs, the success of British arms, and necessary legislation. The House had no intention of considering any of these matters until they settled the Gadsden election issue. In the first order of business Speaker Smith appointed a Committee on Privileges and Elections to consider all aspects of the issues raised in the controversy. Named to the committee were the top echelon of House leaders: John Rutledge, Rawlins Lowndes, Peter Manigault, Charles Pinckney, William Wragg along with Gadsden himself and three others.[66] Their report, adopted a week later by the House, declared "That it is the undeniable, fundamental and inherent Right & Privilege of the Commons House of Assembly, of this Province Solely to examine and finally determine the Elections of their own Members." It found nothing illegal in the disputed election, holding that the initial oath of church wardens was sufficient to the demands of the law: "it would be both unnecessary and unreasonable, to require their taking an Oath several times for the same Purpose." The people's right to representation derived from the British Constitution rather than from a provincial statute, they said, and pronounced the governor's interference an unconstitutional violation of their "Sacred and Essential Privi-

65. September 13, 1762, ibid., p. 158.
66. November 24, 1762, ibid., CO5/480, p. 12.

leges," a dangerous threat to free elections and the independence of the legislature.[67]

When Boone read the remonstrance on December 6, his surly reply began, "It is with some reluctance, I give you any Answer at all," and concluded without yielding a single point.[68] Another remonstrance, drawn up and delivered personally to him on December 11 by the entire Committee on Privileges and Elections, drew from the governor a response even more insulting:

> Gentlemen,
> I must here refer you to my former Answer, if you think that forty such Messages can be of any Service to the Province, I am ready to receive them, but give me leave to rely solely & absolutely on the Inefficacy of any thing you can do or Say to Sully my Character or Conduct.[69]

James Glen could have told Boone the folly of such behavior, for Lowndes and his colleagues had long since learned how to assert their authority and prerogatives against even the most imperious governor. The House sent their remonstrances and Boone's replies to the *Gazette* and resolved on December 16 not "to enter into any further Business with Him until his Excellency shall have done justice to this House on this important point." Then William Wragg, Lowndes, and several others formed a Committee of Correspondence and began drawing up a full account of the dispute for the colonial agent, while the Assembly settled down to daily adjournments without business, waiting for the governor to yield.

Determined rather to quit his office than concede to the House, Boone remained silent, and the government of South Carolina ground to a halt. With the House meeting daily but conducting no business, Boone prorogued it for a month on December 28 and afterwards tolerated the daily adjournments for nine consecutive weeks before interrupting the monotony with a week's prorogation. The House resumed its perfunctory sittings on April 6, then on April 19 ceased meeting altogether. Without so much as asking his leave, the legislators returned to their private affairs; Speaker Benjamin Smith even went "off the Province," leaving Gover-

67. November 30, 1762, ibid., pp. 18–20.
68. December 7, 1762, ibid., pp. 35–37.
69. December 11, 1762, ibid., p. 46.

nor Boone alone in impotent possession of his government for the next four months. Finally on August 18, Boone issued a proclamation calling the Assembly into session on September 1, 1763.

Since Benjamin Smith had not returned to Carolina by September, the first order of business was the selection of a new Speaker. Isaac Mazyck nominated Rawlins Lowndes, "long a Member of the House, . . . very Conversant in the Business thereof, & extremely capable of discharging the duty of that Important Office, to the General Satisfaction of the Assembly."[70] Mazyck knew Lowndes well, had been with him in London, and had served with him in the House for several years. Without division or further nominations the House resolved that Lowndes take the chair. Thomas Wright and James Parsons "took him out of his place and conducted him to the Chair." In a short speech Lowndes thanked his colleagues for the "High Honor" they had conferred on him, and assured them that "tho' conscious of his own Inabilities to discharge the duties of so great a Promotion; Yet as the Lott by their choice had fall'n on him, he should make it his peculiar Attention to acquit himself (in the best manner he was Capable of) in so Important a Station."[71] He then took the chair and thus assumed direction of the contest with Governor Boone.

Receiving a routine approval from Governor Boone the next day, the new Speaker promptly demonstrated to his colleagues the wisdom of their choice. Boone sent down a curt message scolding the House for its neglect of public business, then added: "In consequence to the King's Mandamus, I some time ago issued a Commission to Thomas Skottowe, Esq. to be your Clerk, he has taken the Oaths, & now requires Admission to his office."[72] Skottowe, a placeman, was in complete sympathy with the governor, who obviously intended to use him not only to irritate the Commons but to spy on its proceedings. When the new clerk presented himself before the House, Lowndes promptly ordered him outside until the House decided what to do with him. The Assembly immediately reaffirmed the December resolutions but agreed to accept Skottowe's appointment since it could not be rejected with-

70. September 2, 1763, ibid., CO5/478, p. 13.
71. Ibid.
72. September 2, 3, 1762, ibid., pp. 14, 15.

out directly violating the royal mandamus. In the meantime Skottowe had gone home in a huff, so Lowndes ordered him to appear on Monday. Skottowe duly appeared and "by the Sense of the House" was sworn in as clerk. No sooner was Skottowe sworn than Lowndes "prayed the Indulgence of the House that Mr. Bromley, who had for sometime past discharged the duty of the Office of Clerk, might be admitted Clerk Assistant to the House. . . ." The members were "pleased" with the Speaker's expedient, so Bromley also was sworn.[73] The Commons thus kept its own clerk in spite of the mandamus. The placeman might attend its meetings if he wished, but he would do so without pay.

Rebuked in this move, Boone contrived new insults for the Assembly. In a routine action Lowndes sent representatives Gadsden and Moultrie to witness the governor administer the usual state oath to Sir John Colleton, recently returned a member by St. John's Parish, Berkeley County. Not finding Boone either in his office or the council chamber, the party proceeded to the governor's house. There Boone rudely ordered Gadsden and Moultrie out and administered the oath to Colleton privately. On learning this Lowndes sent immediately for the clerk of the crown to administer the state oath before witnesses according to law. But the crafty governor had anticipated the Speaker and appropriated the required documents.[74] Boone had also seized the accounts of the Public Treasurer, so that no action could be taken concerning the public credit without first coming to him. Then on September 12 James Parsons and Sir John Colleton escorted four more members up to be sworn. This time Boone refused even to hear Parson's routine report, stating that he would take no man's word, but would send for the journals; so none were sworn.

This was the last straw. Resolving that the governor was "Guilty of a New Insult to, & breach of Privileges of this House," the Commons declined to conduct any further business whatever with him and ceased meeting four days later. Three months went by before an Indian attack that took fourteen lives among the Long Canes settlers on Christmas eve gave Boone an excuse to call the

---

73. September 3, 5, 7, 1762, ibid., pp. 14–16, 19–20.
74. September 7, 9, 1762, ibid., pp. 20–21.

Assembly into session in January 1764.[75] Boone now condescended to administer the state oaths in the usual manner. The House met but refused to budge from its previous resolutions. With Lowndes presiding no business was transacted, and before the month was out the members had drifted away again. The arrival of a large group of needy French Protestants in April was Boone's second excuse for recalling the Assembly, to furnish the immigrants some assistance. Speaker Lowndes convened the House on April 23 and kept the members in session only two days, just long enough to table the governor's message with a promise to consider it "as soon as they can consistently with their former Resolutions. . . ."[76]

Boone was beaten and he knew it. To admit defeat, however, was more than he could bring himself to do. In the meantime the Assembly's detailed petition to the Crown had achieved its object, and orders were being prepared for Boone's recall. But the governor had already decided to vacate his office; before the orders arrived, he had quietly packed his belongings and sailed from the colony.[77] The triumph of the Commons was complete.

The Gadsden election controversy proved in many respects to be a rehearsal for revolution. The Commons' success in this dispute encouraged resistance to the tightening of imperial control over the colonies, the principal feature of Crown policy from 1763. The two-year struggle reminded the colonists how to wage such warfare in defense of constitutional rights, and had furnished several of their leaders numerous opportunities to display their mettle.[78]

Speaker Lowndes had acquitted himself quite satisfactorily during the controversy. His leadership was steady and his handling of Thomas Skottowe and the House clerkship was particularly pleas-

75. December 30, 1763; January 4, 1764, ibid., CO5/482, p. 1, 3.
76. April 23, 1764, ibid., p. 13.
77. Governor Boone to Lords of Trade, April 19, 1764, SCPRO, XXX, 141; William Bull to Lords of Trade, May 16, 1764, ibid., p. 143; Lord Halifax to Governor Boone, June 9, 1764, ibid., p. 145; Petition of the South Carolina Commons House of Assembly to the Crown, September 13, 1763, ibid., pp. 155–58.
78. For an excellent treatment of this controversy and its larger implications, *see* Jack P. Greene, "The Gadsden Election Controversy and the Revolutionary Movement in South Carolina," *Mississippi Valley Historical Review*, XLVI (December, 1959), 469–92.

ing to his colleagues. At the same time, he was scrupulously careful to refer all questions to the House for decision. He had proved a very capable presiding officer during the controversy, and had every reason to expect his colleagues to be satisfied with his service. Many were, but he would discover soon enough that some preferred a younger, more colorful figure in the chair.

CHAPTER VI

Reversal

CAROLINIANS could watch with undisguised pleasure as the *Dorset*, with Governor Boone aboard, dropped down the bay on May 11, 1764, crossed the bar, and spread full sail for London.[1] Rancor seemed at once to dissolve in a spirit of cooperation, for political affairs returned to normal as soon as he was gone. Within twelve days Lieutenant Governor Bull and Speaker Lowndes had set in motion legislative machinery that had been idle for the past two years. Members of the House began once again to refuse their seats, who throughout the controversy with Boone had been most diligent in attendance. Even so, a quorum was easily achieved and the Assembly set to work.

Speaker Lowndes named Peter Manigault chairman of the Committee on Public Accounts, which immediately began to calculate the public debt run up over the past two years and to find means for its discharge, while other committees drew up several emergency measures. When news came that Boone had been officially recalled, the Commons House rejoiced in their victory and their Speaker wrote to the colonial agent, Charles Garth, expressing their thanks for his success in presenting their case to the Crown. In short order the House authorized payment of interest on the debt for 1762 and voted £500 sterling to assist the needy French protestants neglected in the struggle with Boone. To promote a better population balance, further importation of slaves was discouraged by a new tax ranging up to £100 per head, to be paid by the purchaser. The House completed its emergency mea-

1. William Bull to Lords of Trade, May 16, 1764, SCPRO, XXX, 143.

sures on June 5 by authorizing a company of rangers to secure the Long Canes settlements from further Indian depredations and to aid the French immigrants now moving toward the frontier.[2]

On July 3, Peter Manigault brought in a superb report on the public debt, much better organized than previous reports, and for the first time, in clear alphabetical order. Two items in the report were particularly noteworthy. One granted to Thomas Bromley the full salary of the House Clerk's office while the placeman Skottowe received only the fees. The other provided no salary for Governor Boone. Approving the schedule, the House sent it on to the Council only to have the placemen there insert an item for £7000 to pay Boone his salary. This blatant challenge to their traditional control over provincial finance drew from the House the expected response. It also set the tone for relations between the two bodies over the last decade of royal government in the colony.

With Skottowe now sitting on the board, the Council extolled the virtues of the departed governor, threatening to reject the tax bill if his salary were not included. In a spirited reply Chairman Manigault rejected their presumed authority to alter the bill to pay Boone or anybody else. It was not a salary, he exclaimed, but a gratuity from the people "which it would be Stupid in them to bestow upon a Governor who had endeavored to deprive them, of what ought to be valued by every Englishman, more than even Life itself." The House would not pay it, "No! not even for your favorite Governor!"[3] But cooler though equally determined heads prevailed. The sum was simply struck out of the bill which was then returned to the Council "for your Concurrence." When the Council retaliated by rejecting both the tax bill and the revival bill as well, the whole House was as mad as Manigault. They exploded to Lieutenant Governor Bull on this "shock" to the public credit by the board, "*a Majority such as are Altogether Placemen, And have no Natural Tie or Connection whatever with the Province.*"[4] Speaker Lowndes ordered a complaint sent to agent Garth

2. May 29, June 2, 1764, Commons Journal, CO5/482, pp. 41, 43, 52-53, microfilm, S.C. Archives.
3. August 22-23, 1764, ibid., pp. 244-46.
4. August 25, 1764, ibid., pp. 250-51.

along with a report on the Council's fiscally irresponsible behavior. Bull prorogued the Assembly to September, employing in the meantime his rare gift for diplomatic persuasion to settle the issue. The Council finally approved the two bills although Boone's salary remained unpaid.

From January to April 1765 Lowndes had the satisfaction of presiding over the first serious efforts in a decade to establish courts outside the capital. The outbreak of war with France in 1754, followed by the Cherokee War, and then the protracted stalemate with Boone had diverted the Assembly's attention from this issue. Now the necessity for judicial reform was building in direct proportion to the volume of settlers swarming down from the more northerly colonies to take up lands in the Carolina piedmont. On the crest of this human tide rode lawless elements that always seem to make their way to frontier regions where law enforcement is weakest. Finding South Carolina's highly-centralized system peculiarly suited to their purposes, they prowled unhindered through the backsettlements, committing all manner of depredations and stimulating a flurry of petitions from the responsible settlers imploring the government in Charles Town to restore order.

Lieutenant Governor Bull in January called on the Assembly "seriously to consider of the Distribution of Justice in Criminal and Civil Matters . . . in those remote parts . . . to Suppress in a great degree Idlers and Vagabonds, who now infest and Injure the Industrious remote Settlers too often with Impunity."[5] Accordingly Speaker Lowndes appointed Christopher Gadsden, John Rutledge, Charles Pinckney, James Parsons, Thomas Lynch and three others to write a bill setting up courts throughout the colony. The committee simply rewrote the old District Court Bill of 1754, which Gadsden brought in for its first reading on March 15. On scheduling the second reading one week hence, the Speaker ordered all members to attend on pain of a ten pound fine. But the penalty could hardly overcome lowcountry indifference to backcountry problems; with only two-thirds of the members attending, the bill narrowly passed its second reading, sixteen to fifteen.[6]

5. January 10, 1765, ibid., CO5/483, p. 2.
6. March 15, 28, 1765, ibid., pp. 62, 74.

To remedy a closely related problem, Bull submitted on April 1 a plan for a prison to be built at public expense. Speaker Lowndes immediately referred the matter to a special committee headed by William Wragg. Wasting no time, Wragg reported that very day that the business was an "absolute necessity" and asked for an appropriation of £10,000 to build the gaol. Unfortunately the House majority saw neither reform measure as particularly pressing and postponed both to the July session. By July the issue was again lost in problems attending a crop-killing drought and mounting furor over the Stamp Act, while patience in the back-country neared exhaustion.[7]

The rights and privileges of the South Carolina Commons House of Assembly and all other provincial legislatures were now being challenged by the British Parliament itself. Even before the war ended in 1763, imperial control over the colonies had begun to tighten; then with the Sugar Act of 1764 the British Parliament began to pass laws for the specific purpose of raising money in the colonies for the Crown. The challenge to their traditional authority over provincial taxation was felt by every colonial legislature, opening the crucial debate on whether Parliament had the right to tax colonials for revenue rather than for the regulation of trade. While the Sugar Act provoked great excitement in the northern colonies where foreign molasses was necessary to the rum industry and the slave trade, it had little real effect on South Carolina since no rum distilleries operated here.[8] But here as in other continental colonies, the law created an opposition which crystallized after the passage of the Stamp Act in 1765.

When news of the proposed Stamp Act reached America in 1764, opposition began to grow, centered in New England and spreading southward. In spite of mounting colonial protests Parliament passed the law in March 1765 to become effective six months later on November 1. The six months' delay allowed time for opponents to create a groundswell of sentiment for resistance to the measure that reached the point of open defiance by November. The Massachusetts Assembly keyed the movement by sending

7. April 1, 4, 6, 1765, ibid., pp. 75–76, 78, 84, 86; William Bull to Lords of Trade, May 3, 1766, SCPRO, XXXI, 32–34.
8. William Bull to Lords of Trade, November 28, 1764, ibid., XXX, p. 215.

out a call for delegates from the various colonies to meet in convention at New York in October to consider a "general united dutiful and loyal Representation to His Majesty and Parliament and implore Relief" from parliamentary taxation.[9]

South Carolina's first reaction to the proposed law in 1764 was characteristically moderate. The Commons House instructed agent Garth to remonstrate against it,[10] for they saw no way to avoid compliance should it become an act of Parliament. Even after the Stamp Act passed, sentiment for compliance remained substantially unchanged. Carolinians, through the summer of 1765, according to Lieutenant Governor Bull, "though they conceived it too great a burthen, seemed generally disposed to pay a due obedience to the Act and at the same time in a dutiful and respectful manner to represent to His Majesty the hardships which it would lay them under, and to pray relief therein."[11] This was the prevailing sentiment when Speaker Lowndes convened the House on July 19, 1765, to consider the Massachusetts proposal for a Stamp Act Congress.

The Commons journals are silent on the views expressed in discussion of the Stamp Act this session, but the House resolved to send three delegates to the New York Congress, Thomas Lynch, Christopher Gadsden, and John Rutledge, and advanced them £600 sterling for expenses. Speaker Lowndes was to keep the delegates informed of developments at home until they should return and deliver their report. This done, the House adjourned on August 9, and shortly afterwards Bull routinely dissolved the Assembly for new elections.[12] Before the delegates returned or the Stamp Act went into effect, Rawlins Lowndes suddenly discovered he had been maneuvered out of his job as Speaker.

This is how it happened. In the October elections following the dissolution, Lowndes was returned by the voters of St. Bartholo-

9. July 19, 1765, Commons Journal, CO5/483, p. 89, microfilm, S.C. Archives.

10. August 25, 1764, ibid., CO5/482, p. 252.

11. William Bull to Lords of Trade, November 3, 1765, SCPRO, XXX, 281–82.

12. July 19, 25, 26, August 2, 8, 1765, Commons Journal, CO5/483, pp. 89, 93–94, 97–98, microfilm, S.C. Archives.

mew's Parish, but then a most peculiar development occurred. When the new House met on Monday, October 28, the election return from St. Bartholomew's was still out, an odd circumstance considering the proximity of the parish to Charles Town. The missing return prevented the representatives of this parish from being seated, including the late Speaker. With a quorum present on Tuesday, Lieutenant Governor Bull directed the House to organize and choose a Speaker "immediately," although the missing return still had not come in.[13]

At this point some discussion arose on the propriety of proceeding in such unprecedented circumstances. A request for further delay could easily have been made on the grounds of a thin House, notwithstanding the quorum present, and the unusual holdup on the late Speaker's election return. According to Lowndes, one member, apparently Isaac Mazyck, argued against further delay, urging that tradition be set aside and the Speaker's chair be filled through a new policy of periodic rotation among members of the House.[14] In any event, the lieutenant governor's order stood, so Mazyck nominated Peter Manigault. The majority present approved, and Manigault was elected late Tuesday afternoon.

The new Speaker waited until Wednesday to summon before the House James Skirving, the warden responsible for the missing return. When the warden brought it in on Thursday, October 31, and was asked why he had not delivered it sooner, Skirving answered that he had been sick. Apparently satisfied with this excuse, Manigault let him go and the investigation was closed. Lowndes was convinced that a group of Manigault's admirers had engineered the whole affair.[15] Now that the delegation could be seated, Lowndes came in first, indignantly refused his seat and stalked out. Following his example, three more of the delegation came in,

13. October 29, 1765, ibid., CO5/484, p. 4; *South Carolina Gazette*, October 12, 1765.

14. Charles Town, S.C., *South Carolina Gazette and Country Journal*, February 28, 1769; October 29, 1765, Commons Journal, CO5/484, p. 4, microfilm, S.C. Archives.

15. October 30–31, 1765, ibid., pp. 8–9; *South Carolina Gazette and Country Journal*, February 28, 1769.

refused election, and withdrew, leaving only James Parsons to represent the parish during the Stamp Act crisis.[16]

While the available evidence shows clearly enough how Lowndes lost the speakership, it leaves historians more to their own devices, who attempt to explain why it happened. Maurice Crouse, the authority on Manigault's career, agrees with Lowndes that he was the victim of a coup. Crouse suggests that the House must have had a real grievance against Lowndes, probably his urging submission to the Stamp Act during the July session, that caused them to turn to the high-spirited and equally capable Manigault for a more vigorous response to the law.[17] The theory is certainly consistent with Lowndes' political views.

Lowndes was basically a moderate with conservative leanings, a political independent rather than factional partisan. With regard to the Stamp Act his most important characteristic was a habitual respect for British law developed through almost twenty years of close association with law enforcement in the colony. For nine of those years he *was* the law to colonials who ran afoul of it. Since then he had demonstrated repeatedly a thorough knowledge of the law and how to protect individual rights within its framework, for he was involved in numerous suits over these years and never lost a case.[18] It should not be inferred, however, that Lowndes was an uncompromising legalist. On the contrary, he felt the letter of the law should be tempered with reason in all cases,

16. October 31, November 26, 1765, Commons Journal, CO5/484, pp. 10–11, 14, microfilm, S.C. Archives.

17. Crouse, "Cautious Rebellion: South Carolina's Opposition to the Stamp Act," *SCHGM*, LXXIII (April, 1972), p. 61. Robert M. Weir, " 'The Harmony We Were Famous For': An Interpretation of Pre-Revolutionary South Carolina Politics," *William and Mary Quarterly*, 3d Ser. (October, 1969), p. 494, discounts the influence of partisan politics, pointing out that "after Manigault resigned because of ill health, a house led by substantially the same men reelected Lowndes to the post. The general policy pursued under the leadership of each was the same and committee assignments did not change significantly." The fact that Isaac Mazyck, who now nominated Manigault, was the same member on whose resolution Lowndes had succeeded Speaker Benjamin Smith, might conceivably be used in support of either case. As for the lieutenant governor, relations between Bull and Lowndes seem to have been consistently formal though cordial, but never close.

18. See Judgement Rolls, S.C. Archives.

as we shall presently see. In defense of colonial rights generally and the prerogatives of the Commons House in particular he was resolute, even formidable, but always careful to operate within the bounds of existing law.

To Carolinians, who had paid scant attention to the Sugar Act, the Stamp Act now represented a new and threatening extension of parliamentary authority over them and a dangerous invasion of their Assembly's traditional control over provincial taxation. Nevertheless, according to Bull, they were in the summer of 1765 generally disposed to obey the law while protesting against it through all legal means. Nor is there any evidence that the House then seriously considered defiance of the law or contemplated stronger measures than the concerted action of the Stamp Act Congress. Their disposition was to take no further action until their delegates returned with recommendations from New York. Since the delegates would not return before the law went into effect, if Speaker Lowndes counseled anything at the July session it was surely compliance with the law; and it would have been most unreasonable of his colleagues to have considered this a serious grievance against him.

But that was in July. By October popular sentiment had shifted radically toward violent resistance. The primary cause of this shift was trading ships arriving from the North in September carrying news of the violent resistance to the Stamp Act that had broken out in Boston and Rhode Island in the middle of August.[19] Encouraged by "some busy spirits" acting behind the scenes, popular resistance in Charles Town reached such intensity that the stamps could not be landed when they arrived on the *Planters Adventure* on October 18. Lieutenant Governor Bull had them first transferred to Fort Johnson across the bay and then to a warship when an unruly mob took to the streets and invaded private homes searching for the stamps. The mob so intimidated George Saxby and Caleb Lloyd, the two agents charged with distributing stamps, that they renounced their commissions on Monday, October 28,

19. William Bull to Lords of Trade, November 3, 1765, SCPRO, XXX, 281–82.

the day set for the new Assembly to convene.[20] A tremendous celebration erupted at the news that the stamp agents had resigned, and since Bull declined to appoint others to replace them, there would be no one to distribute stamps and no stamps to distribute when the law went into effect on the following Friday.

In the midst of all this excitement the new House organized and elected Manigault Speaker in Lowndes' absence. Although the theory of a coup cannot be proved—it must hinge on the veracity of Skirving's statement that his illness had delayed the St. Bartholomew's return, and that can never be certainly determined—the full weight of the evidence strongly suggests collusion. Assuming that Lowndes was the victim of a concerted plan, its strategy was dictated by the fact that the House had never refused reelection to an incumbent Speaker, nor could it be expected to do so now, the present circumstances notwithstanding. Poor attendance could be counted on, since everybody knew no important decisions regarding the Stamp Act would be made, and none were, until the delegates returned from New York. A thin House set the stage where the pro-Manigault men in the Charles Town delegation could exercise a disproportionate influence. The missing return provided an all-too-convenient opportunity to supplant Lowndes, while Bull's order for immediate action furnished the excuse. The radical swing toward resistance since August, coupled with Lowndes' known conservatism, supplied reason enough to select a Speaker more agreeable to the present violent state of the popular mood. No legitimate grievance against his predecessor was necessary; and in the light of later events, none had existed.

The walk from the State House across town to his grand home on West Tradd Street had never been longer than it was on October 31, 1765, when Lowndes refused his seat and withdrew from the House following his loss of the speakership. This was the first serious reversal of his public life, and contemplation of the event over the next four months that he remained absent from the House could only be calculated to feed his rancor. At forty-four he saw himself approaching middle age, an older man, honest and direct, suddenly supplanted through artful maneuver by a

20. Ibid., pp. 282–86.

popular young rival. It was even more galling to consider that he, a self-made and largely self-educated man, had through long and faithful public service finally gained the highest and most prestigious political office available to him only to lose it to a rival not only born to wealth and given the finest education that the Manigault fortune could buy, but whose very qualification for a seat in the House had been a gift from his wealthy father.[21]

Nevertheless, Lowndes was determined that refusal of his seat should be his only protest. He would return to the House, but he would not consider degrading the speakership and embarrassing his colleagues, and possibly himself as well, by contesting Manigault for the chair. Each time a new House was organized Lowndes would delay his appearance until the Speaker had been chosen. This he knew would allow Manigault to continue in the office as long as he wished, leaving himself no prospect for advancement in the House.

Nor were prospects better outside the House. A position on the Council, even had one been available to Lowndes, would have been small compensation to a man who had enjoyed the greater prestige of the Speaker's chair. The only office in the colony that could rival the Speaker's in prestige, and that could possibly be made available to Lowndes, was that of Chief Justice. Of course, he knew as well as anyone that since midcentury the office had been supplied with placemen from England and the appointment of a Carolinian was not to be expected. With his ambition apparently thwarted at every turn, Lowndes nursed his resentment. He had no way of knowing that he was about to be presented with an opportunity to distinguish himself on the provincial bench.

The opportunity grew out of South Carolina's efforts to circumvent the Stamp Act. When the law went into effect on November 1, 1765, there were no stamps available for distribution nor agents to distribute them. After that date no business requiring stamps could be legally conducted. The courts ceased to function, the customs house closed, and incoming vessels began to

21. By an indenture dated January 10, 1756, Manigault Family Papers, South Caroliniana Library, Columbia, S.C., Gabriel Manigault transferred to Peter Manigault 2,470 acres "in order to qualify and enable the said Peter Manigault to take his seat in the Commons House. . . ."

congest the harbor as none could leave without stamped clearance papers. Every transaction requiring stamps was at a stand. The planters had no market, the merchants could make no remittances to Great Britain, and the lawyers could not enter a single writ.[22] Since none of them were willing to defy the law, they sought every means to evade it. The Commons House, now under the guidance of Manigault, made the first attempt.

On the day Lowndes refused election, the House had adjourned to await arrival of the delegates from New York. After they arrived in November, the House reconvened on the twenty-fifth to hear Gadsden read the resolutions of the Stamp Act Congress, adopted a similar set of their own expressing their grievances and denying the right of Parliament to tax the colonies, and adjourned to January 7. In the January session the House engaged in a brief dispute with Lieutenant Governor Bull, attempting to have the law ignored on the ground that official word of its passage had not been received.[23] Bull and the Council turned aside this ploy, then news came from London that Parliament was expected to consider repeal of the Stamp Act, and the House decided to postpone consideration of a tax bill to await further developments. When Lowndes resumed his seat on March 6, reelected by his constituents notwithstanding his recent withdrawal,[24] he could have taken grim satisfaction from the fact that his colleagues had accomplished so little in his absence.

In the meantime the lieutenant governor had opened the port. With most of the rice crop still to be exported, both merchants and planters had been hard hit when the export machinery shut down. Pressure from these two powerful interest groups was applied to Bull to open the port without stamps since Peter Randolph, the surveyor general of customs, had authorized ports to the northward to do so. Bull had furnished a precedent in December when he began to allow ships bearing supplies for troops to the southward to clear the port without stamps. But neither he nor Randolph, who was in town, wanted to assume responsibility

22. William Bull to Lords of Trade, February 6, 1766, SCPRO, XXXI, 23.
23. November 26–29, 1765; January 22–25, 28, 1766, Commons Journal, CO5/484, pp. 15–31, 46–50, 52–53, microfilm, S.C. Archives.
24. March 6, 1766, ibid., p. 80.

for opening the port of Charles Town.[25] By late January the situation was explosive, with ships clogging the harbor and fourteen hundred unemployed sailors roaming the streets of the city.[26] On February 4 Bull adopted the expedient of issuing certificates officially stating that no stamps were available. Thereafter customs officials accepted these certificates in lieu of stamps along with a cash payment equal to the stamp duty. In this way the port opened and the vessels cleared as usual.

Opening the courts promised from the beginning greater difficulty. For one thing, the necessity of conducting court business seemed nowhere near as great as the pressing need to open the port. For another, the consensus among the Charles Town attorneys was that it could not be done legally without stamps. Chief Justice Charles Shinner, an Irish jurist who had for some five years now been presiding virtually alone over South Carolina's civil and criminal courts, conducted business as usual in the Court of General Sessions in late October. After the Stamp Act went into effect, he suspended further business and called a meeting of the Charles Town bar to consider the implications of the Stamp Act in the present circumstances. The attorneys who attended the meeting made a careful analysis of the law but could find no loophole in it that would permit the transaction of any legal business without stamps. His own opinion thus reinforced, Shinner closed the Court of Common Pleas the next day, November 13, "being of Opinion that no Business can [be] proceeded upon until . . . Stamped paper can be procured."[27] Thereafter he convened the court for perfunctory adjournments each return day, turning aside all requests to conduct business, his opinion becoming more rigidly fixed as the weeks went by.

Faced with Shinner's intrasigence, it occurred to the lawyers that a device to open the courts without stamps or Shinner's approval, but fully as legal as the expedient Bull had used to open

25. February 1–3, 1766, ibid., pp. 58–64; William Bull to Henry Conway, December 17, 1765, SCPRO, XXX, 278; Bull to Lords of Trade, February 6, 1766, ibid., XXXI, 22–23.

26. Ibid., pp. 23–24.

27. Crouse, "Cautious Rebellion," pp. 62–63; South Carolina Court of Common Pleas, Minutes, 1763–1770, p. 107, typescript, S.C. Archives (hereinafter cited Common Pleas Journal).

the port, was already at hand. Now lawyers, merchants, and members of the Commons House began to press for its adoption.[28] Carolina law empowered the governor, or the lieutenant governor in his absence, to appoint assistant judges up to the number of four, having an equal voice with the chief justice in general sessions and common pleas, with decisions to be carried by the majority in attendance. Since the only assistant judge, Robert Pringle, seldom attended the courts and never spoke when he did, Shinner usually presided alone. Urged to appoint a full contingent of assistant judges who could overrule the chief justice and open the courts, Bull finally yielded in late February and appointed former speakers of the House Rawlins Lowndes and Benjamin Smith and a former provost marshal, Daniel Doyley. In his presence the lieutenant governor had a magistrate administer the oaths,[29] then handed the three new judges their commissions. Lowndes assumed at once, almost as a matter of course, the dominant role in the work they were to do.

Chief Justice Shinner convened the Court of Common Pleas as scheduled on March 3, apparently anticipating another routine adjournment, and was stunned when Lowndes, Smith, and Doyley came in, produced their commissions already sworn to, and took their places on the bench. Shinner knew instantly what was afoot and "how it was likely to go with him" but he was nonetheless determined to uphold the letter of the law.[30] Thomas Bee and John Rutledge now came forward to bring before the court a test case, *James Jordan* v. *Joseph Law*. No trial was intended since defense attorney Rutledge conceded the case by default. Their sole purpose was to see if a judgment might be entered without the four shilling stamp demanded by the Stamp Act. Arguing for the plaintiff the next afternoon, Bee was supported by a battery of lawyers, Charles Pinckney, James Parsons, Speaker of the House Peter Manigault, and even defense attorney Rutledge, "who tho' not concerned for the Plaintiff in this particular cause said they

28. Speaker Manigault later claimed credit for the appointment of Lowndes: "For he has entirely forgot me, who was the first step to his Rise," *South Carolina Gazette and Country Journal*, March 7, 1769.

29. The three assistant judges were sworn by James Simpson, March 3, 1766, SCPRO, XXXI, 215–16; SCCJ, February 27, 1766, XXXII, 728.

30. March 3, 1766, SCPRO, XXXI, 99–100; Common Pleas Journal, p. 108.

were concerned as Counsel in a great variety of Causes of a similar nature."[31]

Although they considered the Stamp Act unconstitutional,[32] the absence of stamps removed the necessity of arguing this point, and the lawyers built their case on the impossibility of executing the law. They argued that since no stamps were available, the letter of the law must of necessity be broken in order for the judicial system of the province to function. Cases of necessity were always excepted out of the laws of Parliament, even the laws of God gave way to necessity, such as killing another in self-defense. Similarly, the impossibility of performing contracts excused their breach. In short, law did not require impossibilities and would excuse where there was an impossibility of compliance. The stamp distributors having forsaken their office refusing to distribute stamps, compliance with the Stamp Act was impossible. The law would not punish the innocent subject for the fault or neglect of the king's officer. The consequences to the subject were the same whether no distributors had been appointed at all, or being appointed refused to act. It was a reproach to Parliament to suppose they intended the subjects in America to be penalized for the default of an officer. And finally, the long "interruption of Justice" occasioned by closing the courts in November directly violated the "Great Charter of English Liberties" which forbade that justice be delayed or denied.[33]

Attorney General Egerton Leigh challenged the "necessity" of the present case, denying that it constituted necessity in the legal sense, and insisted that "the Stamp Act requires that Judgments should be entered upon Stamp Paper, and that the Act calls upon the Judges to act agreeable to that Law. . . ." With the arguments concluded, James Parsons laid before the court a petition from a number of "Merchants Traders Freeholders and other Inhabitants of the Province" praying that recourse to the courts be no longer denied.[34]

31. Ibid., p. 109.
32. See the "petition of the Practitioners of Law" to Charles Shinner, SCPRO, XXXI, 225-26.
33. Common Pleas Journal, 113-14.
34. Ibid., pp. 109, 113.

The court postponed decision in the case to April 1 when Judge Lowndes delivered the unanimous opinion of the four assistant judges. Drawn up by Lowndes himself,[35] the opinion was based on four points among those raised in the arguments on March 4: the necessity of opening the courts, the impossibility of compliance with the law, the intentions of Parliament in making the law, and the basic purpose of the law itself. Christopher Gadsden, with whom Lowndes had developed a firm friendship in spite of their radically differing political views, had hoped the opinion would challenge the constitutionality of the Stamp Act: "I told my friend, I differed from him in the Principle he went upon, that is, I should have built chiefly on the constitutionalness of the Act and asserted it so, roundly; he, I know thinks it as unconstitutional as I do, But imagined it more prudent and advantageous in our Present circumstances not to touch upon that string."[36] Satisfied that the objective could be attained without the assertion of a radical doctrine, Lowndes wrote a learned and convincing argument for opening the courts without stamps.

With a profusion of citations, Lowndes illustrated how necessity often permitted cases to be construed "contrary to Statutes, contrary to custom, and contrary to the ordinary course of the Common Law. . . ." Reason maintained that persons who break the law out of necessity "shall not be wrong doers." In the necessity of the present case reason dictated that the words of the law be broken in order to avoid greater mischief or greater inconveniences:

It is a fact of Public Notoriety that no Stamp paper is to be had in this Province, and the Governor's Certificate under his Seal and Sign Manual produced in Court confirms it, if it needed any proof; The Stamp Act therefore cannot in the nature of things be compiled with for want of Stamp paper; Whatever cause this may be owing to, the effect and Consequences are the same; If no business is to be done without Stamp paper, and it is absolutely impossible for the Court to procure Stamp paper, the Inference is, that

35. Christopher Gadsden to William Samuel Johnson, April 16, 1766, *The Writings of Christopher Gadsden, 1746–1805*, ed. Richard Walsh (Columbia, S.C., 1966), p. 71.
36. Ibid.

the Stamp Act in such an Exigency would oblige the Courts of Law to be shut up, all business to be remitted and the administration of Law and Justice to be suspended; Can it be presumed the Parliament meant any such thing or is there one word in the Act from the first to the last page of it, that gives the least Countenance to such an interpretation; Could the Parliament intend by this Law to Abrogate and repeal all precedent Acts of Parliament, to unhinge the Constitution of the Colonies, to unloose the hands of Violence and Oppression, to introduce Anarchy and Confusion amongst us, and to reduce us to a State of Outlawry?[37]

Since to be without law and to lack the means of dispensing it were one and the same thing, that train of evils would naturally result from shutting up the courts. "The necessity of the thing therefore, the Law of reason, the preservation and Security of the Province require that such a Construction should be put upon the Act as will prevent such Complicated evils, and excuse even the breaking of the Words of the Act, for the avoidance of so many and great mischiefs."[38]

Beside the urgent necessity for opening the courts stood the impossibility of compliance with the law. No stamps were to be had. The distributors having forsaken their office was responsible for this circumstance, and the circumstance would excuse the subject from compliance with the law:

It is evident from the Act itself that the Obligation to use Stamp paper depends upon an[d] expressly referrs to a previous Condition to be performed by the Commissioners of the Stamp duty; and the penal Clause of the Act must be taken altogether as connected with and having relation to that previous condition. . . . It is indeed altogether superfluous and unnecessary to investigate any other reason for excusing the non Complyance with this Act . . . for it would be the greatest absurdity, and contrary to the clearest principals of reason and Law that any man should be punished for not doing a thing, the doing of which depended on the Act, and concurance of another person, whether that person would or not enable him to do the thing required, for it is implied in the Very Idea of Obedience that the thing required is not only possible but reasonable.[39]

37. Common Pleas Journal, pp. 114–15.
38. Ibid., p. 115.
39. Ibid., p. 116.

While a man's own voluntary act would not excuse him for break-ing the law, "it cannot be supposed in the present Case and ought not to be presumed, that the suitors of this Court are instrumental in causing the necessity which has been so prejudicial to them-selves; besides impossibilities, let them come from what cause they will, are still impossibilities."[40]

Lowndes could not believe that Parliament ever intended that the courts should be closed and justice delayed or denied for want of stamps. He found nothing in the law to warrant such an infer-ence. On the contrary, Parliament had anticipated that "through Accident, neglect, inadvertence, ignorance, or some other Cause the several papers required to be stamped might want that for-mality," and had included a proviso merely postponing the "Effi-cacy and Evidence" of the papers until stamps could be affixed to them.[41] Finally, the basic purpose of the law, to raise a revenue, far from being answered by closing the courts, was actually frus-trated: "Such a Construction of the Act" as required "shutting up the Courts must be absurd and ridiculous, because it would be turning the Act against itself, and making those very means which it has appointed to assist its Execution Subservient to the purpose of defeating it, for without Courts it will be impossible for this part of the Act at least to have Effect."[42]

With a brief summation Lowndes announced that the assistant judges were unanimously of opinion that judgment be entered for the plaintiff "in the usual manner as has heretofore been done, No Stamp paper being to be had." In reply to the petition which Parsons had laid before the court, the assistant judges unani-mously agreed "That the process of this Court be issued out in the usual manner to any person who shall require and apply for the same, that there may be no longer a Complaint, that Justice is either delayed or denied."[43]

At this point Chief Justice Shinner delivered a vigorous dissent. The sole question in the case, he said, was whether the impossi-bility of procuring stamps was a legal one. He held with the at-

40. Ibid., p. 118.
41. Ibid.
42. Ibid., pp. 118–19.
43. Ibid., pp. 119–20.

torney general that it was not legal and cited the common law as proof:

> The Law declares that no man shall avail himself of his wrong. The like law pronounces that no Man shall carve out his own remedy, and it is a principle of equal notoriety that the Laws of England cannot be changed but by Authority of Parliament. From these grounds I reasonably inferr that an impossibility must not be created by Wrong; That if the Subject be agrieved by Law, he must be redressed by Law, and that obedience is due to every Statute from those to whom it extends, until the same Authority, which made the Act, shall graciously see fit, to alter, or annul it. . . . it is absurd to assert 'that a man shall not carve out his own remedy' and yet shall be allowed under a different Rule to prevent for his own private convenience the due operation of a Law.[44]

An utter enemy to innovation, Shinner thought it more prudent to bear a "temporary evil" than to "transgress in any instance against a fundamental Rule of Law." Refusing to give his consent to open the court "in defiance of Law," he charged the assistant judges with denying "the Legislative power of King Lords and Commons," and strictly prohibited "all persons at their peril" from testing any writ or process in his name.[45]

The assistant judges immediately objected to Shinner's interpretation of their opinion, for it had most carefully avoided any reference to the legislative power of Crown and Parliament. Lowndes took notice of the "novel and strange Conclusion" of Shinner's dissent, "the Injunctions he has laid on all the Officers and Ministers of the Court to disregard the Judgment of four of the Judges, in preference to his own single opinion." The chief justice would establish a new precedent contrary to all usage, Lowndes declared, that "the Minority shall conclude the Majority." Lowndes warned all court officers to obey the orders of the court, "always heretofore understood to be the Majority of the Bench present," and directed the clerk, Dougal Campbell, to enter the judgment order in the record.[46]

Campbell was the very model of a dutiful and diligent clerk, always regarding the judges with humility and respect. Now he

44. Ibid., pp. 111–12.
45. Ibid., p. 111.
46. Ibid.. pp. 109–12.

humbly begged leave to decline obeying the order, giving events a most unexpected turn. He explained that under any other law but the Stamp Act it would not have entered his head to disobey the court. In the present circumstances, however, he could not remain passive, for he was by office specifically named in the Stamp Act and stood liable to heavy penalties if he disobeyed the law. The astonished judges dismissed his explanation and reiterated their order, but the mild mannered clerk could not be moved. Repeatedly ordered to enter the judgment, Campbell respectfully persisted in his refusal. Finally a bystander, William Mason, was appointed clerk temporarily, and he recorded the order.[47]

Having secured their primary object of opening the courts, the assistant judges, "from particular tenderness and indulgence on account of his hitherto dutiful and diligent behaviour in Office," took no direct action against Campbell.[48] They nevertheless petitioned Lieutenant Governor Bull for the clerk's suspension. The request threw Bull into a "disagreeable dilemma." He hesitated not to support the authority of the court over the clerk, but to suspend Campbell would probably incur the royal displeasure.[49] He therefore dumped the matter in the lap of the Council. After taking testimony from the chief justice and hearing Campbell's explanation of his conduct, the Council upheld the clerk, and Bull sent his regrets to the judges that he could not comply with their request.

The assistant judges did not press the issue until the clerk refused to issue the writ of venire calling jurors for the May term of court. Thereupon Campbell was pronounced guilty of "endeavouring to wrest from the Court . . . their proper jurisdiction, and to assume and Arrogate to himself a power to supercede and controul their determinations, to the total inversion of all Law, Order, Decency, and Decorum." Judge Lowndes announced the decision; for his "presumptive pretences" the clerk was fined £100 proclamation money.[50] The Commons House conducted a full investi-

47. Ibid., pp. 109–10; April 23, 1766, Commons Journal, CO5/488, pp. 97–98, microfilm, S.C. Archives.
48. Common Pleas Journal, p. 110.
49. May 2, 1766, Commons Journal, CO5/488, pp. 115–16, microfilm, S.C. Archives.
50. Common Pleas Journal, pp. 120–21.

gation of the affair and went in a body to the lieutenant governor to demand Campbell's dismissal. The House particularly objected to Bull's referring the matter to the Council, calling the procedure "highly illegal and unjustifiable, and a Precedent of the most dangerous Nature, as it tends to destroy all Subordination of Ministerial Officers, and to draw the Determination of Causes from the Common Pleas, before the Council in a Summary, Exparte and Extrajudicial way."[51] Nevertheless, Bull adhered to his position, explaining that whenever his conduct was questioned by the king he would have to stand or fall by the propriety of his own judgment: "It will be no excuse to me to have implicitly followed the Opinion of the Assembly if it shall be deemed improper by His Majesty."[52]

When unofficial news of the Stamp Act's repeal came in May, tension over the issue gave way to joyous celebration, and the controversy was shortly settled. Campbell petitioned the court on May 29, expressing his unfeigned sorrow for having incurred the court's censure, and praying relief from the fine imposed on him. Sharing in the general exultation over "the late favourable turn" in American affairs, the court judged that "the Clerk's late conduct proceeded rather from Error in Judgment than any Contempt or want of respect" for its authority and reduced his fine to ten pounds proclamation money.[53]

Chief Justice Shinner did not fare nearly so well. He remained obstinate in his refusal to conduct business until official word of the repeal was received. Thus the full force of the House's anger was directed against him. Moreover, he was all too vulnerable to criticism, for his ignorance of provincial law had been repeatedly demonstrated. In April 1767 the House brought charges against him seeking his dismissal on the grounds of incompetence. Shinner refuted most of the charges in convincing fashion but could not deny his principal deficiency, knowledge of provincial law. On the unanimous recommendation of his colleagues on the Council, he was suspended from office in May by the new governor,

51. May 2, 1766, Commons Journal, CO5/488, pp. 117–18, microfilm, S.C. Archives.
52. May 1, 1766, ibid., p. 113.
53. Common Pleas Journal, p. 124.

Lord Charles Greville Montagu, until the king's pleasure should be known.[54]

Shinner had lost his wife during the Stamp Act crisis and more recently his only child.[55] Now the humiliation and disgrace of his suspension compounded the personal tragedy to bring a swift end to his unhappy career. When he died in the spring of 1768 with his case still pending, Rawlins Lowndes, orphaned thirty years earlier by a similar tragedy, assumed the position of "Chief Judge" of South Carolina.

54. Governor Montagu to Lords of Trade, May 12, 1767, SCPRO, XXXI, 326–27. For the House report of charges against Shinner see ibid., pp. 328–46, and pp. 347–92 for his reply.
55. Charles Shinner Memorial to Governor Montagu, May 2, 1767, ibid., p. 371.

CHAPTER VII

Chief Judge

THE UNEXPECTED turn of events that shunted Lowndes from the Speaker's chair to a subordinate position on the provincial bench could hardly have been better timed to keep him at the center of public interest. This was owing to several factors. The first of these was that intolerable conditions in the backcountry were reaching crisis proportions due to the antiquated judicial and law-enforcement systems. The second was the emergence of an arbitrary ministerial policy that focused on the provincial courts when the colony moved to establish them in the back-settlements. The third was the personality of Rawlins Lowndes, reflected in his disposition to assume authority among the assistant judges, and the disposition of his colleagues to acquiesce in his leadership. Justice Smith had so little interest in the work that he resigned from the bench within six months.[1] Pringle clearly lacked the energy to challenge Lowndes while Doyley possessed neither the judicial experience nor the legal erudition of his more forceful colleague.

Moreover, the uncompromising stubbornness of Chief Justice Shinner opened the way for Lowndes to assume an even larger role. Shinner's obstinate refusal to consider legal any writ or other judicial process issued without stamps had produced in the House a settled determination to drive him from office. Clerk of Court Dougall Campbell, sensing the flow of events, began to consult Lowndes rather than Shinner on court business, often pretending not to notice the chief justice as he passed Shinner's door on the

1. Common Pleas Journal, p. 146. Justice Smith returned his commission to Governor Montagu on November 12, 1766.

way to Judge Lowndes' office.[2] When Shinner was suspended from office the following May, Lowndes took over direction of judicial affairs. He usually charged the grand juries and took it upon himself to make "frequent applications" to Governor Montagu and Lieutenant Governor Bull "for assistance and Support to the Ministers of Justice."[3] The bench desperately needed assistance and support by the summer of 1767. With the whole backcountry risen in defiance of legal authority, the court stood at the vortex of a raging sectional controversy, the South Carolina Regulator Movement.[4]

The South Carolina backcountry at the outbreak of Regulator activity comprised well over half, nearer two-thirds of the land area of the colony not occupied by Indians. It began in the upper pine belt about fifty miles inland and extended across the Fall Line and through the piedmont to the Cherokee frontier in the foothills of the Appalachians. Inital white settlement of the region had been promoted by Governor Robert Johnson's township plan of 1730, which had established within a decade six settled townships ranging eastward across the colony from New Windsor Township on the Savannah opposite Augusta to Queensboro Township on the Pee Dee below Marr's Bluff. Over the next two decades immigrants from the Old World and from the more northerly colonies infiltrated the rolling hills and river valleys of the fertile piedmont until the eve of the Cherokee War when population of the region numbered some twenty thousand settlers. Defeat of the Cherokees removed the Indian menace and stimulated a heavy influx of new immigrants, more than ten thousand

2. *See* the account of proceedings in the Stamp Act Controversy in SCPRO, XXXI, 136.

3. SCCJ, February 3, 1772, CO5/502, pp. 31–32, microfilm, S.C. Archives; William Bull to the Earl of Hillsborough, December 5, 1770, SCPRO, XXXII, 407–8.

4. The following discussion of the Regulator Movement rests squarely on the scholarship of Richard Maxwell Brown, whose *The South Carolina Regulators* (Cambridge, Mass., 1963) carries the long sectional history of the marshalship and the district court movement to its logical conclusion in the Circuit Court Act of 1769. Generalizations on the Regulator Controversy as well as factual information not otherwise supported by notes below are based on this study.

by the middle 1760s, but the Cherokee War left in its wake profound social dislocation in the backcountry.[5]

The fundamental problem that defied backcountry solution in the immediate postwar years was how to effect the transition from a war-ravaged Indian frontier to an orderly society in a region devoid of traditional institutions necessary for the transition. There was no local government above the justice of the peace and his assistant, the constable. Moreover, there was no urban life worthy of the name, no effective religious organization, no criminal courts or law enforcement, and no schools whatever. Ignorance was the common condition, and immorality was all too common. To make matters worse, the war had exerted a brutalizing influence on survivors of the conflict, eroded traditional respect for social institutions generally and the rights of property in particular, and left the region "in a state of anarchy, disorder, and confusion."[6] By the middle 1760s the backcountry was in chaos, spawning gangs of villains of every stripe and inviting others from across the North Carolina border, who plundered the region with impunity.

To the harried farmers of the backsettlements the entire Stamp Act controversy was little more than another distraction that diverted the Assembly's attention from reform legislation long overdue. Actually the Assembly was quite aware of problems in the interior and becoming more sensitive to the settlers' grievances. Backcountry representation had been initiated with the creation of St. Mark's Parish in 1757, which gave the region its first two seats in the Commons House. Others certainly would have followed but for the ministerial prohibition against enlarging House membership. In June 1766, following repeal of the Stamp Act, the Commons House resolved to bring in a bill establishing courts in the backsettlements, but South Carolina's peculiar system of law enforcement made progress painfully slow.[7]

In order to adopt a district or county court system and install county sheriffs to serve the courts, the first necessity was to pur-

5. Brown, *South Carolina Regulators*, pp. 2–11.
6. Ibid., pp. 10–11, 16–19.
7. June 26, 1766, Commons Journal, CO5/488, pp. 181–82, microfilm, S.C. Archives.

chase the office of provost marshal from the patentee. Richard Cumberland had acquired the patent on the death of Hugh Watson in 1759, and Cumberland had sent Roger Pinckney to the colony to serve as his deputy. Through Pinckney, Cumberland let it be known that he was willing to sell the office, and in December 1766 the Commons House authorized agent Garth to negotiate the transfer. The colony was willing to pay £4000 sterling for the office, but Cumberland wanted £6000, so in 1767 the negotiations began in a desultory flow of correspondence between patentee, purchasing agent, and provincial assembly.[8]

In the meantime Marshal Pinckney seldom ventured out of the provincial capital in performing his duties, not through intentional neglect but because the colony had long since outgrown the office and Pinckney had in the local business about all he could manage. His problems were compounded by the hopelessly antiquated criminal court system. Meeting in Charles Town on the third Wednesdays in March and October for sittings that rarely ran longer than a week, the Court of General Sessions attempted to dispense criminal justice for the whole colony. Swollen dockets meant the inevitable carryover of cases, causing delay, expense, serious inconvenience to witnesses, and chronic overcrowding in the provincial prison.

The shortcomings of the outmoded arrangement were strikingly illustrated in December 1766 when seven capital offenders bound over from the October sessions escaped.[9] Judge Lowndes, who continued to serve in the House during his tenure on the bench, thereupon stirred the Assembly to action by introducing and pushing through a bill which increased the annual criminal court sessions to three, to be held the third Mondays in January, April, and October.[10] By the time this bill passed in April 1767,

8. December 10, 1766, ibid., CO5/489, pp. 238-39; Committee of Correspondence to Charles Garth, December 11, 1766, "Correspondence of Charles Garth," *SCHGM*, XXIX (April, 1928), 115; Richard Cumberland to Roger Pinckney, October 1, 1764, *Documents Connected with the History of South Carolina*, ed. Plowden J. C. Weston (London, 1856), pp. 107-10.

9. *South Carolina Gazette*, December 15, 1766.

10. Ibid., April 27, 1767; January 21, 1767, Commons Journal, CO5/489, p. 266, microfilm, S.C. Archives; Cooper and McCord, *Statutes*, VII, 194.

the only measure of judicial reform accomplished this session, conditions in the backcountry had reached a crisis.

The backsettlements had become accustomed to systematic plundering by organized gangs, "stealing horses in one [province] and selling them in the next," as well as the exasperating petty thievery committed by hordes of shiftless poor whites who infested the region.[11] Nevertheless, the industrious settlers were unprepared for the wave of crime and violence that broke over the region in the summer of 1766. A virtual reign of terror spread from the Savannah across the piedmont to the Edisto, the Saluda and Broad, on to the Congarees and the Pee Dee, and even up into the Waxhaws on the North Carolina border. Intimidating, corrupting, or merely defying justices of the peace, the villians robbed, murdered, burned, looted, tortured, assaulted, abducted, and raped their way across the countryside. Even the militia was powerless to restore order. In pitched battles small groups of responsible settlers killed several of the bandits and captured a few others, who were brought down to Charles Town and held for trial.[12]

Five backcountry outlaws came before the Court of General Sessions in March 1767: Ephriam Jones, Solomon Rivers, Anthony Distol, and John Ryan on charges of robbery and larceny, and James Kay for horse stealing. All were found guilty along with Antonio Christian, convicted of murder. Shinner, Lowndes, and their colleagues, impatient with such criminal violence, applied the full rigors of the law, sentencing all six to death by hanging.[13] Christian was promptly hanged, but Governor Montagu pardoned all five of the backcountry outlaws,[14] to the utter consternation of their victims if not their judges as well. This calculated show of clemency by a well-meaning governor all but destroyed what

---

11. *South Carolina Gazette,* August 3, 1767; Brown, *South Carolina Regulators,* pp. 27–29. The great bulk of regulator cases, involving offenses against the king, were heard in the Court of General Sessions, the journals of which for the years prior to 1769 have been lost. *See* note on last page of Court of General Sessions Journal, 1769–1776, S.C. Archives (hereafter cited General Sessions Journal).

12. Brown, *South Carolina Regulators,* pp. 34–35.

13. *South Carolina Gazette,* April 13, 1767.

14. Ibid.; Brown, *South Carolina Regulators,* p. 38.

was left of backcountry confidence in the judicial system and, more than any other single incident, touched off the Regulator Movement.

The crime wave of the previous year had diminished during the winter months, but by spring the outlaw gangs were again on the prowl, "more formidable than ever, as to numbers, and more audacious and cruel in their thefts and outrages." Operating out of hideouts and strongholds, "a chain of communication" between them and "places of general meeting, where (in imitation of councils of war) they formed plans of operation and defence," the gangs ravaged the interior with greater ferocity than ever.[15] Then news of the pardons issued by Montagu came filtering into the backsettlements, turning initial consternation to outrage which soon gave way to a terrible wrath. Already tormented beyond endurance by marauding cutthroats and now thrown completely on their own resources for redress of grievances, the respectable element in the backcountry took the law into their own hands.

A counterwave of retribution against the outlaw gangs broke out almost without warning in the summer of 1767. All through the backsettlements small farmers turned out by the hundreds, took up arms and rode into the outlaw strongholds scattering the rogues in all directions and burning their camps to the ground. Styling themselves "Regulators," the farmers seized and inflicted summary punishment upon such of their tormentors as they could lay their hands on, binding and flogging the petty offenders and sending the more vicious down to Charles Town for trial. When the gangs regrouped and counterattacked, the regulators were forced to form a tighter organization, and the crackling roar of burning cabins, the clatter of hooves and crash of musket resounded through the valleys of the Carolina piedmont.[16]

Reliable reports of the backcountry war began to reach Charles Town in August along with four captured outlaws brought down to the provincial prison.[17] Governor Montagu issued a proclamation offering rewards to those who should bring in others of the

15. *South Carolina Gazette*, August 3, 1767.
16. Brown, *South Carolina Regulators*, pp. 38–41.
17. *South Carolina Gazette*, August 17, 1767.

"set of daring and attrocious villians." [18] By early October a clearer picture of the conflict resulted in another proclamation ordering the regulators to go home and obey the law, but they refused to disperse. Lowcountry sentiment was generally sympathetic to this stage of regulator activity; even Judges Lowndes acknowledged the justice of their cause:

> Memorials and Petitions were repeatedly delivered in to every branch of the Legislature by the freeholders & best Settlers of the back Country, Complaining of the Devastations and ravages committed by Gangs of Robbers, who Burned their houses, Stole their goods Cattle and Horses and inflicted the most cruel and barbarous Tortures on their Persons, Obliging them for their mutual Security to . . . associate together as the only means of defending [themselves], a number of incontestable proofs verified the justice of their Complaints and not a man in the Province entertain'd the least doubt of their grievances. Stimulated by these provocations . . . the regulating Plan was adopted in prosecution of which, they resorted to Arms, Apprehended whom they thought Proper and in General took upon themselves the redress of their own grievances, no other adequate remedy being then afforded them. [19]

Judge Lowndes translated his sentiments into action when the October sessions came on. In this first criminal court session to be held since removal of the chief justice the previous May, Lowndes emerged as the dominant influence on the provincial bench. The session also represented the first harvest of regulator activity. The *Gazette* reported "50 to 55 criminals in custody for trial, mostly for capital offenses, many of them for murder and horse stealing in the back settlements." [20] From sixty-two bills of indictment the grand jury found fifty true bills, out of which no less than thirty-one cases were tried. Twenty-five defendants were found guilty, and twenty-nine others were bound over to the January sessions. [21]

The regulator harvest resulted in four capital convictions for murder and four more for horse stealing. The Lowndes court sentenced the murderers—Mark Nettles, Sylvester and James Stokes,

18. Ibid., August 24, 1767.
19. SCCJ, February 3, 1772, CO5/502, p. 31, microfilm, S.C. Archives.
20. *South Carolina Gazette*, October 26, 1767.
21. Ibid.

and Thomas Floyd—to death by hanging. The court doubtless would have imposed the same on the four horse thieves, but "the act which rendered HORSE STEALING a felony without benefit of clergy being expired," they were branded instead.[22] Sylvester and James Stokes died on the gallows a week later, but Nettles and Floyd, having petitioned for pardon, "were reprieved until His Majesty's pleasure should be known." Six months later both were pardoned and released.[23]

Dividing their time between court and Commons House, Lowndes and Doyley left the courtroom on adjournment and took their seats in the Assembly chamber where prospects for judicial reform had recently soared. Richard Cumberland had reduced his price for the marshalship to £5000, which the Assembly found acceptable, with payment to be made on Crown approval of a bill establishing courts in the interior and sheriffs to serve the courts.[24] The House heard a regulator remonstrance brought down personally by four backcountry leaders calling for "County Courts, Parishes, Churches, Ministers, Schools, and Representatives" for the interior.[25] To meet the immediate need two companies of rangers, fifty-four men altogether, were authorized to operate against the outlaws and drive them from the colony while the House set to work on the circuit court bill. By the following spring both objectives had been accomplished.

Now mounted, armed, and paid, the regulators, who filled the ranks of the ranger companies and furnished its officers, made short work of the outlaws. Scouring the backcountry with a vengeance, they thoroughly routed the gangs, gathered up the stragglers and scattered the others over the border. Pressing on across provincial boundaries in relentless pursuit, the rangers drove one of the gangs all the way into Virginia and another into the mountains of North Carolina where sixteen were captured and hanged on the spot. Within two months the campaign was over, a

22. Ibid.

23. Ibid., October 26, 1767; May 9, 1768.

24. Committee of Correspondence to Charles Garth, April 16, 1768, "Correspondence of Charles Garth," *SCHGM*, XXX (July, 1929), 181–82; November 11, 13, 1767, Commons Journal, CO5/489, pp. 469, 473–74.

25. Governor Montagu to the Earl of Shelburne, November 10, 1767, SCPRO, XXXI, 423–25; Brown, *South Carolina Regulators*, pp. 41–43.

resounding success, and a restless quiet settled over the back-country.[26]

In April 1768 a second motley passel of rogues faced the stern justice of the Court of General Sessions. Apparently most had been hangers-on or operated on the periphery of the outlaw gangs, whose leaders had been summarily dispatched by the rangers. Out of fifty indictments, forty-four true bills resulted in two death sentences, four brandings and miscellaneous whippings and fines for minor offenses. The four branded were backcountry horse thieves, who escaped sentence of death only because the law making their crime a felony had not been revived. Judge Lowndes would have occasion to remember one of them, John Harvey, "burnt in the hand" for stealing a horse.[27]

Meanwhile, the Assembly had done its work equally well, or so it seemed, producing the Circuit Court Act of 1768 which Governor Montagu had signed on April 12, a week before the April sessions convened. The judges apparently had little to do in framing this act, although Lowndes and Doyley had served on William Wragg's committee of thirteen back in November that outlined its basic features.[28] Since then the detail work had been done by others, most notably attorney John Rutledge, who was attempting at the same time to compile a digest of South Carolina law for the convenience of lawyers and judges on the circuit.[29] The act, pending Crown approval, would set up six circuit courts, each meeting twice a year, at Beaufort and Georgetown in the lowcountry, and in the backcountry settlements of Ninety Six, Orangeburg, Camden, and the Cheraws. Sheriffs for each of the districts were to replace the patent office of provost marshal, and the judges were to be paid generous salaries, £500 sterling for the chief justice and £300 sterling for each assistant. A deceptively small provision attached the judges' salaries to their offices on their being appointed during good behavior.[30] Montagu sent the act on to

26. Ibid., 44–46.
27. *South Carolina Gazette*, May 9, 1768.
28. November 10, 11, 1767, Commons Journal, CO5/489, pp. 465, 468, microfilm, S.C. Archives.
29. Brown, *South Carolina Regulators*, pp. 75–76; *South Carolina Gazette*, May 16, 1768.
30. Brown, *South Carolina Regulators*, p. 76.

England, while the Assembly urged Garth and Cumberland to press for Crown approval.

The Circuit Court Act of 1768 was passed scarcely a month after the death of Chief Justice Shinner, and apparently the combination of these two events wrought a discernible if subtle change in the conduct of Judge Lowndes. Shinner's death suddenly made vacant an office that could rival that of Speaker of the House in prestige. Although the post had been a refuge of placemen since midcentury, Shinner's performance had proved the folly of that policy, enormously increasing prospects for the appointment of a Carolinian thoroughly familiar with provincial law and the judicial system. And what better time to institute a new policy than with a new system? In terms of experience, established character, and knowledge of provincial law as well as judicial procedure, it is doubtful that anyone in the colony was better qualified than Lowndes, if indeed his equal.[31] Assuming that the positions on the provincial bench provided for in the Circuit Court Act were to be filled by colonials, the "Chief Judge" had every reason to consider himself the logical choice for chief justice. Already performing the duties of the office, Lowndes apparently set his cap for the commission and began to conduct himself accordingly.

In the summer of 1768 a new and more threatening phase of the regulator movement erupted. From its inception the nature of the movement made inevitable the injury of innocent parties along with those clearly deserving punishment. Now with the outlaw gangs subdued the regulators turned on the nuisance element of the region, the thieving, shiftless "lower people," and through floggings and forced labor attempted to teach them the rudiments of respectability.[32] Since none of these disciplinary measures were sanctioned by law, injured parties began in 1768

31. Carolina lawyers trained at the Inns of Court constituted a sort of aristocracy among the local attorneys, but the training there was far from rigorous. See Rogers, Evolution of a Federalist, pp. 90–92, and Zahniser, Charles Cotesworth Pinckney, pp. 17–18. William Henry Drayton in 1774 singled out Lowndes as one who "has so well digested his reading—although he never eat commons at the Temple—that he was without dispute at least equal to the law learning of the present Bench," Edward McCrady, The History of South Carolina Under the Royal Government, 1719–1776, (New York, 1899), pp. 470–71.

32. Brown, South Carolina Regulators, pp. 46–50.

to bring charges against the regulators individually in the provincial courts. Writs were issued on the charges brought. When the attorney general brought in an indictment and the grand jury found a true bill, process was issued and the case came before the court whether or not the defendant appeared. On conviction by a jury, the court imposed penalty, usually awarding damages in common pleas or imposing fines in general sessions. Regulator reaction was to defy the provincial government, ignore the authority of the courts, and subject to violent abuse anyone who attempted to serve a writ in their domain.[33]

Though initially sympathetic to the regulators, Judge Lowndes showed no tolerance for their latest outrages committed in open defiance of provincial authority. When they were brought before him he was, in his words, "neither Pusillanimous or Passive," subjecting them to heavy fines and other penalties. As his reputation for sternness spread through the backcountry the regulators marked him out, he said, "as an object of their implacable resentment" and devised various schemes to get him "into their power." But Lowndes was not to be intimidated: "I did not at this time of danger Shrink from my Duty, either to my King or to my Country." He had the satisfaction, as he put it, of bringing to justice many of the rogues and thieves as well as "some of the principal Actors in that Scene of Regulating."[34]

The rigid inflexibility of Judge Lowndes stood in sharp contrast to the lenient policy of Lieutenant Governor Bull, whose humanity and conciliatory disposition were among his most admired qualities. Pointing out their limited means and the extreme provocations suffered by most regulators charged, Bull suggested that charges against all but eight ringleaders be dropped. The attorney general complied only to see one of the judges negate the plan by issuing several more warrants.[35] The focus of subsequent regulator hostility points to Lowndes as the offending judge. But the judge did not always have the last word.

---

33. Ibid., pp. 51–52. For reports of regulator violence typical of the summer of 1768, see *South Carolina Gazette*, June 13, July 11, 25, August 8, 15, 22, September 12, 1768.
34. SCCJ, February 3, 1772, CO5/502, pp. 31–32.
35. Brown, *South Carolina Regulators*, p. 53.

Sentences imposed by the Court of General Sessions were subject to review by the chief executive, usually the lieutenant governor during this period; Governor Montagu went North for the
summer in 1768 and took a two-year leave the following spring.
In his absence Bull frequently pardoned offenders or reduced
their fines, employing the powers of his office to moderate the sectional dispute.[36] By the fall of 1768 the worst was over, although
incidents would continue to flare up from time to time until
courts were established in the region.

Rigorous application of the king's justice by the wealthy lowcountry judge was not easily forgotten. Two years later Benjamin
Farar, member of the Assembly and former regulator, was reprimanded by the House for "very unbecoming and gross Expressions against [Lowndes] in his Judicial Capacity."[37] Bull himself
never criticized Lowndes for his conduct on the bench, as if he
understood the possibility of a strategy behind it, perhaps an effort to convince a reactionary ministry that a native Carolinian
could be trusted with the post of chief justice. Judge Lowndes
would never have permitted such inferences to go unchallenged
in his court, but his next move provides further evidence.

Routine elections in the fall of 1768 returned Lowndes as
usual along with most of the old House. Organizing on November 17, they reelected Manigault Speaker and set the following
afternoon for consideration of the controversial Massachusetts
Circular. Because it called for opposition to the Townshend
Acts, Lord Hillsborough, the Colonial Secretary, had condemned
the circular and ordered dissolution of any provincial assembly
that approved it. Lowndes appeared on the floor the next morning and refused to qualify. The reason he gave was a vaguely
worded statement that "various reasons which now concur" made
it "indispensably necessary for him to retire from a Public Scene
of Business."[38] Only twenty-six members appeared that afternoon

36. See General Sessions Journal, pp. 66, 87–88, 91–93, 130–31, 154–56;
South Carolina Gazette, November 7, 1771.
37. March 2, 1770, Commons Journal, CO5/495, pp. 295–96, microfilm, S.C.
Archives.
38. November 17, 1768, ibid., CO5/491, p. 8; South Carolina Gazette, October 10, 1768; South Carolina Gazette and Country Journal, March 7, 1769.

to endorse the circular and suffer the expected dissolution, while eighteen others besides Lowndes found reasons sufficient to themselves for failing to take a stand.[39]

The public press lauded the courage of the "UNANIMOUS TWENTY-SIX," condemning by implication the timidity of their colleagues, but no criticism ever seems to have been directed at Lowndes for his refusal.[40] It did him not the slightest bit of political damage. Speaker Manigault stood ready to appoint him to the usual positions of influence whenever Lowndes should decide to return to the House; and his colleagues, even the unanimous twenty-six, were prepared to give him their unanimous vote for Speaker should his younger rival decide to vacate the chair. This would never have been possible had they entertained a suspicion of cowardice in the conduct of their former Speaker, which might have happened had he simply delayed his appearance until the critical vote had been taken. But he came before them, stated as honestly and openly as circumstances would permit the indispensable necessity of his refusal, and to a man they seem to have understood.

Rather than evidence of timidity, refusal of his seat was an expedient of clear necessity if Lowndes were to retain any hope of consideration for the appointment of chief justice. Nor was the appointment of a Carolinian an idle dream, for the Hillsborough ministry had decided the idea had possibilities and were in the process of considering Carolinians for the post. This was a goal the colony had cherished since midcentury when their beloved Charles Pinckney had been forced to yield the office to a placeman without any cause shown for his removal.[41] The colony actually had more

---

Activities of the provincial legislature are treated in more detail in the following chapter.

39. *South Carolina Gazette*, November 24, 1768. The twenty-six who attended are listed in this issue.

40. Ibid. The exception was Peter Manigault who made a critical reference to Lowndes' refusal to qualify when the two engaged in a newspaper debate four months later. See *South Carolina Gazette and Country Journal*, March 7, 1769.

41. Zahniser, *Charles Cotesworth Pinckney*, pp. 5–6. When Charles Pinckney sailed for England the *South Carolina Gazette*, April 11, 1752 praised him thus: "We cannot omit saying, that he was a true Father of his Country . . . ."

to gain from a change in policy than did the Carolinian who won appointment to the office. Judge Lowndes had every reason to believe that, if the ministry had learned anything from the Shinner debacle and based the appointment on merit, he had earned the right to primary consideration. But Crown policy all too often failed to follow the dictates of common sense. Sometime during the next three months Lowndes learned to his utter dismay that the policy had indeed changed but the criteria had not: he was to be passed over in favor of William Wragg.[42]

The thinking behind Wragg's appointment seems obvious enough. Of an old and well-established Carolina family, Wragg held the British view that men of substance and property by virtue of their standing in the community were entitled to hold the reins of government. Independence of mind was his most outstanding quality. He had served on Governor Lyttelton's Council until his summary removal for outspokenness in 1756 destroyed the prestige of the Upper House. Moving immediately into the Commons House, he became one of its most active leaders until 1765 when his single vote kept the House from giving unanimous approval to the Stamp Act resolves, which denied the right of Parliament to tax the colonies.[43] Moreover, following the Stamp Act case, Governor Montagu had warned the ministry about the growing power of the assistant judges.[44] These were all the facts necessary for Hillsborough's decision. The mysterious workings of the ministerial brain were not always easy for colonials to fathom, but everybody knew Lord Hillsborough put a premium on obedience to royal authority.

There seems little doubt that it was Hillsborough's decision to

42. The author realizes he makes an important assumption here, that Lowndes learned of the ministry's intentions some weeks before official receipt of the news, but this was not at all uncommon, as examples such as early information on the Stamp Act's passage and repeal indicate. The assumption provides the only plausible explanation for Lowndes' subsequent behavior. Formal announcement of Wragg's appointment came in a letter from Lord Hillsborough to Governor Montagu, March 25, 1769, SCPRO, XXXII, p. 75.

43. Rogers, *Evolution of a Federalist*, pp. 38, 39, 50–51; Wallace, *South Carolina, A Short History*, p. 232; November 28, 29, 1765, Commons Journal, CO5/484, pp. 25–31, microfilm, S.C. Archives.

44. Governor Montagu to Lords of Trade, August 6, 1766, SCPRO, XXXI, p. 86.

appoint Wragg rather than Lowndes that drew from the latter a reaction which stands as one of the most revealing episodes in a long public career. If his indignation drove Lowndes to inquire about recommendations for the appointment, a supposition by no means unlikely, he would have been told that provincial opinion had not been solicited.[45] Faced with the utter futility of lashing out at the ministry, Lowndes apparently brooded over the matter. Finally he turned on the scapegoat nearest at hand.

On February 28, 1769, an essay appeared in the *South Carolina Gazette and Country Journal* over the name "Bobbedel," offering some thoughts on the upcoming general election. Bobbedel proposed to the voters "an Alteration in their Conduct" that he expected would have a beneficial effect on political affairs. To illustrate his point, he selected an incident that he had "either heard, read or dreamt of," taking place in a certain political club:

> The next that stood up was Lawyer Scout, and he spoke to the Following Effect,—"Sir, the Business now under our Consideration, is the choosing a proper Person to preside in this Club, and I move that Mr. Peter Pounce may take the Chair; it is true Mr. Friendless was our late Chairman, and he behaved well, no man has any Thing to object to him, his Character is well established, and if we were to follow Precedents, he certainly should have the Precedence; but, Sir, it is time to depart from such Precedents, this Club have few Opportunities of distinguishing its Members, and it is very just and reasonable that *our Favours should not be confined to one Man*, but that *every* Member should have a Chance of succeeding to that honorable Station by Rotation, and therefore, Sir, I hope my Motion will have the Approbation of the Club, and that Mr. Peter Pounce may be our Chairman."

Bobbedel remembered that these arguments had convinced a majority in the club to approve the scheme. He now suggested that the same principle be applied in the upcoming election:

> Perhaps a few formal precise People may still hold odd Notions, that it is ungenerous, if not dishonourable, to discard or abandon old trusty Servants, who have faithfully and conscientiously done their Duty, and that to Affront them unnecessarily in so public and undeserved a Manner, is neither agreeable to Humanity or good Breed-

---

45. Official correspondence in SCPRO contains no reference to the appointment of Shinner's successor before the appointment was announced.

ing; but these Niceties and Scruples are more suitable to the old fashioned antiquated Times, in which our Fore-fathers lived, than the refined enlightened Taste of the present Generation, and if we have but a Majority for the Thing, we will Laugh at such chimerical Stuff. I hope to see in the next House 50 new Members of our young Friends and boon Companions, who will afford us many Opportunities of sacrificing to Bacchus, and I doubt not will soon evince the Propriety of the Measure, and do honor to the Penetration and Sagacity of Lawyer Scout.

It was a rare Charlestonian who did not recognize in Bobbedel and Peter Pounce the former Speaker of the Commons House and his successor, Peter Manigault.[46]

No one expected the high-spirited Manigault to suffer in silence such aspersions on the honor and breeding of his friends and himself. If he was shocked at the attack he quickly recovered. One week later his response appeared over the signature of Demosius. It was immediately apparent that in this contest Lowndes was overmatched, at least in terms of cleverness, wit, and literary style, as Manigault employed the weapon of ridicule with telling effect:

The World in general seems to think that Friendless is the Author of the Letter signed Bobbedel, and published in your last Paper. But I, who am well acquainted with the Man, am by no Means of this Opinion; and that for two Reasons; 1st, Because the Letter has some Strokes of Humor in it, which are inconsistent with *the Pomposity of his Character, the affected Austerity of his Manners, and his Ideas of his own Importance*: And 2dly, Because the Stile is very different from that of Friendless.[47]

To illustrate, Manigault thus quoted a recent advertisement placed by Lowndes: "Strayed from my Plantation, the beginning of May, a Pair of Sorrel or Chestnut Horses, very much alike, only one carries himself closer behind than the other, they are long sided, *has* Silver Manes and Tails, lately trimmed, etc."

It is observable [he continued], that the above Description of the Horses, especially the one that goes *Close*, suits the Owner so exactly, that it is impossible for any Man who reads it, to Mistake his

46. *South Carolina Gazette and Country Journal*, February 28, 1769. Richard J. Hooker was the first historian to identify them; *see* Hooker, ed., *Woodmason*, p. 268 and note.
47. *South Carolina Gazette and Country Journal*, March 7, 1769.

Person. And so striking is the Resemblance, that if he were a Deserter from one of his Majesty's Regiments, tis odds, that he would be carried to *Head Quarters,* or brought to *my Quarters,* (which indeed would be only returning him to his *Old Quarters*) by the first Person who met him. It is merry enough too, that he has left it to the Sagacity of his Readers, to find out whether the Horses are *Sorrel* or *Chesnut*; the Owner being content, as he had lost a Pair of Horses, to have either *Chesnuts or Sorrels* in their Room, provided they both HAS *Silver Manes and Tails."*

Manigault went on in the same vein making sport of the way Lowndes revealed the limitations of his provincial education: how *"mechanically* he . . . learned to spell his own name," how "a certain Paper of his writing [was] corrected in a Dozen different Places, before it was admitted on the Journals of his favourite Club," and how, even in his recent essay, he had misspelled the fictitious name "BOBADIL." [48]

Manigault attributed Lowndes' ill humor to envy and disappointed ambition. He expected the former Speaker one day to "burst himself with Envy," like the frog in the fable. Moreover, "Disappointed in his ambitious Views, he looks upon every Man to be his Enemy, who in the Club he raves about, does not express the same lofty Ideas, of his *Parts and Penetration,* as he has formed of them himself." Having pointed out Lowndes' "Foibles," Manigault could find no merit in the man: "that Side of his Character, presents a perfect Blank." Furthermore, Lowndes was lacking in gratitude, "For he has entirely forgot me, who was the first Step to his Rise. But perhaps! he will recollect me, when I prove, to be the last, to his Elevation." [49]

For all his display of wit and literary skill, Manigault had sidestepped the issue and delivered an uncharitable personal attack on his antagonist. He had been at great pains to ridicule Lowndes for ignorance, vanity, and envy with never a reference to the propriety of his removal. There was enough sting in Manigault's remarks to provoke a response from Lowndes over the pseudonym "Friendless" on March 23. He admitted authorship of the "Bobbedel" piece and his lack of literary grace, but he was by no means chastened.

48. Ibid.
49. Ibid.

It is now certain, that although *Friendless* has not sense enough to advertise a horse, yet without a LATIN Motto or even studying *Orthography*, he could write intelligibly in some other Cases, so as to be understood by, and provoke the resentment too, of one of the Literati, who it appears has not yet *learnt* philosophy enough to bear with patience the Truth, tho' put into a disguised habit.

. . . You have indeed PETER, very incautiously convinced the world that you have taken uncommon pains to rake into old News-Papers and musty Journals, not to find precedents to justify your conduct, but to pick out something that your '*good nature*' might turn against me, if peradventure . . . some little inaccuracy or literary error, might turn up to gratify a mean, pitiful, captious spirit; and behold, 'the mountain has brought forth a mouse!' The poor little monysyllable 'HAS', is, with great pomp and triumph, produced in evidence against me . . . and from this only proof . . . am I arraigned of ignorance, envy, ambition, and such like petty names . . . refined down into the gentle term of 'foibles.'[50]

His critic might rest his case on grammar and orthography but Lowndes preferred to concentrate on conduct in office. He chided Manigault for a reluctance to join the speakers of other colonial assemblies, who had written open letters against British policy, "wrote in such a stile, with much ardour, energy and spirit," that in Lowndes' opinion reflected credit on themselves and their constituents.[51] Regarding the criticism of his own style, he challenged his critic to "publish *the whole of both our works or failings* together, and I will be at half the expense: Your industry in searching into News Papers, will better qualify you for the office of Editor . . . but observe before hand, I object to *scraps* and *pieces*." He denied the allegation of envy: "I am thankful to Providence for the portion of its goodness and favour it has allotted me, sincerely, Sir, *envying* no man his superior '*abilities*,' or the advantages he derives from them." He could read a good performance with pleasure, he said, and from a due sense of his own imperfections, he

50. Ibid., March 23, 1769.
51. Manigault had shown a prudence worthy of Lowndes himself in declining to commit his legislative colleagues to support policies originating in the northern colonies. A letter from Thomas Cushing vigorously defending colonial rights had been published in the *South Carolina Gazette* on May 2, 1768. Montagu had not responded until late in July, and then only to say the matter would be taken up by the Assembly at its next sitting. *See South Carolina Gazette*, September 12, 1768; Rogers, *Evolution of a Federalist*, pp. 48–49; Crouse, "Manigault Family," pp. 215–16.

could overlook and excuse the incorrectness of others. But Manigault had simply attempted to divert public attention from the issue which Lowndes had raised:

> It is not, Sir, whether a *fictitious* name is rightly spelled; it is not whether an advertisement is wrote 'Orthographically;' it is not about '*Literary talents*' neither; if it had, I should have given up the point, or rather I would never have made a *point* of it at all: No, Sir, it is not the 'propriety' of WRITING, but the 'propriety' of ACTING, that is the primary and known cause of our difference; keep to that mark, Sir, and let us take the opinion of the public upon it . . . whether your fable of the frog is applicable to me—whether envy, ambition &c. on my part, or an ungenerous, unprovoked insult on yours, is the source of the present contention, and the reason that we are not now, as we heretofore were, good friends.[52]

Here Lowndes concluded his essay. At this point he should have left well enough alone. His effort had been quite able and his arguments well made, so that for the present he appeared to have possession of the field. But he fancied he had caught Manigault himself in violation of the rules of grammar and could not resist adding this postscript: "Be pleased to let me know, whether the word 'WERE,' applied to a 'deserter from one of his Majesty's regiments,' is, in your idea, agreeable to Grammatical strictness; if it is not, 'why beholdest thou the mote in thy brother's eye, but considerest not the beam that is in thine own eye!'"[53] Manigault never replied; indeed he might well have been too thoroughly amused to respond, for Lowndes had just proved his case. The postscript exposed Lowndes to all the world as an utter stranger to the mysteries of the subjunctive mood.

Neither Lowndes nor Manigault ever again resorted to the public press to air a personal quarrel. After their tempers had cooled both had reason to regret that they had done so this once. The sensitive pride of Lowndes had obviously generated what can only be described as self-pity fed by a festering resentment. Manigault was doubtless correct in his accusation that Lowndes was suffering from "disappointed ambition" but missed the mark in branding him with envy. What burned in the soul of Rawlins

52. *South Carolina Gazette and Country Journal*, March 23, 1769.
53. Ibid.

Lowndes was clearly something deeper, a firm conviction that his
personal merit had been disregarded, first by House members who
maneuvered Manigault into his chair in 1765, and now by a reactionary ministry that cast aside "old trusty servants" in favor of
the only member of that House who refused to challenge parliamentary authority. References to his pompous behavior and
affected austerity of manner suggest that Lowndes was more than
a little pretentious, a common human failing expecially among
men who have overcome humble circumstances to achieve wealth
and status without finding opportunity to acquire the trappings
of culture and taste appropriate to their new station in life.

Manigault's essay was even more revealing of himself. On the
surface he merely toyed with Lowndes, treating him, as Woodmason remarked, like a "meer School Boy [who] deserved Whip-
ping." [54] With stinging wit and literary dash he eluded his stolid
opponent and, thrusting straight for the jugular, dispatched him
to his own satisfaction. Only upon reflection did the triumph become hollow when arrogant presumption of superiority gained
through circumstance of birth and family fortune began to show
through the clever facade.

A notable difference in attitude between members of the South
Carolina oligarchy could be detected by the knowledgeable observer, a difference that would become more apparent when it began
to influence political alliances in the next decade. Both Lowndes
and Manigault undoubtedly considered themselves members of
the provincial aristocracy, but the difference lay in their assump-
tions. Lowndes and his peers had assumed the pretensions of an
aristocratic class along with its responsibilities, the duty of public
service. They competed among themselves for public honors available to them and uniformly resented the advantages that English
placemen brought with them into the contest. Manigault and the
younger men who shared his outlook, the Rutledges, Middletons,
and Pinckneys, appeared to be taking on the presumptions of
aristocratic status. Manigault himself, who seems to have exerted
a moderating influence on the younger men, was removed from
the political scene before this attitude was translated into revolu-

54. Hooker, ed., *Woodmason*, p. 268.

tionary politics of the next decade. By then it had evolved into something approaching the British prerogative of aristocratic status, the right to govern.[55] The result would be a contest over the nature of state government and the limits of its republican form.

Their public quarrel having proven to the average Carolinian that his most trusted leaders were as human as himself where personal pride was concerned, Lowndes and Manigault soon recovered their composure and returned to public business. It was to the credit of both that neither seems to have permitted their personal antagonism to affect their official conduct. Lowndes merely continued the practice of waiting for each new House to organize and elect Manigault Speaker before taking his own seat. Speaker Manigault for his part continued to recognize through committee appointments Lowndes' standing in the House.

New elections held early in March 1769 returned Manigault, Lowndes, and most incumbents to the House, but a series of prorogations kept the Assembly from meeting. In the meantime official word of Wragg's appointment arrived only to be greeted by a polite rejection from the most independent-minded man in the colony.[56] Wragg's refusal may well have been a subtle rebuke to the Hillsborough ministry if not part of a concerted plan. Wragg was just the sort to take exception to ministerial condescension, especially when all his peers knew why he had been singled out. He stated his reasons to several members of the bar and conveyed by private letter his apologies to Hillsborough, but both went unrecorded.[57] With Wragg removed from consideration the ministry was faced with a choice between naming Lowndes or some other provincial Whig to the post or giving up the new policy altogether and reverting to the practice of appointing

55. One of the best analyses of this attitude among future political leaders of South Carolina, the Rutledge-Pinckney faction, is in Zahniser, *Charles Cotesworth Pinckney*, pp. 102–6. *See also* Edward Rutledge to John Jay, June 29, 1776, *Letters of Members of the Continental Congress*, ed. Edmund Cody Burnett, 8 vols. (Washington, 1921–1936), I, 518; Edward Rutledge to John Jay, November 24, 1776, *The Correspondence and Public Papers of John Jay*, ed. Henry Phelps Johnston, 4 vols. (New York, 1970, 2nd ed.), I, 94.

56. Governor Montagu to Lord Hillsborough, June 30, 1769, SCPRO, XXXII, 80.

57. Ibid.; *South Carolina and American General Gazette*, July 4, 1769.

placemen. On the objectionable point of challenge to parliamentary taxation, Lowndes clearly had the best case behind Wragg's. The chief judge had not voted on the Stamp Act resolves, and his opinion on *Jordan* v. *Law* had confined the issue to the unavailability of stamps and consequent impossibility of executing the law, carefully avoiding any challenge to parliamentary authority.

Following Wragg's refusal in June 1769, the South Carolina Association was formed with the purpose of forcing repeal of the Townshend duties. Judges Pringle and Powell subscribed the Association, but Lowndes again avoided giving offense to Hillsborough, explaining that his signing would be "incompatible with his [judicial] office, in case any matters relative thereto might come in judgement before him. . . ."[58] The provincial government if not the entire population of Charles Town was in full cooperation with Lowndes. Unrestrained abuse fell on other nonsigners but Judge Lowndes went unscathed, both publicly and politically.

Meanwhile the Circuit Court Act of 1768 had run afoul of the royal prerogative and come back disallowed. The ministry had found particular fault with the clause attaching salaries to judicial offices contingent upon the appointment of judges during good behavior.[59] Ignoring the fact that judicial tenure in England was dependent on good behavior, the ministry considered the clause as insult to the Crown and demanded its deletion, along with some other minor changes in the act. Lowndes took his seat after the House organized the last week in June, and Manigault named him to the committee that made the necessary revisions.[60] Completing their work by the end of July and adjusting the date to 1769, the House yielded all points demanded by the Crown, even the essential one of judicial tenure, in order to meet the pressing need for courts in the backsettlements.[61] Governor Mon-

58. Bull to Hillsborough, December 5, 1770, SCPRO, XXXII, 408.
59. Matthew Lamb to Lords of Trade, July 22, 1768, SCPRO, XXXII, 24–25; Hillsborough to Bull, October 12, 1768, ibid., pp. 51–53, found the provision "altogether inadmissible."
60. July 1, 1769, Commons Journal, CO5/495, p. 25, microfilm, S.C. Archives.
61. Brown, *South Carolina Regulators*, pp. 96–98.

tagu signed the bill on Saturday evening, July 29, and the next day sailed for England taking the act with him for delivery to Hillsborough in person.[62] Finding the colony had capitulated to its demands, the ministry offered no real objection to the act so it became Carolina law in November 1769.

Actually the law would not go into effect until courthouses and jails were built and officers were appointed to serve the courts. Since construction would take well over a year to complete, Hillsborough and Bull opened an unhurried correspondence on the matter of selecting circuit judges. If Hillsborough had tipped his hand with the abortive appointment of William Wragg, he openly revealed it when he asked Bull in December 1769 for recommendations on assistant judges, clearly intending to select a chief justice without provincial advice.[63] There was no longer a probability, if there ever had been, that a Carolina Whig would receive the appointment.

Bull pondered the matter until the following March before sending his response. In some of the most diplomatic language that ever passed between continents the lieutenant governor suggested that Hillsborough might find lawyers in England that had failed to meet the competition there, who might be persuaded to close their mediocre careers riding circuit through the Carolina wilderness for £300 a year.[64] The idea had merit, and Bull was persuasive in arguing its advantages. His point that the present bench consisted of laymen "not bred to the Law," who would be on the circuit without ready counsel of more learned men was particularly convincing. Bull also spoke of the difficulty of finding lawyers here willing to leave off other business to serve on the bench.[65]

The current bench, however, could have offered several valid counterpoints that the lieutenant governor failed to mention. If they were considered adequate to the demands of the capital they surely were competent to meet the more limited needs of the interior. Moreover, it was unreasonable to expect Carolina judges

62. Bull to Hillsborough, August 12, 1769, SCPRO, XXXII, 91.
63. Hillsborough to Bull, December 9, 1769, SCPRO, XXXII, 131.
64. Bull to Hillsborough, March 7, 1770, SCPRO, XXXII, 206–8.
65. Ibid.

who had served for years in Charles Town without pay, to decline an additional responsibility that paid £150 sterling for riding each circuit of the new provincial courts. Of greater importance was the fact that conspicuous honors were becoming more scarce in a provincial government increasingly staffed by placemen. Finally Bull's known sentiments, his peculiar circumstances and his innate sagacity must be taken into account.

Although Bull's loyalty to the Crown was beyond question, his apparent plea for placemen seems inconsistent with his sympathetic understanding of provincial sentiment during the Stamp Act controversy. It is difficult to conceive of his being now so insensitive to provincial opinion that he would recommend without other cause a program calculated to embitter his fellow Carolinians. The explanation seems to lie in his circumstances.

Four months before Hillsborough's request for recommendations the lieutenant governor named George Gabriel Powell, a planter and an outspoken critic of ministerial policy, to Benjamin Smith's vacant seat, making a full complement of assistant judges.[66] Then in December the South Carolina Commons House quietly made a grant of public funds to aid the notorious Crown critic, John Wilkes.[67] The grant was supported by Lowndes, Doyley, and Powell in spite of the fact that it was certain to incur the royal displeasure. On reading Hillsborough's December letter a few weeks later Bull could not but have realized the earl's apparent determination to have his own man in the post of chief justice. In view of the recent Shinner debacle and the temper of the present bench, it was not too difficult to predict another wrangle in the courts. Bull apparently felt it his duty to suggest a practical alternative. Furthermore it seemed only prudent to test ministerial reaction to the Wilkes grant before proceeding further. When the earl replied in April with a reiteration of his initial request, the responsibility for difficulties that might develop in the future shifted to London.[68]

In June the lieutenant governor recommended the bench then

---

66. Miscellaneous Records, PP, pp. 175–76, S.C. Archives. Powell was appointed August 10, 1769.
67. This subject will be treated more fully in the following chapter.
68. Hillsborough to Bull, April 14, 1770, SCPRO, XXXII, 253–54.

presiding as fit persons to receive commissions under the new law. Doyley had dropped out after the January sessions and John Murray, a lawyer from North Britain, had replaced him.[69] Bull described Lowndes, Pringle, and Powell as "men of integrity, understanding and propriety," who were "as well qualified as most who would consent to act in that office," presumably including second-rate lawyers from England.[70] By the time Hillsborough returned to the subject four months later the Wilkes Fund Controversy had made its impact on the Crown. On October 3 the powerful earl firmly set criteria for the South Carolina bench. They must be "well qualified . . . , attached to His Majesty's Person and Government . . . , true friends to the Constitution [and] free from factious connections and unconstitutional prejudices."[71] In one stroke Hillsborough eliminated from consideration every man of standing in South Carolina except the lieutenant governor himself.

Under these strictures the lieutenant governor withdrew the names of Lowndes, Pringle, and Powell, retaining Murray whose politics were "unexceptionable." After making inquiries among those who might be suitable, Bull reported, "Some have wholly declined, others object to the fatigue of the Circuits to which three hundred pounds is not equivalent." Besides Murray the best he could come up with were three candidates. The first was Wellins Colcott, a forty-two-year-old English lawyer recently arrived in Charles Town with a character recommendation from a London clergyman. His legal training would "give him importance on the Bench" since the other two knew next to nothing about the business. George Milligan was a surgeon "at small pay" to the king's troops in South Carolina which, being gone from the colony, had left him unemployed: "His education renders him as capable of acquiring knowledge as others not bred to the Law." The last was William Henry Drayton, recommended, despite his youth, for his liberal education and the fact that he was related to the lieutenant governor.[72]

69. General Sessions Journal, p. 48, March 5, 1770.
70. Bull to Hillsborough, June 13, 1770, SCPRO, XXXII, 290.
71. Hillsborough to Bull, October 3, 1770, ibid., pp. 334–36.
72. Bull to Hillsborough, December 5, 1770, ibid., pp. 407–9, 410–15.

On reading Bull's letter Hillsborough realized he would have to find suitable men himself. He set aside the recommendations except for Murray's and began to send over new judges one by one, provoking growing resentment in the colony and an apparent slowdown in construction of the new courthouses and jails.[73] In 1771 Pringle stepped down to admit Edward Savage, and by October the new chief justice, Thomas Knox Gordon, a Dublin lawyer reputed to be "a Gentleman of Eminence in his Profession," had arrived.[74] Lowndes and Powell still held their commissions.

A fundamental difference in approach separated Lowndes from the new judges. Unfamiliar with provincial custom and circumstances they tended to adhere strictly to the letter of the law in rendering decisions, while Lowndes relied as often on common sense and reason as on the law. This difference was illustrated in one case when Lowndes remarked that "their opinion might be law but he was Sure it was not Reason," evoking a raised eyebrow from Chief Justice Gordon.[75] Their "officious arrogance" and uncompromising legalism contrasted sharply with the homespun approach of Judge Lowndes. These factors combined with colonial resentment to make a clash inevitable.

A regulator incident occurred in 1769, dragged through the Court of Common Pleas for two years, and eventually resulted in a spectacular clash between Judge Lowndes and Chief Justice Gordon. On September 26, 1769, at Noble's Creek in Granville County a group of settlers caught John Harvey in possession of a stolen horse. Seized and held in confinement for three days, Harvey was then taken out, tied to a tree, and in the presence of a large crowd of people from the neighborhood, was given a sound thrashing and released.[76] Four days later in Charles Town Harvey swore out a warrant for David Robinson, one of the group who had abused him, seeking damages in the amount of £1000.[77] Since Harvey was suing for damages, the case was to be tried in

73. Brown, *South Carolina Regulators*, p. 109.
74. *South Carolina Gazette*, January 3, 1771.
75. SCCJ, February 3, 1772, CO5/502, p. 39.
76. Judgement Rolls, 1771, no. 135A, S.C. Archives.
77. Ibid.

common pleas rather than in the Court of General Sessions where offenses against the king were heard. This fact was important, for whatever damages the jury awarded could not be remitted by the governor but would have to be paid in the full amount.

By the time the case came to trial in October 1771 the composition of the court was the most important factor. Chief Justice Gordon was now presiding along with three assistant judges, John Murray, Edward Savage, and Rawlins Lowndes, the only native judge among them. Having recently arrived in the colony, Gordon and Savage were unfamiliar with circumstances in the province at the time the offense was committed, a fact which could be expected to prejudice the case against the defendant. David Robinson had the further misfortune to secure the services of a lawyer, not identified in the records, who made an initial appearance in his behalf, then abandoned him to prosecution.[78] As Robinson failed to appear in his own defense, guilt was presumed and judgment went by default to the plaintiff, John Harvey. The only question for the jury to determine was the amount of damages to be awarded.

Since no witnesses appeared for the defense, Harvey's attorney, James Parsons, was able to compile a damning indictment against Robinson. This disturbed Judge Lowndes, who recognized Harvey as "one of those Vagrant Rogues who infested the back Country" during the 1760s. Lowndes noted the behavior of the plaintiff, standing by as his friends gave testimony in his behalf, "with a pitious, distressed, mellancholy Countenance, Calculated very opportunely to excite Compassion, and with the presumption in his favour of being a very good harmless Creature."[79] Through questioning of witnesses Lowndes established that Robinson was a poor man of good character, but it was clear the case was going heavily against him and the damages would be large.

Chief Justice Gordon, with nothing more to go on than the testimony he had heard, was incensed at Robinson's conduct. In charging the jury the chief justice denounced the flogging of Harvey as "an audacious insult against the Laws of the Country and

78. SCCJ, February 3, 1772, CO5/502, p. 28.
79. Ibid., pp. 33–34.

the Public Peace" and recommended that full damages be awarded.[80]

Convinced that a miscarriage of justice was about to occur, Judge Lowndes felt constrained to offer for the jury's consideration some valid points that had not been brought out in the testimony. He declared that had Robinson's attorney not abandoned him, several extenuating circumstances might have been brought out that would serve to mitigate the damages to be awarded. He recounted in great detail the violence and disorder that plagued the settlers in the backcountry during the time the offense was committed, circumstances that the chief justice could not be expected to be acquainted with, but which drove men of good character such as Robinson to seek redress by committing violence on rogues and vagabonds infesting the region. While Lowndes could not excuse the regulators' illegal proceedings and applied to them the rigors of the law, the government in consideration of their provocations remitted their penalties, in order "To draw a Vail over all past Transactions." [81] But since this was a civil case, he said, the governor had no authority to intervene so that whatever damages were awarded must be paid. Lowndes observed that the character of the parties at suit was a fit subject for the jury's inquiry, and that he was "warranted to Say from the record of the Court of Sessions, That the plaintiff's stood in no very favorable point of view in that Respect." [82]

At this point Chief Justice Gordon interrupted and told the jury to disregard what Lowndes was saying, that it had not been entered in the evidence nor was the character of the plaintiff the point of issue in the case. Enraged at Gordon's arrogance in presuming to interrupt him while he was addressing the jury, Lowndes shot back that he was not to be called to order in giving his opinion "when Judicially required of me" and that on the bench he had an equal voice with the chief justice. Gordon replied, according to his account of the affair, that he had no intention of disputing Lowndes' right to sit on the bench, but that he considered it his duty to prevent anything from being laid

80. Ibid., p. 20.
81. Ibid., pp. 27–29.
82. Ibid., p. 29.

before the jury that had not been entered in evidence. Lowndes exploded "That he would prove Harvey to be a Villain and a Rogue, and that he had been tried in that Court and Burned in the hand, and for that purpose desired that Mr. Johnston the Clerk . . . might be sworn, and called for the Book, and said he himself would go off the bench and be sworn and give evidence of it." Judge Savage then joined the argument pronouncing Lowndes' observations on the plaintiff's record immaterial to the case. Lowndes managed to keep silent and the case thus went to the jury.[83] When the jury returned Gabriel Manigault announced their decision: fifty pounds currency damages and court costs.[84]

Gordon immediately left the court, found Governor Montagu, and demanded that Lowndes be dismissed from the bench for conduct "highly improper and unbecoming the Station and Character of one of the King's Judges," and for advancing doctrines that "tended to Stir up the People in this Province to Sedition and Disobedience to His Magesty's Government."[85] Lowndes was forthwith summoned before governor and Council where Gordon repeatedly demanded that he explain his behavior. Notwithstanding Gordon's vehemence Lowndes refused to answer until the charges were put in writing. His accuser had no choice but to comply, and six weeks later submitted the formal charges.

In his defense Lowndes recounted the details of the incident, and while he admitted violating the rules of evidence used in England, he refused to apologize for his conduct:

> I would not on any trivial light occasion interfere in a matter of that sort, I never did it before in any one instance, but where it is of importance in a public as well as a private view, I never did, I never shall think it below the Character of the highest and most exalted Station, or degrading even to a Judge in his Scarlet Robes, in the Cause of truth, to give evidence before a Jury of his Peers. Judge Gascoignes' declaration to Henry the fourth, that he would Condemn a Man in his judicial Capacity, that in his private, he knew to be innocent, is according to my limited Ideas of Justice and Law, absurd & inhumane.[86]

83. Ibid., pp. 21–22, 29.
84. Ibid., pp. 36–37; Judgement Rolls, 1771, no. 135A, S.C. Archives.
85. SCCJ, February 3, 1772, CO5/502, pp. 22–23; ibid., November 14, 1771, XXXVI, Part 1, 218, S.C. Archives.
86. Ibid., February 3, 1772, CO5/502, pp. 30–31.

Actually Lowndes was well within the bounds of Carolina custom when he offered evidence in behalf of the defendant. Bull had written to Hillsborough in 1770 explaining that "the Judges are considered as Counsel for the Prisoners."[87] When the Council dismissed the charges, Lowndes had won a small triumph to the applause of friends like Henry Laurens: "Mr. Lowndes . . . came off in the dispute with the chief justice and appeal to the Council, without Censure and he certainly deserved none."[88]

The Lowndes-Gordon affair was only another in a growing list of incidents that caused South Carolinians in increasing numbers to call into question the wisdom of ministerial authority and colonial policy in general. If customs racketeering drove the moderate Henry Laurens into the arms of more radical leaders like Christopher Gadsden, arbitrary ministerial policy regarding the courts pushed Lowndes in the same direction.[89] Nor was he alone in his resentment. The bitterness of Carolinians over loss of their native judges lingered for years afterwards, a fact that has been well documented.[90] Courts like taxes touch the lives of every citizen, and the manner in which those in South Carolina were given over to men whose chief recommendation was obedience to an arbitrary ministry sent many a Carolinian down the road to revolution.

The new circuit courts were finally completed and set to open for the October sessions of 1772, but Justices Lowndes and Powell would never ride circuit. The commission for their replacements, John Fewtrell and Charles Croslett, had arrived the previous April. Judge Lowndes donned his judicial wig and scarlet robe

87. Bull to Hillsborough, November 30, 1770, SCPRO, XXXII, 377.
88. Henry Laurens to John Lewis Gervais, May 29, 1772, Henry Laurens Papers, microfilm, SCHS.
89. Rogers, *Evolution of a Federalist*, p. 48. On the importance of an independent judiciary in the ideology of colonial America, *see* Bernard Bailyn, *The Ideological Origins of the American Revolution* (Cambridge, Mass., 1967), pp. 74–75.
90. Brown, *South Carolina Regulators*, pp. 108–9; Rogers, *Evolution of a Federalist*, pp. 74–75. On October 24, 1771, the *South Carolina Gazette* with a fine edge of sarcasm referred to the new judges as "Gentlemen of Fortune, Abilities and Character." A more plaintive note may be detected in the announcement that the last placeman had taken his seat on the bench, "so that all our present Justices are from Abroad," ibid., April 30, 1772.

for the last time on April 21, 1772, and made a final appearance on the bench. Two days later, "without any cause assigned or misbehavior imputed to [him], contrary to the Spirit of the English Constitution," his commission was revoked.[91] He had not heard his last case, however, for the most important decision of his judicial career lay in the future.

91. Ibid.; General Sessions Journal, pp. 160, 184-87; Miscellaneous Records, PP, pp. 171, 175; October 27, 1772, Commons Journal, CO5/504, p. 14, all in S.C. Archives. Justice Powell's commission was revoked the same day.

CHAPTER VIII

Speaker

COLONIAL OPPOSITION, united and powerful, forced repeal of the Stamp Act. No law in the history of the English colonies had provoked such a universal outcry of protest. Everywhere the law was met with violence, preventing its operation and eventually forcing Parliament to retreat. During the controversy, traditions of loyalty were profoundly disturbed. Afterwards the colonies came to rely increasingly upon each other through intercolonial cooperation in order to defend traditional rights against fresh inroads of ministerial and parliamentary authority. South Carolinians developed a particular sensitivity to reports of how the struggle was being carried on in the more northerly colonies and in England as well. Their reaction to these reports provoked a series of conflicts with the representatives of royal authority that from 1768 onwards formed an unbroken "bridge to revolution."[1]

At first it seemed the dawning of a new day. In the general exultation over the Stamp Act's repeal, South Carolinians ignored the Declaratory Act and indulged themselves in effusions of loyalty to the Crown. Even before official receipt of the news, the Commons House, on the motion of Rawlins Lowndes, voted £7000 for a statue of William Pitt to be erected in Charles Town at the intersection of Broad and Meeting streets in gratitude for Pitt's exertions for repeal. Shortly afterwards the Commons House unanimously voted "that a Dutiful and Loyal Address of Thanks,

1. Jack P. Greene, "Bridge to Revolution: The Wilkes Fund Controversy in South Carolina, 1769–1775," *The Journal of Southern History*, XXIX (February, 1963), pp. 19–52; *see also The Nature of Colony Constitutions*, ed. Jack P. Greene (Columbia, S.C., 1970), pp. 5–55.

be Presented to His Most Gracious Majesty on the Repeal of the Stamp Act." One week later the House greeted the new governor, Lord Charles Greville Montagu, with expressions of congratulation on his safe arrival and promises of cooperation to make his administration a success. Even when Montagu announced an additional instruction requiring the Commons to pay him a "Salary" instead of the usual "Gifts or Presents" granted to former governors, the news was accepted without protest. So expansive was the prevailing mood that the House readily granted to Montagu's predecessor, the despised Thomas Boone, more than £8000 in back pay.[2]

It scarcely troubled Carolinians that the Sugar Act had not also been repealed, for molasses had never become a significant article of their trade. But they were encouraged to believe that other restrictive laws might be removed. One act of Parliament in particular, the Currency Act, had hampered commerce in South Carolina since 1751 by limiting issues of local currency to £106,500. Hence a petition calling for repeal of the Currency Act was submitted in November 1766.[3] The refusal of Parliament to take action on this petition had a dampening effect on Carolina spirits. Then with the passage of the Townshend duties in 1767, the brief honeymoon in South Carolina came to an end.

Opposition to the Townshend duties, which taxed the colonies on imports of glass, paint, lead, paper, and tea, first developed in New England. The law went into effect on November 20, 1767, and during the following February the Massachusetts Assembly adopted and sent to the lower houses of all continental colonies a circular letter urging them to unite in opposition to the new law. Governor Francis Bernard promptly dissolved the Massachusetts Assembly, and Colonial Secretary Hillsborough ordered Bernard to dissolve the next one if it refused to rescind the letter. Hillsborough further directed other colonial governors to take similar action should the various assemblies attempt to support the Massachusetts circular.

2. May 8, June 14, 17, 25, 1766, Commons Journal, CO5/488, pp. 122, 154, 160–61, 175, microfilm, S.C. Archives; D.E. Huger Smith, "Wilton's Statue of Pitt," *SCHGM*, XV (January, 1914), 18–25.

3. November 26, 1766, Commons Journal, CO5/488, pp. 216–17, microfilm, S.C. Archives.

Although primarily concerned with the effort to establish courts in the backsettlements during the early months of 1768, the South Carolina Commons joined the resistance effort in April when it directed Charles Garth to cooperate with other colonial agents in pressing Parliament to repeal the Townshend duties.[4] Garth followed his instructions, but Parliament could not be moved despite the concerted effort of the colonial agents. In the meantime, as we have seen, the South Carolina Commons passed the Circuit Court bill of 1768 which was approved by the Council and Governor Montagu shortly before he prorogued the Assembly to September and departed for New York for the recovery of his health. By September Montagu had not returned, and as the present Assembly had been in existence almost two years, Lieutenant Governor Bull dissolved it and called for new elections to be held in October.

It was after the elections of October 1768 that Lowndes refused his seat in order to avoid jeopardizing his chances for judicial preferment through involvement in the controversy surrounding the Massachusetts circular. Governor Montagu, who had recently returned to his duties, dissolved the Assembly according to Hillsborough's orders when the "UNANIMOUS TWENTY-SIX" in the House endorsed the Massachusetts proposal. Lowndes returned to the House following new elections in March 1769, but through repeated prorogations Governor Montagu kept the new Assembly from meeting pending instructions on what to do next. In the meantime a series of public meetings in June and July resulted in the formation of the South Carolina Association on July 22 with an executive committee of thirteen merchants, thirteen planters, and thirteen "mechanicks," who commenced enforcing a boycott of certain British imports in an effort to force repeal of the Townshend duties.[5]

Governor Montagu finally received instructions from Hillsborough authorizing the Assembly to meet in July to revise the

4. April 12, 1768, ibid., CO5/491, p. 691.
5. Governor Montagu to Hillsborough, November 21, 1768, SCPRO, XXXII, 61–64, said the House locked its doors admitting no one while voting on the circular; Wallace, *South Carolina, A Short History*, pp. 240–41; Rogers, *Evolution of a Federalist*, pp. 50–51.

Circuit Court Act, which was returned along with the instructions. Besides serving on the committee that rewrote the disallowed act to conform with Crown objections, Lowndes joined another committee that denounced Montagu for permitting the House to sit only five days in fourteen months, "contrary to the spirit of the Election Law of 1721."[6] The governor, however, avoided further contention over the Massachusetts circular by departing for England at the end of July where he was to remain for the next two years. In his absence the House created a much more serious controversy by voting £1,500 sterling in public funds to support the English gadfly and the Crown's most outspoken critic, John Wilkes.

Wilkes had first gained notoriety in April 1763 when he published in his periodical, the *North Britain*, No. 45, an attack on George III's speech from the throne.[7] Charged with libel against the government, Wilkes had fled to France. Upon his return to England in 1768, he was convicted of various charges and imprisoned, becoming to many Englishmen and Americans as well a celebrated martyr of English liberty. To finance his cause and pay the debts he had incurred in pursuing it, a group of his supporters in London formed the "Society of Gentlemen Supporters of the Bill of Rights" and began to solicit funds in England and the colonies. The only colonial legislature to respond was the South Carolina Commons House of Assembly. On its authority alone, without submitting the matter to either the Council or Lieutenant Governor Bull for approval, the House on December 8, 1769, quietly ordered Treasurer Jacob Motte to advance to a House committee headed by Speaker Manigault £10,500 currency "for the Support of the just and Constitutional Rights and Liberties of the People of Great Britain and America."[8] The committee promptly forwarded the money, amounting to £1,500 sterling, to the society supporting Wilkes in England.

In seizing this opportunity to demonstrate their generosity and

---

6. June 28, 1769, Commons Journal, CO5/495, p. 17, microfilm, S.C. Archives.

7. Reprinted in *South Carolina Gazette*, July 23, 1763. For an excellent discussion of this entire controversy, see Greene, "Bridge to Revolution," pp. 19–52.

8. December 8, 1769, Commons Journal, CO5/495, p. 214, microfilm, S.C. Archives.

zeal in the cause of liberty, the Commons, according to Bull, had acted "in a very hasty manner," and many members soon wished the grant had never been made.[9] Informed of the grant, the ministry considered it an insult to the Crown; and notwithstanding the fact that the South Carolina Commons House had on several previous occasions ordered the expenditure of funds on its sole authority, the practice was declared to be in violation of the constitution of Carolina. On April 14, 1770, Hillsborough sent to Lieutenant Governor Bull a list of additional instructions destined to become the focal point of the developing controversy. The additional instructions prohibited the South Carolina Commons from granting any monies without the approval of the governor and Council and specifically restricted the expenditure of public funds to local purposes which were to be clearly stipulated in all future tax bills. The governor and colonial treasurer were strictly enjoined on pain of removal and other penalties from giving effect to any House measure which deviated from the instructions. But the ministerial order destined to become the central issue in the Wilkes Fund Controversy barred repayment of the grant to the provincial treasurer.[10] The South Carolina Commons was determined to reimburse the treasurer, while the lieutenant governor and the Council proved equally adamant in resisting repayment.

Even before Hillsborough's additional instructions arrived the Council took unilateral action to block repayment of the grant. On April 5, 1770, the Council sent back to the House the annual tax bill, pronouncing it neither fit nor decent, as it contained an item for reimbursement of the treasurer in the amount of the grant. Highly insulted, the House ordered the offensive message expunged from their journal, and in a critical series of resolutions passed on April 10, vigorously asserted their exclusive right and their determination to control money matters in the colony.[11] When the Council refused to yield, Bull initiated a series of prorogations to await Hillsborough's advice. Receiving the additional

9. Bull to Hillsborough, August 23, 1770, SCPRO, XXXII, 317–18.
10. August 16, 1770, Commons Journal, CO5/499, p. 405, microfilm, S.C. Archives.
11. April 7, 10, 1770, ibid., CO5/496, pp. 382, 390–91.

instructions in August, Bull presented them to the House on the sixteenth. The Commons, of course, found completely inadmissible the ministerial invasion of its traditional control over fiscal affairs in the colony. The next day the members reaffirmed their resolves of April tenth and defiantly inserted the disputed Wilkes grant in the tax bill. The Council upheld the ministry, however, and again rejected the tax bill on September 7.[12] Thereafter the refusal of either house to yield produced a deadlock that would prevent for the duration of royal government in South Carolina the passage of any tax bill. Faced with the impasse, Bull prorogued the Assembly on September 8 to the following January.

Rawlins Lowndes, who had taken a secondary part in supporting the prerogatives of the House in this controversy, suffered during this prorogation a great personal loss. On December 19, 1770, the *South Carolina and American General Gazette* proclaimed the solemn news that "After a long and tedious illness, which she bore with truly Christian Patience and Resignation, Mrs. [Mary Cartwright] Lowndes, Wife of the Honorable Rawlins Lowndes, Esquire," had died. For the second time Lowndes had been widowed by the great wife-killer of the age, the complications of child birth. During their marriage Mrs. Lowndes had presented her husband with three sons and four daughters; and for two years after her death their home on Tradd Street would be without the care and guiding influence of a mother until Lowndes found another to take Mary's place.

Following hard upon this melancholy event came news that exploded whatever hopes Lowndes still entertained for judicial preferment. The *South Carolina Gazette* announced on January 3, 1771, the appointment of Thomas Knox Gordon to the post of Chief Justice for South Carolina. Lowndes was certainly disappointed and had just cause to be even more bitter than his contemporaries over this development. But it failed to effect a basic alteration in his fundamentally moderate political position or his consistent adherence to principle. He doubtless considered ministerial policy ill-advised at best and stupidly blundering at worst, and he was spirited enough to give vigorous expression to his

12. August 17, 29, September 5, 7, 1770, ibid., CO5/499, pp. 406–7, 434–38, 450, 453–54.

anger, resentment, or disgust when he felt the occasion warranted. But no royal policy or ministerial ukase, however absurd or ill-advised, proved sufficient to drive him from his basically moderate position to the radical stance assumed by his friend Christopher Gadsden. Lowndes proved a resolute defender of the rights and privileges of the Commons House and the colony in general, but he would not easily give up hope of an accommodation with the mother country. He was ever ready, however, to check the pretensions of the Council, and with judicial preferment now closed to him, Lowndes now took a more active role in the House leadership.

As the deadlock in the provincial legislature continued, the House elected to present no tax bill in March 1771.[13] Thereupon Bull initiated another series of prorogations which kept the Assembly from meeting again until Governor Montagu returned to the colony in September. Montagu's first message to the Commons on September 17 emphasized Hillsborough's additional instructions, clearly demonstrating that ministerial policy had not changed. Representative Lowndes chaired a committee which answered the governor's message, declaring that the Commons preferred to risk the consequences of having no tax bill at all rather than sacrifice "the established mode of Proceedings, and the proper Rights of the People," by acceding to the instructions.[14] Even so, the House consented to frame a new tax bill covering the years 1769 and 1770, with Christopher Gadsden, Rawlins Lowndes, and James Parsons selected to draft it. Reported by Lowndes on September 25, the tax bill was amended on a motion from the floor so that the £10,500 currency was "entered in the Schedule Generally and not particularly" under the heading of "Extraordinary Expenses" in the provincial treasurer's accounts.[15] The Council was not taken in by the ruse, and on November 2, sent back the bill for lack of specifics and for failure to comply with the late instructions. This drew from the Commons a determined statement of their position: "Honorable Gentlemen, We have read your

13. March 20, 1771, ibid., CO5/498, p. 516.
14. September 17, 18, 1771, ibid., pp. 520–22.
15. September 23, 25, October 11, 16, 1771, ibid., pp. 525, 527, 556, 563.

Message of the 2ᵈ Instant for answer to which we assure you, that, We never shall regard any Ministerial Instruction in the framing of a Money Bill, nor alter any part of the Schedule upon your requisition, And we are firmly persuaded that these will be the Sentiments of every future Commons House of Assembly."[16] And so they were.

Nevertheless, the Commons altered the schedule when a more devious alternative was proposed. Jacob Motte, the provincial treasurer, had died in June 1770, owing the public £124,734, which was to be recovered out of Motte's estate and turned over to Benjamin Dart and Henry Perroneau, the joint-treasurers appointed to succeed Motte. The tax bill included a provision for more than £28,000 due Motte's estate for funds the treasurer had advanced for various purposes, including the Wilkes grant. The House now resolved to alter the schedule to reduce by £10,500 currency the amount due to be paid to Motte's estate by the public, at the same time reducing by the identical sum the amount due the public from his estate.[17] The effect would be to repay the advance without having to make a specific appropriation for it.

The next day, before the Council had time to act on this measure, the session was abruptly ended. The joint public treasurers, like their predecessors in the office, were regarded as servants of the House who traditionally obeyed its orders without question. But Dart and Perroneau now refused to comply with "an Order of the *Commons House* of Assembly *alone*, to advance the Sum of Three Hundred Pounds Currency to the Committee on the Silk Manufacturers." The outraged Commons dismissed their plea that compliance would be a blatant violation of Hillsborough's orders, and after Lowndes gave them a tongue-lashing for their refusal, ordered them committed to prison for contempt.[18] Here Governor Montagu intervened with a dissolution on November 5 that set the stubborn treasurers free. Up to this point the Council had very effectively defended ministerial authority, but

16. November 4, 1771, ibid., pp. 577-78.
17. November 4, 1771, ibid., p. 579.
18. *South Carolina Gazette*, November 7, 1771; Henry Laurens to John Lewis Gervais, May 29, 1772, Henry Laurens Papers, microfilm, SCHS.

Montagu's entry into the fray was followed by a series of blunders that eventually cost him his office. In the process his principal antagonist emerged as Rawlins Lowndes.

Having committed Dart and Perroneau "with but one dissenting Voice to the Resolution," the House maintained its unity following the dissolution. March elections returned Lowndes and an overwhelming majority of the late House to their seats.[19] The new House met in April 1772, with Lowndes as usual delaying his appearance until Peter Manigault had been reelected Speaker, then taking his seat on the ninth. When the Commons again refused to submit to the instructions, adamantly insisting on its right to frame tax measures free of ministerial restrictions, Montagu angrily proclaimed another dissolution on April 10.[20] Within two weeks of the dissolution Lowndes' commission as assistant judge was finally revoked, leaving him free to concentrate on legislative affairs. Before the year was out he had been reelected Speaker of the House and had assumed direction of its quarrel with the governor.

Montagu delayed four months his decision to issue writs for a new election. The temper of public opinion was revealed in June when Charlestonians celebrated the king's birthday "with but *one* Illumination," which the *Gazette* explained "possibly may be owing to the Scarcity of Tallow."[21] The governor displayed a scarcity of good judgment and delivered another shock to public opinion in August when he issued writs returnable at Beaufort, some fifty miles down the coast from Charles Town.

The obvious intention of this maneuver was to deter the attendance of many of the more radical representatives of Charles Town by holding the session at this inconvenient location. The result, though, was quite the opposite. Determined not "to make the Choice a mere Compliment," the people returned virtually all members of the late House in the September elections;[22] and an unprecedented number of thirty-seven members appeared on the first day of the Beaufort Assembly. Perhaps better than any other

19. *South Carolina Gazette*, March 22, 26, 1772.
20. Ibid., April 9, 16, 1772.
21. Ibid., June 11, 1772.
22. Ibid., September 17, October 1, 1772.

member, Rawlins Lowndes illustrated their determination to put aside personal considerations for the public good when he broke his own personal rule and took his seat with his colleagues on the first day of the session. By unanimous vote Peter Manigault was again chosen Speaker. Faced with this unexpected display of unity, Montagu waited three days, then prorogued the Assembly to meet in Charles Town on October 22. Booming cannon greeted the bumbling governor on his return from the Beaufort fiasco, but the church bells were rung only when the representatives arrived in town.[23]

In the middle of this crisis, Rawlins Lowndes became Speaker of the House. On October 28, Manigault, who had been in poor health for some time, resigned the speakership. When Manigault could not be persuaded to reconsider, Christopher Gadsden moved that, as Rawlins Lowndes "had formerly been Speaker of the House . . . and had acquitted himself in that Office to the General satisfaction of the Assembly," that Lowndes be elected Speaker.[24] The motion, seconded by James Parsons and unanimously approved by the House, completely vindicated Lowndes' conduct over the past seven years by returning him once more to the Speaker's chair. Within a fortnight Montagu found the new Speaker's conduct cause for another dissolution.

This incident grew out of Governor Montagu's growing sensitivity to criticism. Rapidly losing control of events in the colony and fearful of losing his office as well, Montagu had taken to examining the journals of the House to prevent the representatives from passing resolutions critical of his conduct. On October 29, Gadsden's Committee on Grievances condemned Montagu's decision to call the Assembly at Beaufort as "a most unprecedented Oppression, and an Unwarrantable Abuse of a Royal Prerogative," fairly roasting the governor for his arbitarary behavior.[25] With the report still under consideration, the House adjourned for the day, and Speaker Lowndes took the journal home with him. When

23. October 8–10, 1772, Commons Journal, CO5/504, pp. 1–6, microfilm, S.C. Archives; *South Carolina Gazette*, October 15, 1772.

24. October 28, 1772, Commons Journal, CO5/504, pp. 15–17, microfilm, S.C. Archives; *South Carolina Gazette*, October 29, 1772.

25. October 29, 1772, Commons Journal, CO5/504, pp. 20–26, microfilm, S.C. Archives.

the governor sent for the journal, his messenger was informed that Lowndes had it. In the meantime, as luck would have it, the Speaker had gone out to dine with friends and consequently was not advised of Montagu's order until quite late in the evening. The next morning Lowndes sent the journal to the House clerk for delivery to the governor, but another delay resulted from a sudden illness of the clerk.[26]

By the time Governor Montagu received the journal the House was ready to resume consideration of Gadsden's scathing report. Scanning the proceedings of the previous day confirmed Montagu's suspicions, and he sent word for the House to attend him immediately. When the governor's order arrived the House was on the point of passing the resolutions from Gadsden's committee. Heretofore the receipt of such an order automatically and immediately suspended all House business until the governor had been attended. But on this occasion Speaker Lowndes read the order, then "desired to know whether it was the Pleasure of the House to attend His Excellency immediately." [27] The House answered by ordering the Speaker not to quit the chair "until the Question be put on the above Motion." So the business was completed and the resolutions passed including instructions for the colonial agent to seek Montagu's removal. The members then attended the governor, who prorogued the Assembly to November 9.

Montagu's anger turned to rage when he read the latest proceedings of the House. As soon as a quorum was secured on November 9, he called the House before him and severely castigated the conduct of Speaker Lowndes:

> It is highly proper to me to observe to you, that the Commander in Chief of this Province has a Right at all Times, to inspect the Journals of the General Assembly, And I am sorry that I must charge the present speaker of the Commons House, of having acted in an unprecedented Manner; It seems then that the Commons House of Assembly having upon their Journals a Report of a violent and unconstitutional Nature; the Speaker took the Journals into his Possession; and although I wrote to him to demand them, I could not procure them until the next day, and

26. *South Carolina Gazette*, November 12, 1772.
27. October 30, 1772, Commons Journal, CO5/504, pp. 25–26, microfilm, S. C. Archives.

then only a very short space of time before the meeting of the House. It is in such a Manner that violent Measures in a Commons House of Assembly are to be concealed from a Governor, until almost the Moment of their being carried into Execution. . . .

But having perused the Journals of the Commons House of that Day on which the last Prorogation took Effect, I find that after they had received my Commands then immediately to attend me, they did continue to sit, to put a Question, to form Resolves and Orders.

Charging the House with violations of parliamentary procedure and attempts to delude the people, Montagu again dissolved the General Assembly.[28]

Lowndes was never the sort to permit his side of a controversy to go unheard, and he proved entirely capable of defending his actions. Two days later the *Gazette* published the Speaker's explanation of the incident. Lowndes defended the propriety of taking the House journal home with him in order to examine it for mistakes by the clerk and to prepare himself for the next day's business. He explained the circumstances that delayed delivery of the journal on the night in question as well as the clerk's illness the next morning. But with firmness and a sense of dignity that contrasted sharply with Montagu's emotion-charged outbursts, Lowndes denied the governor's accusation of deliberate deception:

My idea is, and my Sentiments are known to many Gentlemen, that if the Governor has a Right to inspect the Journals, it is below the Dignity of the House, or its Speaker, to use any Shifts or Evasions to keep them from him; if he has no Right, his Claim ought to be disputed upon its proper Grounds. What I did was of my own mere Motion, I had no Authority or Sanction of the House for it.[29]

Montagu was now determined that Lowndes should not serve again as Speaker. The Commons on the other hand could hardly have been more pleased with Lowndes and absolutely refused to select another in his stead, giving him their unanimous support through two successive dissolutions and elections over the next three months.[30] Finally Montagu gave up the struggle, and on March

28. November 10, 1772, ibid., pp. 27–29.

29. *South Carolina Gazette*, November 12, 1772.

30. November 9, 1772, Commons Journal, CO5/504, p. 29, and February 17, March 11–12, 1773, ibid., CO5/506, pp. 1–5, microfilm, S.C. Archives; *South Carolina Gazette*, January 7, 14, February 14, 22, 1773.

10, 1773, sailed from the colony. Thus for the second time, a Commons House presided over by Rawlins Lowndes had driven an arbitrary and unpopular governor from South Carolina. And fittingly enough, Montagu's last public appearance was at a concert given by South Carolina's most prestigious social organization, the St. Cecilia Society, which had just chosen Rawlins Lowndes as its president.[31]

Following Montagu's untimely departure, the Council took upon itself the responsibility of forcing the Commons to submit to the controversial instructions. The effort produced a collision that shook the Council "to its very foundation."[32] The Powell case, as it came to be called, developed in August 1772 when it appeared that the Commons wanted the general duty law to expire in the hope that the ministry would consent to withdraw the instructions rather than see the colony succumb to fiscal chaos. The Council decided to compel the House to renew the general duty law by refusing to act on any other leigslation until the law was revived.[33] Two native colonials on the Council, John Drayton and his son, William Henry Drayton, objected to this policy and entered a formal protest on August 26 against the Council's refusal to act on a much needed law to curb counterfeiting. The younger Drayton then gave a copy of the protest to Thomas Powell with the request that he publish it in his paper, the South Carolina Gazette. Accordingly Powell published the document without comment on August 30.[34] Highly indignant, the Council then issued an order for Thomas Powell's arrest for a "high Breach of Privilege and Contempt," and had him confined to the common gaol "during the pleasure of the [Upper] House."[35]

Powell's arrest produced a sensation in the colony and brought the historic running quarrel between House and Council to a

31. McCrady, South Carolina Under the Royal Government, p. 529; South Carolina Gazette, December 3, 1772; February 22, 1773.
32. McCrady, South Carolina Under the Royal Government, p. 717.
33. Greene, ed., The Nature of Colony Constitutions, p. 31; August 11–13, 1773, Commons Journal, CO5/506, pp. 33–37, microfilm, S.C. Archives.
34. September 8, 1773, ibid., p. 79; South Carolina Gazette, August 30, 1773.
35. Ibid., September 2, 1773; September 8, 1773, Commons Journal, CO5/506, pp. 79–80, microfilm, S.C. Archives.

head. The popular editor engaged a rising young lawyer, Edward Rutledge, to handle his case. Rutledge promptly applied to Rawlins Lowndes and George Gabriel Powell (not related to the prisoner) for a writ of habeas corpus. The attorney's strategy here is abundantly clear. He did not apply to the Court of General Sessions as the hearing then would have come before a bench occupied entirely by placemen and presided over by Chief Justice Gordon, himself a member of the Council and one of the majority who ordered Thomas Powell's commitment. Lowndes and George Gabriel Powell, besides being members of the Commons House, were also justices of the quorum, a special category of justices of the peace, any two of whom were empowered by a provincial act of 1712 to constitute a court to hear such pleas as the present one.[36] Moreover, a decision from justices Lowndes and Powell, by virtue of their prior years of service on the provincial bench, could be expected to carry great weight among the people, much embittered over the replacement of their native judges by English lawyers.[37]

The writ of habeas corpus was duly issued and the hearing was held on September 3. In pleading for Powell's release, Rutledge rested his case on arguments developed through at least a quarter century of controversy over the legislative powers of the Council.[38] The Council claimed the right of commitment for breach of privilege on the ground that they were the provincial counterpart of the House of Lords and therefore possessed equivalent powers. Rutledge rejected the comparison and denied the Council possessed any such power, since they, unlike the House of Lords, were not independent men but subject to the King's pleasure for their positions. They were, in short, "Nothing more than merely a Privy-Council, to assist the Governor with their Advice."[39]

Justice Lowndes' opinion utilized several of the points ad-

---

36. Ibid., p. 83. Justices of the quorum listed in *South Carolina Gazette*, November 7, 1767, October 16, 1769, included the principal officers of provincial government.

37. McCrady, *South Carolina Under the Royal Government*, p. 539.

38. For the text of Rutledge's argument, *see South Carolina Gazette*, September 13, 1773; for a much earlier discussion of the powers of the Council, see ibid., May 13, 1756.

39. Ibid., September 13, 1773.

vanced by Rutledge, as both drew upon the same familiar source for their arguments. But Lowndes' opinion was a more thorough analysis, superior to the attorney's argument both in legal erudition and logical force.[40] Lowndes opened by reviewing the circumstances of the case, then expressed his regret that the matter had come before him. He admitted a bias in favor of the Commons House, but he trusted that it was "no Propensity to exclude from any other body of men or any other part of the Community any Right, Privilege or Immunity whatever, which they may, on a fair Inquiry be found to be Intitled to."[41]

Proceeding to the legality of the commitment, Lowndes cited several acts of Parliament and statutes of the realm to show that "no Freeman shall be taken or Imprisoned but by the Judgment of his Peers or by the Law of the Land." No judgment of his peers had been given in the Powell case, "for Judgment by his Peers, means a legal course of Tryal by Jury." Turning then to the question of whether the law of the land warranted commitment, he demonstrated that both houses of Parliament had exercised such powers from time immemorial and had been upheld in that exercise by the courts. But for the Council to assume equal power was quite another matter, as the law of the land gave them not "the least colour of right" to do so.

To exercise the power of commitment, then, the Council, according to Lowndes, must found their claim on the usage and practice of the House of Lords. Hence it became necessary to inquire "what Affinity or Resemblance there is between them, to intitle the Council to a derivative right to this high Privilege exercised by the Lords." Here Lowndes went to the heart of the matter and laid bare the basic differences between the two bodies:

> The Lords are a permanent body, inheriting the right of Legislation independent of the Crown. They are the hereditary Councillors to the King and Guardians of the State. The Power of Judicature resides in them in the dernier resort, they try their own Members on Life and Death, without being under the Obligation of an Oath, and

40. Lowndes' opinion may be found in ibid., September 13, 15, 1773, and in September 8, 1773, Commons Journal, CO5/506, pp. 82–86, microfilm, S.C. Archives.

41. See ibid., for all citations from Lowndes' opinion quoted below.

all these and many other high Privileges they inherit from the best of Titles, Prescription and Usage from time immemorial, indeed they are of the very essence of the Constitution.

Compare the Constitution of the Council with that of the Lords and where shall be found cause to inferr that they Possess or ought to Possess the powers of the latter. The Council are appointed during the Pleasure of the Crown, removable at Pleasure, and may be Suspended by the Governor; they hold their Office and all the Appendages to it, at Will, and therefore want that most essential Requisite of Independency to constitute them a branch of the Legislature, or in any respect to Assimilate them to the Lords, unhappy for the People it is so, much to be wished it were not so . . . the People have nothing to fear from the Lords, they are their Guardians and a Bullwark of defence against Oppression and Tyranny, they are numerous as well as Independent, no private pique or personal resentment can influence them—here the most Important Concerns of the Province are often, very often determined at a meeting of three of the Members of the Council, very seldom that they exceed four, and the object of their care is more particularly, the Prerogative.

Nor was the Council to be considered an Upper House of the provincial legislature, in Lowndes' opinion. He declared that from the single circumstance of their acknowledged right to "concur in the passing of Provincial Laws," which was "in Consequence of Instructions from the Crown," the Council had "created themselves an Upper House." They now claimed powers equal to those of the House of Lords, powers which Lowndes judged to be "dangerous and unnecessary to be exercised by the Council. . . ."

Toward the close of his remarks, Lowndes delivered a ringing declaration of his views on the basic rights of the accused, regardless of circumstances:

The Freedom and Liberty of an English Subject is of so high estimation in the Eye of the Law, that to deprive him of them it is incumbent upon those that would do it, to show their right clearly and incontestibly; loose and Vague reasoning, Fallacious Conclusions, Specious Inferences or bold Assertions will not do, the Judgment of his Peers, or the clear voice of the Law of the Land must Justify, and nothing else can Justify the Commitment of any free Subject whatever.

He agreed with Rutledge that the commitment of Powell was "merely as a Commitment by the Privy Council" with no more force than that of a private magistrate. Pronouncing the Council's action a "dangerous . . . Usurpation of Power . . . destructive of sound Law and every principle of Justice," Lowndes, with the concurrence of his colleague, ordered the prisoner freed.[42]

The Council was furious. On September 6, they resolved that "the said Justices have been guilty of the most attrocious Contempt of this House, and by their Public avowal and declaration . . . that this House is no Upper House of Assembly . . . they have as far as in them lay, absolutely and actually abolished one of the Branches of the Legislature, and in so doing, have subverted the Constitution of this Government. . . ."[43] The Council then demanded that the Commons "direct your said Members to Wave their Privilege in order that we may proceed" against them.

Justices Lowndes and Powell immediately volunteered to waive the immunity they enjoyed as members of the Commons, but their colleagues would not hear of it. Instead the House conducted a full investigation of the affair and announced their findings on September 8. They declared the commitment of Thomas Powell to be "unprecedented, unconstitutional and Oppressive, and a Dangerous Violation of the Liberty of the Subject." They thanked judges Lowndes and Powell "for their able, upright and impartial Decision," pronounced the reasons which they gave for discharging the prisoner "extremely satisfactory to this House," and ordered their opinions to be printed and made public. The House further declared that the Council's latest resolutions contained "a partial Judgment, and indecent Reflection on the Conduct of Mr. Speaker and Col. Powell, and [were] a gross and unparalleled Insult to this House." Finally the Commons directed the colonial agent to seek the dismissal of the Council members responsible for the outrage and urged Lieutenant Governor Bull to suspend them pending word from the Crown.[44]

With strong popular support and the unanimous endorsement of the Commons House, the decision in the Powell case dealt a

---

42. Justice Powell followed Lowndes' opinion with a brief one of his own which supported that of his colleague but failed to approach it in quality or thoroughness; see September 8, 1773, ibid., CO5/506, pp. 86–87.

43. Ibid., pp. 77–79.

44. Ibid., pp. 79–80, 87–88.

severe blow to the pretensions and prestige of the governor's Council. Although minor disputes between the two bodies would occasionally flare up during the two remaining years of royal government in the colony, the decision virtually closed the historic struggle between House and Council in South Carolina. The councillors took what consolation they could from three subsequent developments in the case: Bull declined to suspend anyone from the board as the House had requested; Garth's petition for removal of the offending councillors failed; and Thomas Powell lost his suit against President of the Council Egerton Leigh, on whose order he had been arrested, when Chief Justice Gordon ruled that the Council was indeed an upper house with power to commit for contempt.[45] But the opinion of Gordon was rejected and that of Lowndes upheld by several members of the House of Lords, who declared on May 11, 1775, that the American councils had "not the least resemblance to the House of Peers, That a Council in which the Majority are Placemen from England cannot but in common Language be called a Council of Placemen. . . ."[46] Equally embarrassing to the Council was the royal silence which followed their appeal to the Crown for support in November 1773. Sixteen months went by without a word from the Crown on the subject.[47] By then, the spring of 1775, the question was no longer of any consequence, having been lost in the larger issues of the movement toward revolution.

No one could have realized at the time, not even Lowndes himself, that the Powell case had brought him to the zenith of his public career. He was more than merely admired by his friends and respected by friend and foe alike; solidly backed and warmly praised by the Commons, he was also the recipient of enthusiastic popular support and wide public acclaim. Although he was destined to hold even higher office, the highest in fact in the government of South Carolina, never again would Lowndes enjoy such universal popularity and public esteem, nor have his opinions so

45. September 13, 1773, ibid., p. 96; March 4, 1775, ibid., XXXIX, 265, S.C. Archives.
46. March 4, 1775, ibid., p. 255.
47. Ibid., p. 262.

widely quoted nor his name so firmly joined in the popular imagination with the cause of colonial rights.[48]

The explanation behind this fact seems simple enough. Through the past decade, as Speaker and judge, Lowndes had been contending against arbitrary royal governors ,against what he considered to be unconstitutional acts of Parliament, against arrogant and officious British judges, and against pretentious placemen dominating the governor's Council. The controversies he joined were thus popular causes, so that he had always enjoyed strong public support. Furthermore, none of them had required that he transgress the limits of English law or the framework of imperial government. Following the Powell case, however, the struggle in South Carolina began to assume a character increasingly extralegal. At the same time events began to move more rapidly toward a break with royal authority than Lowndes wished to go, forcing upon him the inevitable difficulties of a moderate in the midst of revolution.

48. Lowndes' fame spread to London when the controversy was removed there. Egerton Leigh wrote a pamphlet in defense of the Council's claims which was published in London in January 1774 under the title, *Considerations on Certain Political Transactions of the Province of South Carolina.* This pamphlet provoked another, an *Answer to Considerations on Certain Political Transactions of the Province of South Carolina,* by Arthur Lee, who defended the position taken by the Commons House. Lee relied heavily on Lowndes' opinion in the Powell Case, quoting it in full in his *Answer,* and calling it "irrefutable Argument and Conviction." See the definitive treatment of this subject in Greene, ed., *The Nature of Colony Constitutions,* and especially pp. 176–81 for Lee's use of Lowndes' opinion. William Henry Drayton also relied on this opinion, basing the defense of his conduct on it in protesting his removal from the Council in March, 1775. See March 4, 1775, Commons Journal, XXXIX, 262, S.C. Archives.

CHAPTER IX

Moderate in Revolt

SINCE 1770 the Wilkes Fund Controversy had claimed first attention among South Carolinians, superseding the issue of
parliamentary taxation. This was due in substantial degree to the
repeal of all Townshend duties that year except the tax on tea.
Now in December 1773, scarcely three months after the Powell
case, the taxation question displaced the Wilkes Fund Controversy as the major issue in South Carolina. The Powell case itself,
since it resolved none of the difficulties surrounding the Wilkes
grant, had little bearing on this change. With stubborn persis-
tence the Council continued to block all efforts to repay the grant
or to pass a tax bill until the House complied with the additional
instructions. An even more resolute House refused to capitulate,
but soon discovered a way to circumvent the Council. In March
1774 the House ordered its clerk to issue certificates of indebted-
ness to creditors of the public, which were the same as promissory
notes that would be redeemed on passage of a new tax bill. These
certificates, being accepted by virtually everybody, relieved the
pressure for a tax bill and enabled the House to accomplish its
purpose without submitting to the additional instructions.[1] The
Wilkes grant remained unpaid, but by this time the controversy
surrounding it had been lost in the storm over the Tea Act.

Intended as a measure to save the East India Company from
impending ruin, the Tea Act allowed the company for the first
time to ship tea directly to America where it could be profitably
sold at a price lower, even with the tax, than smuggled tea or

1. March 24, 1774, Commons Journal, CO5/478, p. 164, microfilm, S.C.
Archives.

company tea sold in England. Nevertheless, most Americans tended to view the law as a trick designed to lure them into paying the tea tax which would amount to an admission of Parliament's right to tax the colonies. Moreover, the monopolistic features of the law drove normally conservative merchants to join their more radical neighbors in resisting its implementation. The violent reaction to the Tea Act, especially in Massachusetts, and the Coercive Acts which that violence provoked brought the colonies to the final turning point on the road to revolution.

In South Carolina two simultaneous and compensating developments took place. From December 1773 the business of the Commons House began to wind down, diminishing in frequency and consequence until August 1775, when it ceased altogether. At the same time extralegal organizations, created one after another to assume the powers being relaxed by the Commons and directed for the most part by its leadership, steadily evolved into the revolutionary government of South Carolina.

Even so, most leaders in the House, Speaker Lowndes among them, made the transition from royal to revolutionary government with considerable reluctance. They hoped for redress of grievances and restoration of pre-1763 autonomy, but hardly considered permanent separation or independence. They also knew that each transfer of power would increase the potential for radical influence on political affairs so that many, most notably Speaker Lowndes, began to assume a more conservative stance than they had taken on earlier issues. The natural result was a division of sentiment between radical men like Gadsden and their more cautious friends such as Lowndes over the pace of revolutionary activity. And Speaker Lowndes became all but submerged in the flow of events leading toward revolution.

Local controversy over the Tea Act came sharply into focus on December 1, 1773, when word flashed through Charles Town that a tea ship had arrived in the harbor.[2] A controlled though nonetheless powerful reaction spread through the population resulting in a great "general meeting" of the citizenry two days later. Their

2. John Drayton, *Memoirs of the American Revolution*, 2 vols., (Charleston, 1821), I, 97.

immediate decision was to revive the moribund Association with resolutions neither to import tea nor to buy any. At a second mass meeting the issue was debated more fully, revealing deeper divisions on the subject than had first appeared. They resolved to meet again, but for the time being recommended no stronger measures. A few days later Lieutenant Governor Bull was able to forestall a tea party such as occurred in Boston, by having the controversial cargo, 257 chests of tea, quietly unloaded and stored in the basement of the Exchange.[3]

From the first general meeting occasioned by the arrival of this cargo of tea can be traced the revolutionary government of South Carolina. Two subsequent mass meetings on January 20 and March 16, 1774, proved too cumbersome to conduct business efficiently and brought about the election of a standing "General Committee" to act as an executive body. Among the first to be named to the General Committee were Speaker Lowndes, Gadsden, John Rutledge, and several other leaders of the Commons House.[4] Over the ensuing weeks tea consumption suffered a sharp decline as the General Committee carried out the public mandate to enforce the Association.

Then in the early summer came news of a far more dangerous threat to colonial liberties than mere taxation by Parliament. The Boston Tea Party had so angered king, lords and commons that they retaliated in May and June 1774 with the Coercive Acts, closing the port of Boston, radically altering the administration of justice there, and taking from the people their control of the civil government and turning it over to men appointed by and subservient to the Crown. Spreading southward from Boston the news struck a sympathetic chord in every colony and rallied them to the support of Massachusetts. On May 27 Virginia issued a call for a congress of delegates from all continental colonies to meet at Philadelphia in September to consider the alarming developments.

In South Carolina the General Committee responded by sending out a call for popular election of delegates throughout the colony

3. Ibid., pp. 97–100.
4. Wallace, *South Carolina, A Short History*, p. 252.

to assemble in the capital the first week in July. The election returned 104 delegates who met in Charles Town on July 6. Here
they were joined by the General Committee representing the city
along with many interested Charlestonians. Proceeding directly
to their task, the delegates approved without serious division resolutions professing their loyalty to the Crown, condemning the
Coercive Acts and asserting their traditional colonial rights.[5]
But in taking up the issue of a continental congress, the first serious
contest between radicals and moderates took place.

Provincial opinion was virtually unanimous on the matter of
sending a delegation to the First Continental Congress, but a
"warm debate arose as to the number of Deputies, who should be
appointed, and the powers with which they should be invested."[6]
After some debate the assembly decided to send five delegates,
who should be elected by ballot among the people, which meant
essentially the population around Charles Town. On the question of what powers to bind South Carolina should her delegates
be granted, a resolution was introduced to vest the delegation with
unlimited authority. At this point Rawlins Lowndes rose to urge
the assembly to proceed with caution, striking a conservative theme
that he was to reiterate repeatedly in the years ahead.

Reminding his fellow citizens that their northern friends took
a more radical view of colonial rights than Carolinians had demonstrated, he was unwilling to trust southern interests to the more
populous and less prudent northern colonies. It was well known,
he said, that

> the Northern Colonies in general, totally denied the superintending
> power of Parliament; a doctrine, which no one here admitted. And,
> unless the Deputies from this colony, appeared in Congress with
> limited powers; being outnumbered by the Northern Deputies,
> they, and consequently their constituents, would be bound by votes
> upon points, which they at present absolutely denied. But, to obviate
> this danger, the Resolution vesting the Deputies with power, was
> so worded; that no vote in Congress could bind this colony, but
> such as was agreeable to the opinion of our Deputies.[7]

5. Drayton, *Memoirs*, I, 128–29.
6. Ibid.
7. Ibid., p. 130.

John Drayton, writing his *Memoirs* from notes left by his father, William Henry Drayton, maintained that "This sentiment from Mr. Lowndes . . . declared the prevailing opinion of the Colony."[8] Drayton might have added that the sentiment expressed a provincial view of what were essentially national problems that Lowndes maintained through the Revolution and well beyond. But the delegates were voted broad discretionary powers in spite of his opposition.

The selection of delegates now assumed much importance. The merchants of Charles Town were especially concerned that the policies of non-exportation and non-importation, which they had just defeated in the General Meeting, should not be given up at the Continental Congress. To prevent this they put forward a slate of five candidates agreeable to their views: Henry Middleton, Lowndes, Charles Pinckney, Miles Brewton, and John Rutledge. The merchants committed a tactical blunder, though, when they rounded up their clerks and marched in a body to the polls. This action stirred the radical faction to rally their own supporters with the result that Lowndes, Pinckney, and Brewton were defeated by Thomas Lynch, Christopher Gadsden, and Edward Rutledge; John Rutledge and Henry Middleton proved acceptable to both groups.[9] The radicals thus won this contest, and their delegates shortly departed for Philadelphia. But before the General Meeting adjourned, a new General Committee of ninety-nine was chosen with the defeated candidates named to important positions on it. Vested with broad executive powers and presided over by Charles Pinckney, the committee of ninety-nine virtually became the temporary government of South Carolina.[10]

The Commons House of Assembly had not yet ceased to meet but had almost ceased to function, as royal government in the colony slowly disintegrated. Speaker Lowndes convened the House in August long enough to arrange for borrowing funds to pay the expenses of the delegates to Philadelphia before Lieutenant Governor Bull again prorogued the Assembly to September. Two

8. Ibid.
9. Ibid., pp. 131, 138–39.
10. Weir, "*A Most Important Epocha*," p. 55.

more prorogations prevented their meeting again until January 1775 when Lowndes convened the House only to be told that Bull had "nothing in command from the King."[11]

Business of much greater moment was being transacted by the extralegal government of the colony. The five delegates to the Continental Congress had returned in November to deliver a report that confirmed the worst fears of the mercantile community and many others as well. They had committed the colony to support a continental Association pledging non-importation of British goods, as of December 1, 1774, and non-exportation of products to Britain, with the exception of rice, effective September 10, 1775.[12] The General Committee considered these matters of such gravity that a call for a provincial congress was issued, to consist of thirty representatives from Charles Town, six from each parish and ten from each of the four large interior districts.[13] Interest ran high during this election, especially in the interior regions where indigo and grain production was heaviest.

The 184 delegates to the Provincial Congress met at the Exchange in Charles Town on January 11, 1775, and almost immediately a heated controversy erupted over the exception of rice from the Association. According to Drayton, "This exception, had created an alarming disunion, throughout the whole Colony," had "given so general a disgust, that the whole interior of the province, considered their interests as sacrificed to the emolument of the rice planters. . . ."[14] The indigo planters in particular were angered that the rice planters of the lowcountry had been favored over themselves and moved that the exception be "expunged." Christopher Gadsden announced that he had opposed the exception all along and lent his support to its repeal. At this point John Rutledge defended the measure, pointing out that the northern and middle colonies, exporting very little of their produce to England anyway, would be only slightly inconvenienced by the non-exportation Association, while the economy of South Caro-

11. August 2, 1774, January 24, 1775, Commons Journal, XXXIX, 172–73, 177–78, S.C. Archives.
12. Drayton, Memoirs, I, 168, 190–91.
13. Ibid., p. 155.
14. Ibid., p. 168.

lina, so heavily dependent on the rice trade to the mother country (two-thirds of the total crop), would be ruined without the exception. He would never consent that South Carolina should thus become the "dupes to the people of the north." Rutledge closed by stating that it was the intention of the delegation that some means might be worked out to compensate the indigo planters for the virtual embargo of their product.[15]

As others joined the debate, the question took on sectional and class overtones, and the whole day was consumed in argument. Thomas Lynch, William Henry Drayton, and Edward Rutledge were outspoken in support of the exception, while Christopher Gadsden, Rawlins Lowndes, and the Reverend William Tennent, in leading the opposition, defended the interests of the small farmer.

By these latter gentlemen, it was contended, the compensation scheme was impracticable. That if it were to operate in favor of the indigo planter, it should afford in justice also relief to the hemp-grower, the lumber cutter, the corn planter, the makers of pork and butter, etc; for, why should this benefit be confined to the indigo maker, in exclusion of other classes of citizens, whose commodities were their means of support, and would equally, nay more, be unsaleable by the association? That as we were all one people; we should all suffer alike; and then, all would struggle through difficulties, which might arise. That union among ourselves was a *sine qua non*; and this odious distinction had cruelly convulsed the Colony.[16]

Advocates of the controversial exception insisted that a compensation scheme was practical; but their most convincing argument was that public disavowal of measures recommended by the late Continental Congress would be bad policy, as the appearance of unity among the colonies at this time was of the utmost importance.[17]

---

15. Ibid., pp. 169–71. The South Carolina delegation had insisted on the exceptions of both rice and indigo in the Continental Congress, even withdrawing at one point, but eventually had to compromise. See Edward Rutledge to Ralph Izard, October 29, 1774, *Correspondence of Ralph Izard of South Carolina*, ed. Anne Izard Deas, 2 vols. (New York, 1844), I, 21–22, microfilm.

16. Drayton, *Memoirs*, I, 171.

17. Ibid., p. 172.

The Provincial Congress was persuaded. They approved the Association, worked out a reasonably satisfactory compensation plan and emphasized their satisfaction with the conduct of their five late delegates by reelecting them to represent the colony at the Second Continental Congress in May. Before adjourning, the Provincial Congress ominously warned all inhabitants of the colony to learn the use of arms and directed that committees be established to enforce the Association. Shortly afterwards the Commons approved the transactions of the continental and provincial congresses and again agreed to pay the expenses of the colony's representatives to the Second Continental Congress.[18]

The more radical element in the population saw to it that a rigorous enforcement of the Association was swiftly implemented. In February a cargo of coal, tiles, and salt was dumped in the Hog Island channel, and a cargo of three hundred slaves was refused admission and sent out of the colony. In March, however, the arrival of another ship carrying the merchant Robert Smyth and his family home from England along with their personal property provoked another clash between the radicals and moderates. The issue turned on the question of admitting Smyth's two horses which had been purchased and used in England before being brought in on this vessel. When Smyth applied to the General Committee for permission to land his furniture and horses, the committee by a narrow margin held that importing such property was not in violation of the Association and consented to its being landed.

Popular reaction to the decision shocked many of the conservatives and alarmed the moderates generally. All over town the cry went up that by landing the horses, "*The Association was broken.*" So great was the public clamor that the committee hastily agreed to reconsider their decision. Two days later in the presence of a great throng of noisy radicals the question was reopened. Gadsden, ever sensitive to the popular mood, moved to reverse the decision on the ground that it violated the Association and the people opposed it. Even William Henry Drayton swung over to the radical

18. Ibid., pp. 174–80; January 26, February 3, 7, 1775, Commons Journal, XXXIX, 182, 189–93, S.C. Archives.

side, proclaiming that "Upon all public and general questions, the people are ever in the right." The Rutledge brothers, John and Edward, joined Thomas Lynch, Thomas Bee, and Rawlins Lowndes in an attempt to curb the popular will.[19] They argued that the constituted authority of the General Committee must be maintained to prevent its falling into contempt, a certain consequence of popular repeal of its decisions. Temporizing, they warned, did not become honest men and statesmen, who ought to follow the convictions of conscience rather than yield to popular clamor. But the pressure proved just strong enough to carry the day. The decision was reversed by one vote, marking the first time the people had rejected a major decision by their traditional leaders.[20]

The incident served as an ominous warning to men like John Rutledge and Rawlins Lowndes that the movement toward the unstable realm of revolution could easily race beyond their control. Lieutenant Governor Bull clearly recognized the radical potential. He observed to the Earl of Dartmouth on March 28, 1775, "The men of Property begin at length to see that the many headed power, the People, who have hitherto been obediently made use of by their numbers and occasional riots to support the claims set up in America, have discovered their own strength and importance, and are not now so easily governed by their former Leaders."[21]

For the lieutenant governor himself the colony was becoming each day more impossible to govern. An encouraging event had occurred in February when the Council at long last abandoned recalcitrance and approved a House bill to prevent counterfeiting, then in March also approved the revival bill.[22] But the receipt of news from England that Lord North had refused to recognize the authority of the Continental Congress, intending to deal with the colonies separately, again spurred revolutionary activity. On

19. Drayton, *Memoirs*, pp. 182–84.
20. Ibid., pp. 184–86.
21. Bull to Dartmouth, March 28, 1775, SCPRO, XXXV, 79–80.
22. February 15, March 3, 1775, Commons Journal, XXIX, 217, 250, S.C. Archives.

the night of April 21 both the colony's magazines were raided under orders of a secret committee appointed by President Charles Pinckney of the Provincial Congress, and all arms and powder stored in them were carried away. When Bull reported the affair to the Assembly, Speaker Lowndes sent back a reply professing ignorance, but added that "there is reason to suppose that some of the Inhabitants of this Colony may have been induced to take so extra-ordinary and uncommon a step in consequence of the late alarming Accounts from Great Britain."[23]

One week later the Commons House closed its doors and went into secret session to consider a motion to raise troops and funds to support the Continental Association. The motion had been offered by Thomas Lynch, one of the delegates now preparing to leave for the meeting of the Second Continental Congress in Philadelphia. Speaker Lowndes again expressed the moderate viewpoint. In doing so, he stated his own philosophy regarding the proper authority of Parliament over the colonies.

> Mr. Lowndes . . . hoped the Delegates would be cautious; as it was yet too early to proceed to extremities; and he thought we had best trust a little to the plans of non-importation and non-exportation. He said, he did not think the parliament had any right to take money out of the pockets of the colonists; but excepting that particular, he thought parliament had a right to legislate for them, in all national and commercial cases.[24]

In this statement the Speaker revealed the fundamental difference between the views of radicals and moderates concerning their basic rights. As an authority on colonial South Carolina has phrased it, "The radicals based their case on the rights of all men, the moderates on the rights of Englishmen."[25] Content with having stated his views, Lowndes withdrew his objection and the resolution passed unanimously.

When news of Lexington and Concord reached Charles Town on May 8, revolution became a virtual certainty, and the best the moderate men could hope for was to restrain their more radical

23. April 25, 27, 1775, ibid., pp. 272–73, 279.
24. Drayton, *Memoirs*, I, 228–29.
25. Rogers, *Evolution of a Federalist*, p. 77.

neighbors from adopting measures that would make an accommodation with the mother country impossible. For more than a year they were successful. This was owing in no small degree to the fact that the people in general seemed to share their views. Moving into the unknown and unpredictable terrain of revolution, the ordinary citizen of South Carolina turned for guidance to his trusted and proved leaders, moderates such as John Rutledge, Henry Laurens, Charles Pinckney, and Rawlins Lowndes, who could restrain the Gadsdens and Draytons among them. But ultimate success depended on a reciprocal moderation of British colonial policy, and when it became all too evident that such was not to be, the moderate position became untenable and a full-scale war for independence loomed.

The news from Lexington and Concord again set the revolutionary government in motion. When the Provincial Congress met on June 1, 1775, Henry Laurens was unanimously elected president of the congress. Laurens straightway named Rawlins Lowndes to head a committee to draw up a general statement of association to be signed by all adult males in the colony. Reported by Lowndes on June 3, the statement was by no means a declaration of independence, but expressed their grievances as well as their hopes of an eventual accommodation with the Crown.

> The actual commencement of hostilities against this continent, by the British troops, in the bloody scene on the 19th of April last, near Boston, the increase of arbitrary impositions from a wicked and despotic ministry, and the dread of instigated insurrections in the colonies, are causes sufficient to drive an oppressed people to the use of arms: We therefore, the subscribers, inhabitants of *South Carolina*, holding ourselves bound by that most sacred of all obligations, the duty of all good citizens toward an injured country, and thoroughly convinced, that, under our present distressed circumstances, we shall be justified before God, and man, in resisting force by force; DO UNITE ourselves, under every tie of religion, and of honour, and associate, as a band in her defense, against every foe: Hereby solemnly engaging that, whenever our Continental or Provincial Councils shall decree it necessary, we will go forth, and be ready to sacrifice our lives and fortunes to secure her freedom and safety. This obligation to continue in full force until a reconciliation shall take place between Great Britain and America, upon

constitutional principles, an Event which we most ardently desire. And we will hold all those persons inimical to the liberty of the colonies, who shall refuse to subscribe this association.[26]

The association was adopted, and the next day all members signed, beginning with President Laurens. Next the congress moved to put the colony in a posture of defense, authorizing the raising of three regiments and placing rice under embargo until September 10.

To act as an executive body after this congress adjourned, a Council of Safety was created and vested with extraordinary power. The council was to "direct and regulate the operations of troops; to stamp, sign and issue certificates"; it was granted "full power to suspend officers, order courts martial and have direction . . . of all military affairs." It also had authority over "all such matters and things relative to the strengthening, securing, and defending the colony, as shall by them be judged and deemed expedient and necessary."[27] To wield such far-ranging authority, the people's representatives turned to their traditional leaders. The first three named to the Council or Safety were Henry Laurens, president of the Provincial Congress, Charles Pinckney, its former president, and Rawlins Lowndes, Speaker of the Commons House; they were followed by Benjamin Elliott, Arthur Middleton, Miles Brewton, James Parsons, Thomas Ferguson, William Henry Drayton, Thomas Heyward, Jr., Thomas Bee, John Huger, and William Williamson. By mid-July it became evident that Drayton, Middleton, Ferguson, and Pinckney could be counted on to support more vigorous measures, while Laurens, Lowndes, Parsons, Brewton, Heyward, and Bee were more disposed to proceed with caution. Huger, Elliott, and Williamson held the balance of power, swinging to one side or the other depending on circumstances. Laurens explained these divisions of sentiment: "Some are Red-Hot and foolishly talk of Arms and there is another extreme who say that implicit obedience is the Surest Road to redress of Griev-

---

26. *Extracts from the Journals of the Provincial Congresses of South Carolina, 1775–1776*, eds. William Edwin Hemphill and Wylma Anne Wates, (Columbia, S.C., 1960), pp. 35–36 (hereafter cited Hemphill and Wates, *Extracts*).

27. Ibid., pp. 50–51, 54–56.

ances, the great majority of members lie between, and are men of wealth and consideration."[28]

The Provincial Congress was still in session when the new colonial governor, Lord William Campbell, arrived on June 18. With his arrival attention shifted to the Commons House. Campbell's first message after Speaker Lowndes convened the House on July 10 was enough to dispel any hope of immediate accommodation with the Crown. The governor had no positive suggestions but only expressed grief and disappointment at finding the colony in such a "distracted state" with "the most Dangerous Measures adopted, and Acts of the most outrageous and illegal Nature publicly committed with impunity."[29] In response, the Commons declared their surprise that the governor had no recommendations as to how their grievances might be redressed and voiced their disappointment that he should censure measures which they had been forced to adopt "for the preservation of their Liberties, and the Liberties of Generations yet unborn."[30] Convinced this early in Campbell's administration that further efforts to resolve their differences with the Crown through traditional channels would be fruitless, the Commons abandoned the effort. On July 12 they resolved to defray the expenses incurred by measures recently adopted by the Provincial Congress, including the issuance of one million pounds current money.[31] This was to be the last positive action taken by the Commons House of Assembly. On July 18 the House asked leave to adjourn, and being denied, continued meeting day to day with Speaker Lowndes until August 30, 1775, when they held their last meeting under the authority of the Crown. The next day, when neither Speaker Lowndes nor any other member of the House appeared, the legislative branch of royal government in South Carolina came to an end.[32]

Within two weeks more the last vestige of royal government in the colony was removed. The judicial branch as well as other offices had already been cleared of Crown appointees when they

28. Drayton, *Memoirs*, I, 318–19; Henry Laurens to Richard Oswald, January 4, 1775, Henry Laurens Papers, microfilm, SCHS.
29. July 10, 1775, Commons Journal, XXXIX, 290, S.C. Archives.
30. July 11, 1775, ibid., pp. 292–94.
31. July 12, 1775, ibid., p. 295.
32. July 18, 21, 29, August 18–30, 1775, ibid., pp. 299–300, 305, 311–14.

refused to subscribe the South Carolina association. Then Lord William Campbell himself was trapped into revealing his dealings with loyalist elements in the backcountry. Already fearful for his personal safety, Governor Campbell on September 13, 1775, confided to a Whig, who pretended to be a Tory from the interior, his plans for arming the loyalists in the backcountry against the revolutionary government on the coast. Receipt of this news "excited universal indignation; and it was strongly urged, on the motion of Arthur Middleton, that Lord William Campbell should be taken into custody."[33] The proposal was rash in the extreme, as arrest of the royal governor by the revolutionary government would doubtless have been followed by strong retaliatory measures, perhaps war. The moderates rallied support in the Charles Town General Committee, however, and "a strong opposition headed by Mr. Lowndes, prevented the motion from succeeding."[34] When Governor Campbell realized the full extent of his error, he abandoned his office, took refuge on board the *Tamar* sloop-of-war, and never returned.

The withdrawal of Governor Campbell left the government of the colony in the hands of three revolutionary bodies: the Charles Town General Committee, the Council of Safety, and after it convened in November, the Provincial Congress. The Council of Safety, charged with the direction of military operations, authorized the immediate seizure of Fort Johnson which was accomplished without bloodshed on September 15. Two weeks later radical elements on the Charles Town General Committee succeeded in pushing through a resolution that the British men-of-war in the harbor should be "*secured, destroyed, or removed.*" But moderates on the Council of Safety led by Lowndes and Parsons advocated defensive measures only and effectively blocked all efforts to carry the resolution into effect.[35] To strengthen their defensive

33. Drayton, *Memoirs*, II, 31–35.
34. Ibid., pp. 34–35.
35. Ibid., pp. 35–37, 55–57, 76. Drayton identified the two opponents of this measure simply as "Mr. L——— and Mr. P———" (p. 76), but elsewhere (p. 70) clearly identified the opposition spokesmen as Lowndes and Parsons. It seems extremely unlikely that he could have meant Laurens and Pinckney, as the latter usually supported such measures and the former rarely spoke out, though he might cast his vote against them.

posture the council on October 19 authorized an attempt to block the Hog Island channel of the Cooper River to prevent British warships from moving upstream without passing under the guns of the city's defenses. Led by William Henry Drayton on November 11, the attempt drew fire from the *Tamar*. In a harmless booming of carriage guns, the Revolutionary War began in South Carolina.

Under the pressure of these rapidly changing circumstances the need for a constitution and regular frame of government to replace the extralegal organs that had been erected rather haphazardly over the past two years became increasingly evident. The Second Provincial Congress elected in September met on November 1 to consider the proper steps to be taken. Rawlins Lowndes and conservative James Parsons were foremost among those members who hoped that a reconciliation with the Crown could still be reached without the necessity of organizing under a new constitution. To silence William Henry Drayton, the leader of the radicals at least while Gadsden was in Philadelphia, the moderates elected Drayton president of the congress. The scheme backfired, however, as Drayton utilized his position to advocate more vigorous measures. Lowndes and Parsons protested that Drayton's conduct was contrary to the custom of the chair, but the congress declined to rule against their president.[36]

Nevertheless, the congress appeared content for the time being to delay action on the constitution question. They resolved on November 10 explaining that the royal proclamation of August 23 which declared the colonies to be "in avowed rebellion" had "sunk deep in the minds of the people" and had driven them to the necessity of taking up arms. Urging the citizens to improve the colony's defenses, the congress elected a new Council of Safety with Lowndes, Laurens, Parsons, and other moderates among its members.[37] On November 29 the congress adjourned to February 1, 1776, the date set for consideration of a new frame of government. In recognition of his leading the moderate oppo-

36. Ibid., p. 70.
37. Other council members were David Olyphant, Thomas Savage, Charles Pinckney, Henry Middleton, Thomas Ferguson, Arthur Middleton, Thomas Heyward, Jr., Thomas Bee, Benjamin Elliott, and President Drayton.

sition his colleagues selected Lowndes on the last day of this session to deliver a speech of thanks to President Drayton for his service in the chair.[38]

The second and last session of the Second Provincial Congress met as scheduled on February 1, 1776, and took up the question of framing a constitution. On February 10 in Committee of the Whole the question was under consideration when Christopher Gadsden, recently returned from Philadelphia with a copy of Thomas Paine's *Common Sense*, "boldly declared" not only in favor of a new form of government but "for the absolute Independence of America." Gadsden's declaration "came like an explosion of thunder" upon the members. They were totally unprepared to consider so decisive a step; "neither had the majority of members at that time, any thoughts of aspiring at independence." John Rutledge asserted that he "abhorred the idea; and that he was willing to ride post, by day and night, to Philadelphia, in order to assist, in re-uniting Great Britain and America." The reaction of Rawlins Lowndes was apparently an explosion of profanity. Lowndes voiced his contempt of Thomas Paine in terms so strong that John Drayton, who recorded the incident in his *Memoirs*, prudently left the passage blank. Even those few who desired independence were shocked at Gadsden's sudden declaration, and he was universally condemned for his imprudence.[39] So it was made clear even before its foundations were laid that the new government would be a temporary expedient, to be abandoned upon reconciliation with the mother country.

That same day the congress agreed that "the present mode of conducting public affairs is inadequate" and proceeded to ballot for members to draw up a constitution. Charles Cotesworth Pinckney, John Rutledge, Charles Pinckney, Henry Laurens, Christopher Gadsden, Rawlins Lowndes, Arthur Middleton, Thomas Bee, Thomas Lynch, Jr., and Thomas Heyward, Jr., were chosen.

38. For Lowndes' gracious remarks on this occasion, *see* Hemphill and Wates, *Extracts,* pp. 167–68.

39. The quotations above may be found in Drayton, *Memoirs,* II, 172–73, but Drayton failed to identify those who responded to Gadsden. For their identity see unpaged manuscript written by William Lowndes, Rawlins' son, titled "Historical Anecdotes" in Lowndes Papers, Library of Congress.

Curiously, Lowndes was sent with James Parsons and Thomas Savage on a mission to Savannah five days later to encourage the reluctant Georgians to support the continental non-exportation resolution. This mission, which eventually produced the desired effect, kept Lowndes and Parsons out of town to March 1, so that they were able to contribute little if anything to the new constitution.[40] Lowndes' opposition to the whole idea of pulling down the old government of the colony was so well known that one suspects those who favored the move might have conspired to get him out of town while the document was being drawn.

When the new plan of government was presented for consideration on March 5, Lowndes "and those members who were with him in opinion, strongly contended putting off what they thought the evil day."[41] They argued that procedure had been faulty; the recommendation of the Continental Congress stating that constitutional conventions should be specially elected to frame the state governments, had not been followed in South Carolina. A motion was therefore introduced, apparently by Lowndes, to postpone the question to May in order that a special election might be held. The proposal was brushed aside with assurances that the Provincial Congress was sufficient for the purpose, as it "aimed at the happiness and good order of the Colony—that it was a full and free representation—and if a new Congress were called, it would not be more so. In short, that time pressed—and, we had none to lose."[42] So the motion to postpone lost, and discussion on the constitution opened on March 8.

Resistance continued over the next two weeks, generally delaying progress, as the constitution was considered, debated, and modified in one particular after another. Henry Laurens was especially distressed to see "that many of those who were most forward, most violent, are now languide," and remarked that if he were an enemy to this country he would write to Lord North,

40. Hemphill and Wates, *Extracts*, pp. 184–85, 191, 218–19, 222.
41. Drayton, *Memoirs*, II, 175–76. Here again the author identified the speaker simply as "Mr. L———," but the evidence is overwhelming that it was Lowndes.
42. Ibid.

" 'My Lord give your Self no trouble about the people in Carolina let them alone and they will ruin themselves.' "[43] But resolution stiffened with the arrival of news that Parliament on December 21, 1775, had declared the colonies in a state of actual rebellion and consequently subject to the severest penalties. This news "silenced in a great measure, the moderate men, who wished a reconciliation with Great Britain," and ended further attempts at postponement.[44] Three days later, on March 24, John Rutledge indicated the degree to which moderate sentiment had shifted when he offered a long preamble to the constitution, which detailed their grievances but also described the constitution as a temporary expedient designed to serve only until an acceptable form of the royal government could be revived. The preamble was promptly approved, and with their intentions thus clarified, the congress adopted the constitution on March 26, 1776.

That South Carolina moderates approved the constitution of 1776 was due not only to its temporary nature, but also because it continued in effect many of the basic features of the old government, while others were modified to conform to old ideals and new circumstances. The old Commons House became the General Assembly, at first composed of, and afterwards based on, the membership of the Second Provincial Congress. A new Legislative Council, consisting of thirteen members elected by the General Assembly from its own membership, took over the legislative duties of the defunct governor's Council. To the General Assembly was reserved the right to initiate all money bills, which the Legislative Council might approve or reject but could not amend. These two bodies balloted jointly to elect a President of the colony, a Vice-President, a Privy Council to advise but not bind the chief executive, and other principal officers of the government. A separation of powers was implicit in the provision which outlawed plural office-holding, and a system of checks and balances in the presidential veto.[45] Thus constructed the new constitution

43. Henry Laurens to James Laurens, March 1, 1776, Henry Laurens Papers, microfilm, SCHS.
44. Drayton, *Memoirs*, II, 176–78.
45. Hemphill and Wates, *Extracts*, pp. 256–63.

represented considerably less change from old familiar forms of government than Lowndes and other moderates had feared might be the case. On the whole the document reflected the prevailing spirit of moderation among those who framed it. The majority continued to hope that the best features of the new government might eventually be blended with the best of the old under the restored authority of the Crown. This sentiment was nowhere more clearly expressed than in the preamble, which declared the constitution established "until an accommodation of the unhappy differences between Great Britain and America can be obtained (an event which, though traduced and treated as rebels, we still earnestly desire)."[46]

In this period of transition from royal government through irregular revolutionary government to self-government under a regular constitution, Rawlins Lowndes had acted as the leading advocate of moderation in public measures. In so doing he gained rather than lost respect among the majority of his contemporaries. This fact was best explained by John Drayton, son of the radical William Henry Drayton, one of Lowndes' most persistent opponents. Analyzing the role of the moderate opposition during this period, the younger Drayton stressed that they acted from the purest motives, then asserted,

> Besides, it must not be forgotten that the citizens of South Carolina, did not lead, but followed the American Revolution. They had been mildly treated by the Royal Government and therefore did not hastily lose sight of British protection. Hence, the public mind weighed how far it should support violent measures against the ancient Government and did not give way until the revolutionary troubles, and revolutionary principles thence arising, led them step by step to concede points as proper and patriotic which, a short time before, they had thought disloyal and unadviseable. For these reasons, the opposition members were always kept in place; as eliciting by their opposition, more prudent measures. And, that their conduct in so doing was not disapproved, the high public stations to which many of them were called during the most critical times of the revolution will be the best assurance of the public approbation.[47]

46. Ibid., p. 256.
47. Drayton, *Memoirs*, II, 88–89.

The best assurance of Drayton's accuracy was the election of John Rutledge to be the self-governing colony's first president and Rawlins Lowndes to be its second. Rutledge's experience in the office would increase his conservatism, while that of Lowndes would make it all too plain that the fruits of moderation could be bitter indeed.

CHAPTER X

President

HAVING ADOPTED THE CONSTITUTION in the morning of March 26, 1776, the Second Provincial Congress of South Carolina convened at five o'clock that afternoon as the General Assembly of South Carolina. In the first order of business Charles Pinckney, Henry Laurens, Rawlins Lowndes, Henry Middleton, and nine other members were selected to constitute the Legislative Council. These two bodies then balloted to fill the two principal offices of government. Moderates were chosen for both positions. Two ballots proved necessary to elect John Rutledge president and one sufficient to choose the reluctant Henry Laurens vice-president. Another moderate, James Parsons, was unanimously chosen Speaker of the General Assembly. The irrepressible William Henry Drayton was selected to fill the office of chief justice.[1] In this apparent effort to silence Drayton, the moderate leadership failed to appreciate what he saw immediately: the potential for espousing radical doctrine through the traditional charge to the jury.[2] On March 28 the president and other officers of the government were sworn and formally proclaimed. Other necessary details of organization were completed by April 11, when this first session of the General Assembly adjourned.

Rawlins Lowndes took no part whatever in these proceedings. He neither appeared to take his seat in the General Assembly nor

1. *Journals of the General Assembly and House of Representatives, 1776–1780*, eds. William Edwin Hemphill, Wylma Anne Wates, and R. Nicholas Olsberg, (Columbia, S.C., 1970), pp. 3–5 (hereafter cited Hemphill, et al., *Journals*).

2. William M. Dabney and Marion Dargan, *William Henry Drayton and the American Revolution* (Albuquerque, N.M., 1962), pp. 177–92.

to be sworn a member of the Legislative Council. His failure to lend assistance in organizing the new government leads one to suspect that he wished to avoid assuming a greater share of responsibility for putting into operation a government he disapproved of. On the other hand, his absence during this time could easily be explained in terms of priorities, in which personal affairs took temporary precedence over public service, for Lowndes had just bought Crowfield.

It appears that Lowndes had been aiming toward the purchase of an elegant country seat such as Crowfield, if not throughout his life, at least through a quarter century of land acquisition and speculation. It will be remembered that before he left the office of provost marshal in 1754 he had acquired two rice plantations, one in Colleton County and another at Goose Creek. As his affairs prospered into the 1760s he broadened his activities to include extensive speculations in real estate. Evidence of his skill in land speculation is seen in two examples. In June 1771 he purchased for £2227 currency a sixteen-acre tract one mile north of the city. Subdividing it into lots, he sold off eight lots at £350 each, then in December 1772 disposed of the remainder for £2700, clearing a profit, excluding expenses, of £3273 currency.[3] Again in February 1772 he bought for £20,000 currency four tracts in Craven County amounting to 1,130 acres, held them for a year, then sold them for £25,000, realizing a clear profit of £5000 on the transaction.[4] So successful were his various dealings in real estate that by 1773 he owned at least 15,000 acres in the lowcountry parishes and held a warrant for more than 7000 acres in Georgia.[5] In addi-

3. Charleston County Deeds, W–3, pp. 218–22, 230–38; ibid., C–4, pp. 423–27; ibid., 4–R, pp. 70–73; ibid., Y–3, pp. 49–52, 52–56; ibid., 4–W, pp. 337–40; ibid., 4–E, pp. 130–34; ibid., Q–6, pp. 353–56; ibid., 4–T, pp. 115–19, S.C. Archives; South Carolina Gazette, August 22, September 12, 19, 26, 1771.

4. Charleston County Deeds, A–4, pp. 167–70; ibid., C–4, pp. 241–47, S.C. Archives.

5. Deeds to most of the Carolina lands included in these figures may be seen in the Charleston County Deed Book, S.C. Archives, covering the period from October 30, 1762, through February 1773. See also South Carolina Colonial Plats, Vol. 9, p. 61, S.C. Archives, for his 3,300-acre tract on the Edisto River acquired in 1767, and Quit Rents, Receipts and Disbursements, 1760–1768, Part I, p. 104, S.C. Archives, for records on 3,420 acres belonging to him in Berkeley and Colleton counties.

tion he had come into possession of at least five houses in Charles Town and numerous lots in and around the city.[6]

Aside from his holdings in real estate, Lowndes possessed sufficient liquid capital to loan the state government £16,000 currency in 1777, more than £35,000 in 1778, and after the severe depreciation began in 1779, he advanced the state £10,000 more.[7] His slave property must have numbered well above one hundred, for in 1778 he hired out to the state sixty-two of his slaves, who may be presumed to have been mature males, to work on fortifications from April through December.[8] It seems not unreasonable to estimate that the number of female slaves along with those considered unsuitable for such gang labor or needed to maintain his three plantations during the gang's absence, would at least have equaled the number hired out. He later estimated his annual income in the years before the war at more than £3500 sterling.[9]

A recent change in his domestic life doubtless had a bearing on his decision to buy Crowfield. His second wife having died in December 1770, Lowndes waited two years before marrying again. The third Mrs. Lowndes, the former Sarah Jones of the distinguished Jones family of Georgia, was sixteen and her husband fifty-two when they married in January 1773.[10] Despite the difference in their ages and the fact that thenceforth she would preside over a household of stepchildren some of whom were older than herself, the marriage seems to have been a happy one in every respect. With an attractive, "dark-eyed, rosy-cheeked" young wife and a growing family,[11] all that was needed to realize what must have been the dream of his earlier years was a country seat befitting a Carolinian of his public standing and material success. The property known as Crowfield "truly was one of the hand-

6. Charleston County Deeds, V-4, pp. 107-10, 140-46; ibid., ZZ, pp. 574-78; South Carolina Colonial Plats, Vol. 11, p. 382; Judgement Rolls, 1765, no. 493A; ibid., 1767, no. 493A; ibid., 1770, no. 78A; ibid., 1772, 198A, all in S.C. Archives.
7. See South Carolina Treasury Records, Audited Accounts, Revolution, no. AA 4695, Rawlins Lowndes, S.C. Archives.
8. Auditor General's Accounts, 1778-1780, pp. 15, 36, 97, S.C. Archives.
9. See below, chapter eleven, at footnote eleven.
10. Ravenel, *Lowndes*, p. 2; *South Carolina Gazette*, January 28, 1773.
11. Mrs. Lowndes gave birth to her first child in January, 1774, "Extracts from the Journal of Mrs. Ann Manigault," *SCHGM*, XXI (January, 1920), 66.

somest estates in colonial South Carolina."[12] Originally a 1440-acre tract of forest and swamp lands located on Goose Creek, the property was acquired by William Middleton in 1729.[13] Over the next decade Middleton developed the wilderness tract into a profitable rice plantation, built a sixteen-room "brick capital mansion" upon it, and converted the grounds surrounding the house into a showplace that could rival in beauty and grace the family estate in England, for which Crowfield was named. Visiting the place in 1743, Eliza Lucas left a vivid description of the house and grounds that were to serve as Rawlins Lowndes' principal residence during the American Revolution:

> The house stands a mile from, but in sight of the road, and makes a very hansoume appearance; as you draw nearer new beauties discover themselves, first the fruitful Vine mantleing up the wall loading with delicious Clusters; next a spacious bason in the midst of a large green presents itself as you enter the gate that leads to the house, which is neatly finished. . . . From the back door is a spacious walk a thousand foot long; each side of which nearest the house is a grass plat ennamiled in a Serpentine manner with flowers. Next to that on the right hand is . . . a thicket of young tall live oaks where a variety of Airry Chorristers pour forth their melody. . . . Opposite on the left hand is a large square boleing green sunk a little below the level of the rest of the garden with a walk quite round composed of a double row of fine large flowering Laurel and Catulpas which form both shade and beauty. . . . [At] the bottom of this charming spot . . . is a large fish pond with a mount rising out of the middle—the top of which is level with the dwelling house and upon it is a roman temple. On each side of this are other large fish ponds properly disposed which form a fine prospect of water from the house. Beyond this are the smiling fields dressed in Vivid green. Here Ceres and Pomona joyn hand in hand to crown the hospitable board.[14]

Middleton sold the place in 1754 when he returned to England to take possession of the family estate there, and afterwards Crowfield changed hands several times. Finally in 1774 Samuel Carne bought it; but he, too, decided to leave South Carolina as the revo-

---

12. *The Letterbook of Eliza Lucas Pinckney, 1739–1762*, ed. Elise Pinckney, (Chapel Hill, N.C., 1972), p. 61, note.
13. Charleston County Deeds, E–5, p. 196, S.C. Archives.
14. Pinckney, *Letterbook*, p. 61.

lution approached, and advertised the property in February 1776.[15] Lowndes bought it from Carne for £2000 sterling on March 19, 1776,[16] exactly one week before the temporary constitution of South Carolina was adopted and organization of the new government took place. The timing of these two events is most remarkable, for one brought about the realization of Lowndes' highest ambition with respect to his private life, while the other set in motion seven days later a train of events that threatened his personal ruin if the colonial struggle failed. Even so, Lowndes proved ready to risk his considerable fortune and to sacrifice such fame as he enjoyed in defense of colonial rights.

Organization of the new government came none too soon for the British had already planned a campaign to seize Charles Town in May. These plans were delayed when loyal Scots in North Carolina, who were counted on to assist in the invasion attempt, failed to force passage of Moore's Creek Bridge and were thus prevented from joining the expedition. The main British force did no better, arriving off Charles Town in June only to fail in their effort to dislodge the stubborn defenders on Sullivan's Island and force entry into the harbor. After lingering about the harbor entrance into July, the British fleet departed, leaving the southern colonies in relative peace for almost three more years.

The abortive attack on Charles Town, followed shortly by news that the Second Continental Congress had declared the colonies independent of Great Britain, rallied South Carolinians to support the "cause of liberty." Rawlins Lowndes was among those to respond. In later years he would remark that originally he was very much "against a declaration of independency," but when it received the approbation of the people, it became his duty, "as a good citizen, to promote [its] due observance."[17] He might have added that the British attack on Charles Town all but destroyed the moderate center in South Carolina politics, driving

---

15. *South Carolina and American General Gazette*, February 3, 1776.
16. Charleston County Deeds, E-5, p. 196, S.C. Archives.
17. *The Debates in the Several State Conventions on the Adoption of the Federal Constitution as Recommended by the General Convention at Philadelphia in 1787*, ed. Jonathan Elliot, 5 vols. (Philadelphia, 1836), IV, 274 (hereafter cited Elliot, *Debates*).

men like Lowndes to abandon the long-cherished hope of reconciliation and to join the cause of independence. It seems to have driven Lowndes himself further than most moderates, for he appears from this time forward to be fully committed to the idea of complete independence from the mother country.

President Rutledge called the General Assembly into session on September 17, a month earlier than scheduled, and two days later submitted a copy of the Declaration of Independence for their consideration. On this date, September 19, Lowndes made his first appearance in the General Assembly and took the required oath to support the constitution of South Carolina. He then declined acceptance of his election to the Legislative Council, preferring to continue his long service in the representative branch of the legislature, and took his seat accordingly. Speaker Parsons promptly named the veteran legislator chairman of the committee charged with bringing in a report on the president's address including a recommendation on the continental declaration.[18]

The committee report which Lowndes brought in and read to the Assembly the next day opened with an eloquent paragraph of praise for the defenders of Fort Moultrie on Sullivan's Island. Their "heroic behaviour" had disappointed "the vain and flattering expectations of our cruel and unnatural foes," the British invaders. Turning to the continental declaration, the report became much more effusive than might have been expected from a committee chaired by a man with Lowndes' reputation for caution in such matters. The report declared:

> It is with the most unspeakable pleasure we embrace this opportunity of expressing our joy and satisfaction in the Declaration of the Continental Congress, declaring the United States free and independent States, absolved from allegiance to the British Crown and totally dissolving all political union between them and Great Britain, an event unsought for, and now produced by unavoidable necessity, and which every friend of justice and humanity must not only hold justifiable as the natural effects of unmerited persecution, but equally rejoice in, as the only effectual security against injuries and oppressions and the most promising source of future liberty and safety.[19]

18. Hemphill, et al., *Journals*, pp. 59, 63–65.
19. Ibid., pp. 66–67.

The Assembly majority proved to be considerably more restrained in their sentiments as well as their support for the declaration. A motion to delete the phrase "most unspeakable pleasure" was defeated. Then the majority removed the superlative from the unspeakable pleasure they felt and expressed "satisfaction" rather than "joy" over the declaration.[20] With these modifications the report was approved, and the government of South Carolina adopted the Declaration of Independence.

Adoption of the declaration suddenly changed the status of South Carolina from a rebellious colony looking toward eventual reconciliation with the mother country to that of an independent state. The change necessarily required that the state constitution be revised so as to form a permanent rather than a temporary frame of government. The effort to accomplish this task would be the principal public service performed by Rawlins Lowndes over the next eighteen months.

The early stages of framing a new constitution were under the direction of Lowndes, and the results of his efforts this session proved to be relatively noncontroversial. He chaired a new committee of eight charged on October 12 with recommending specific revisions in the temporary constitution, and brought in their report two days later. As amended and finally approved by the Assembly on October 18, the report pronounced the dissolution of all political connection with Great Britain and offered eleven specific recommendations for revision. The principal recommendations were that the "style" of South Carolina be changed from "Province or Colony" to "the State of South Carolina," that the Legislative Council be popularly elected with each parish and district electing one member, that no future president of the state serve more than one two-year term within an eight-year period, that the judicial system be liberalized in certain particulars, that representation in the Assembly be reapportioned as soon as practicable on the dual basis of population and taxable property, and that the oath of office required by the constitution be altered so as to omit the words "until an accommodation of differences between Great Britain and America shall take place."[21]

20. Ibid., pp. 67–68.
21. Ibid., pp. 143, 148–49, 162–63.

Although Lowndes' committee was further instructed to bring in a bill to implement the recommendations, the session expired two days later. On October 20, the General Assembly's term of existence as limited by the constitution ended, leaving the task for the next legislature.[22] In the meantime, the restoration of peace on the Cherokee frontier, which left South Carolina virtually free of warfare through 1777, meant that revision of the constitution would be the most important, and the most controversial work of the new legislature.

According to David Ramsay, who participated in these events, the elections held on November 30 and December 1, 1776, "were conducted on the idea that the members chosen, over and above the ordinary powers of legislators, should have the power to frame a new constitution suited to the declared independence of the state."[23] The new legislature, with substantially the same membership as the previous one, took up Lowndes' report in January 1777 and over the next few months made much more extensive alterations than his committee had recommended. By the midsummer adjournment they had written an entirely new constitution. Copies of the document were then printed and submitted to the people for their consideration during the balance of the year, after which the General Assembly would take final action on it. Submitting it to the people, according to Ramsay, and having it receive their general approval, gave to the new constitution "all the authority which could have been conferred on the proceedings of a convention expressly delegated for the exclusive purpose of framing a form of government."[24] But Ramsay's view seems much too sanguine, for opinion on the new constitution was so seriously divided that it produced the first great political crisis in the state's history.

The issue turned on four controversial provisions in the new frame of government. The first grew out of a powerful campaign launched by the Reverend William Tennent and the dissenter

22. Ibid., p. 176, note. The official journal ends here and does not resume until August 31, 1779.

23. David Ramsay, *The History of the Revolution of South Carolina, From a British Province to an Independent State*, 2 vols. (Trenton, N.J., 1785), I, 129.

24. Ibid.

majority in January 1777 that succeeded in disestablishing the Anglican Church.[25] Subsequent provisions obliterated the Privy Council, replaced the Legislative Council with a Senate of twenty-eight members directly elected by the voters of the several parishes and districts, and removed from the president (to be called governor) his veto power.

As could have been expected, strong opposition to these measures arose among the old Charles Town and lowcountry aristocracy who feared the loss of their traditional control over political affairs to the more numerous democracy of the parishes and interior districts. This conservative faction, led by the Rutledges and Middletons, were joined by "the Churchmen," as McCrady calls them, who vigorously objected to the disestablishment of the Anglican Church. Nevertheless, lines were not clearly drawn. Rawlins Lowndes and Charles Pinckney favored the more democratic changes such as direct election of senators, elimination of the Privy Council, and removal of the president's veto power, while both spoke out strongly against disestablishment.[26]

The issue reached a crisis on March 5, 1778, when the bill enacting the new constitution passed the legislature and was submitted along with several others to President Rutledge for his signature. Rutledge signed the other bills; but when Speaker Thomas Bee, heading a joint committee of both houses, made a short speech and handed Rutledge the constitution, "the President took it & laid it before him & took a paper out of his pocket which was a Speech . . . to both houses for refusing his assent to it."[27] Rutledge said that he was under "the absolute necessity" of rejecting the constitution, finding it impossible to give his approval without breaking the oath he had taken to uphold the constitution of 1776. He stated that, even without the difficulty presented by the oath, he would still withhold his approval for other reasons. Here he proceeded to what he considered the principal faults in the

25. Ibid., I. p. 129–32; Edward McCrady, *The History of South Carolina in the Revolution, 1775–1780* (New York, 1902), pp. 206–11 (hereafter cited *South Carolina in the Revolution*, I).

26. Ibid., p. 242.

27. John Lewis Gervais to Henry Laurens, March 16, 1778, Raymond Starr, ed., "Letters from John Lewis Gervais to Henry Laurens, 1777–1778," *SCHGM*, LXVI (January, 1965), 27–28.

new frame of government, and revealed a strong antipathy to its more democratic features.

Arguing from the premise that the constitution of 1776 had been sanctioned by "the people" while its proposed successor had not been, he maintained that the legislature was obliged to "adhere inflexibly" to the original, "not admitting any innovation of it." Consequently he found the new constitution unconstitutional, since "the legislative authority, being fixed and limited, cannot change or destroy itself without subverting the constitution from which it is derived." Without any authority to do so, then, the legislature had removed the president's veto, had annihilated one branch of government and taken the right of electing another out of the General Assembly, giving it to the people themselves. The last he found most objectionable, claiming on his authority alone that the people preferred to keep the Legislative Council, as it was elected out of the General Assembly and therefore more likely to be composed of men of greatest integrity, learning, and ability. He asserted further that the new system tended to enlarge the democratic power which he said experience had shown to be "arbitrary, severe and destructive." Nor was he willing to give up the idea of an accommodation with Great Britain, declaring that it was "as desirable now as it ever was." He had no hope, though, that his opinions could influence the legislature to reverse its position. He therefore thought proper to resign the office of president and forthwith submitted his resignation.[28]

On examination Rutledge's arguments seem hardly convincing. His emphasis on the inflexibility of the constitution of 1776 was not only inconsistent with its preamble which declared it to be temporary, but also completely ignored the fact that the president himself had already approved the first change in it regarding the original oath required of office holders.[29] The whole argument that the authority of the first was derived from the people while the second lacked that prerequisite was simply contrary to fact. The Provincial Congress had on its own authority written the first and the General Assembly the second. Neither had been framed

28. Ramsay, *Revolution in South Carolina*, I, 132–38; McCrady, *South Carolina in the Revolution*, I, 236–39.
29. Ibid., pp. 242–43.

by a specially elected convention. A member of the Assembly stated that the second carried more authority than the first, for "every body knows with regard to the [1776] Election that this Assembly was chosen by the people for the very purpose of altering the Constitution, & that printed reports of the Intended alterations had been sent over the Country previous to the Election."[30] This same point was made by David Ramsay. Finally, the president's claim that accommodation with the mother country was "as desirable now as it ever was," ran counter to public opinion, to the legislature's position, and to his own previous public pronouncements on the subject.[31]

In view of these facts, it appears fairly obvious that Rutledge's fundamental objection to the new constitution was that it would reduce his personal political authority along with the influence of the conservative Charles Town faction in South Carolina politics. The closely guarded secrecy with which he concealed his intention to veto the new constitution and resign his office strongly suggests that his sudden and totally unexpected resignation was a power play of no little arrogance, designed to throw the government into confusion and force alterations in the new constitution that would prevent the limited diffusion of political power it proposed. The success of such a scheme was not at all unlikely. Rutledge was rapidly becoming the most popular man in Charles Town and its most powerful political figure. And he might have had his way had it not been for the leadership of Christopher Gadsden and Rawlins Lowndes.

When the president submitted his resignation the committee was stunned. Taken completely by surprise, they stood there stupefied, staring at one another in wide-eyed amazement.[32] When they recovered their composure sufficiently to withdraw, they returned to the Assembly where the Speaker reported that the president had vetoed the new constitution and resigned his office. The stunning effect of this news left the shocked Assembly sitting some moments in dumbfounded silence as if no one had

30. Gervais to Laurens, March 16, 1778, *SCHGM*, LXVI (January, 1965), 29.
31. *See* Hemphill, et al., *Journals*, p. 84, and McCrady, *South Carolina in the Revolution*, I, 242–43.
32. Geravis to Laurens, March 16, 1778, *SCHGM*, LXVI (January, 1965), 28.

any notion of what to do next. Finally Rawlins Lowndes took the initiative to bring a semblance of order out of what appears to have been almost total confusion. Lowndes said that, although he could not approve the president's reasons for rejecting the constitution, yet he admired Rutledge for acting according to his conscience and judgment, and without fear of the consequences, exercising the power vested in him. Lowndes then moved that a committee be appointed to consider what measures might be pursued in the circumstances. A furious Christopher Gadsden, in seconding the motion, delivered a blistering denunciation of the president's conduct.[33]

Over the next two days Lowndes led the government out of the crisis, and in the process, suddenly found himself President of South Carolina. He chaired the two committees which clarified the issues and outlined a plan of procedure, reporting the resolutions of both. The first, a House committee, justified the controversial provisions in the new constitution, refuted the president's reasoning on it, and moved acceptance of his resignation and election of a new president. He next presided over a joint conference committee of eleven which came to the same conclusions. They decided, by the narrow margin of their chairman's vote, that Rutledge had a right to resign, then adopted the recommendations of the House committee. The legislature approved the plan and on the seventh of March elected Arthur Middleton. When Middleton refused election on the same grounds Rutledge had used, namely the difficulty presented by the oath, the legislature recoiled from the Rutledge faction and turned to the two men who could be counted on to bring the new government into being, Rawlins Lowndes and Christopher Gadsden.[34]

According to John Lewis Gervais, who left in a letter to Henry Laurens the most detailed account of these proceedings, Lowndes really did not want the office of president and only agreed to accept it out of a sense of duty, to prevent further "anarchy & confusion." Gervais wrote that after Middleton declined the office,

33. Ibid.; McCrady, *South Carolina in the Revolution*, I, 239–40.
34. Gervais to Laurens, March 16, 1778, *SCHGM*, LXVI (January, 1965), 28–29.

we had another Election Mr. Lowndes had 54 votes, Mr. Gadsden 48 not a majority. Mr. Lowndes intreated not to chuse him, but requested that those who had honored him with their votes could transfer their favours to his friend who was more Capable of the office than he was, we had another Ballot & Mr. Lowndes had a Majority of Votes, when he found his entreaties availed him nothing he retired, a Committee was sent to acquaint him that he was elected, he accepted considering the situation the State was in.[35]

For reasons of state Christopher Gadsden accepted the office of vice president, despite his settled conviction that his election had been engineered by the Rutledge faction to "get rid" of him and render him ineligible for office in the next election.[36] On the twelfth Lowndes was sworn and proclaimed President of South Carolina and one week later signed the constitution of 1778, to take effect after the fall elections.[37]

That two men of such diverse political views as Lowndes and Gadsden should have joined forces at this time is not as surprising as one might think. They had been very good friends for years, at least since the Stamp Act crisis, and though Gadsden had been an early advocate of independence, both had been thoroughly committed to the cause since 1776. While it cannot be denied that both were politically ambitious, it seems nonetheless true that they were primarily concerned with promoting the public good rather than their personal ambitions. They found the government in crisis in March 1778 and assumed, at no small risk to themselves and to their substantial fortunes, the responsibility for restoring political stability to the state. They were destined to share a common disappointment as well, for their brief ten-month tenure was to be an experience most miserable and mercifully short.

The problems of the Lowndes administration arose from a variety of causes. The Rutledges never forgave him for joining forces with Gadsden and accepting the presidency, and used their influence during his administration to stir popular feeling against

35. Ibid., p. 28.
36. Christopher Gadsden to William Henry Drayton, June 1, 1778, Walsh, ed., *Writings of Gadsden*, p. 126.
37. *South Carolina and American General Gazette*, March 12, 1778.

him.[38] Always conscientious in fiscal matters, he soon came to be disliked also for his strict investigation of the public accounts. John Wells reported that "his dealing out of the Public money with a very heavy hand has given much offense," so that by September he found the "Civil and Military Departments" complaining and the "Gentlemen of the Army" turning against him.[39] Finances were a constant problem, and the heavy taxes laid on in March to finance the war effort produced the resentment that could have been expected from a population largely apathetic to the problems facing their government. Nor was he to be spared personal bereavement and painful illness. Two of his sons died this year, while Lowndes himself was often so severely ill with the gout that he had to prevail upon Gadsden to conduct the business of his office.[40]

In spite of these difficulties, probably no one could have handled the routine administration of his office with more diligence and ability than Lowndes. He established and maintained throughout his tenure a steady correspondence with Henry Laurens, President of the Continental Congress, through which both were kept abreast of the latest developments in state and national governments. Similarly, he corresponded regularly with the governors of North Carolina and Georgia, urging the coordination of their efforts against the common enemy, the British, and cooperation in keeping order on the Indian frontier.[41] His most serious difficulties, though, stemmed not from the way he administered his office but from his reluctance to wield executive authority. He presided over the government much as if he were still Speaker of the House, leaving much of the decision-making to the legislative branch and giving his approval to their measures even though they might

38. John Wells, Jr., to Henry Laurens, September 6, 1778, quoted in part in Walsh, ed., *Writings of Gadsden*, p. 133, note.
39. Ibid.
40. Gadsden to Peter Timothy, June 8, 1778, ibid., p. 130; Gadsden to William Henry Drayton, June 15, 1778, ibid., p. 134.
41. Laurens' Letterbook number eleven in the South Carolina Historical Society bearing dates March 6 through September 23, 1778, contains a number of letters to Lowndes, some of which are cited below. The correspondence between Lowndes and Caswell during this year may be found in volume thirteen of *The State Records of North Carolina*, ed., Walter Clark, 26 vols. (Goldsboro, N.C., 1886–1907).

run directly counter to his own position. In short, it appears that his talents and disposition were not well suited to executive office in the circumstances of 1778. The circumstances themselves caught him directly between contending factions of conservatives and loyalists on the one hand, and radical popular elements on the other.

The first and most serious controversy of his brief administration grew out of the new loyalty oath law. Passed in March 1778, the law required every free male inhabitant of the state above the age of sixteen to take the following oath:

> I, ———, do swear (or affirm, as the Case may be) that I will bear Faith and Allegiance to the State of South Carolina, and will faithfully support, maintain and defend the same against George the Third, King of Great-Britain, his Successors, Abettors, and all other Enemies and Oppressors whatsoever; and will, without Delay, discover to the Executive Authority, or some one Justice of the Peace of this State, all Plots and Conspiracies that shall come to my Knowledge against the State, or any other of the United States of America. So help me God.[42]

Failure to comply within thirty days in the vicinity of Charles Town and sixty days elsewhere would result in the loss of all rights to hold office, to bear arms, to vote, to serve on juries, to sue in the courts, to hold, buy, or sell property, or to exercise any profession or trade. Those who should elect to depart the state rather than take the oath, and should afterwards return, would be subject to trial for treason and suffer death on conviction.[43] The legislature found justification for such stringent measures in the revolutionary circumstances of declared independence and existing war which demanded the discovery and removal of internal enemies. Although the severity of its penalties was contrary to his personal preference for moderation in government, President Lowndes withheld the veto and signed the bill into law on March 28.

Since this was the first law passed in South Carolina that required all citizens to take a public stand on the question of independence, violent disagreement over its execution was in-

---

42. *South Carolina and American General Gazette*, April 2, 1778.
43. Ibid.

evitable. The previous loyalty oath passed in the Rutledge administration applied only to the "late officers of the King of Great Britain, and all other persons whom the President and Privy Council should suspect of holding principles injurious to the right of the State."[44] Lowndes could use no such discretion when the new law went into effect, and the result was widespread disaffection and a growing exodus of loyalist elements from the state.

The law was proclaimed on April 2, and within a fortnight two refusals were reported from the Charles Town regiment.[45] One week later the *South Carolina and American General Gazette* began publishing the announcements of a growing list of citizens who were settling their affairs in Carolina, being "obliged to depart this State."[46] Benjamin Waller expressed the resentment of all loyalists and the defiance of many on April 23:

> As LIBERTY is a blessing which I am fond of enjoying, all persons indebted to me are earnestly entreated to make payment; that by discharging all my debts, a disagreeable incarceration may be as short as possible; also that those law pretenders may not any longer have it in their power to distress me; for if through kindness I happen to give a fop among them a little *shillela*, he immediately sues, and binds me over to the sessions for it.[47]

As the list was enlarged each week with dozens of names such as Pierce Butler, Lachlan Mackintosh, John Grant, James Duncan, Robert Keith, William Walton, and on May 14, even James Parsons, news of widespread disaffection was coming in from the Ninety Six area. At the same time law and order began to break down in the capital city, with numerous break-ins, runaways and an attempt "to burn the remainder of the Town" that had not been destroyed in the great fire of the previous January.[48] In the midst of mounting chaos Lowndes did all he could to preserve order, and offered a reward of a thousand pounds for the discovery of the arsonists who had tried to burn the town.[49]

44. McCrady, *South Carolina in the Revolution*, I, 213–14.
45. *South Carolina and American General Gazette*, April 16, 1778.
46. *See* the issues from April 23 through May 21, 1778, ibid.
47. *South Carolina and American General Gazette*, April 23, 1778.
48. Ibid., April 23, 30, May 7, 14, 21, 1778.
49. Ibid., May 14, 1778.

Then came news that calmed the apprehensions of those who had been inclined toward independence but hesitant to risk everything in taking the oath. On May 26 Lowndes published an announcement that France had acknowledged the independence of the American states and signed a treaty of amity and commerce, the king pledging to support their independence "with every means in his Power." The French were reported preparing for war, with 50,000 troops moving to the coast of Normandy and 270 sail commissioned.[50] According to Ramsay this news fairly turned the tide of sentiment in South Carolina. Now, instead of "that hankering after Great-Britain, which had made a separation painful, the current of popular opinions and prejudices ran strong in the opposite direction."[51] Prospects of victory and independence soared with news of the French alliance, suddenly diminishing the exodus as many former royalists began to come in and take the oath. An even larger number of reluctant Whigs headed by the Rutledge men found their resolution stiffened and their ambitions whetted by the encouraging news.

Shortly afterwards President Lowndes received a communication from the Continental Congress containing two recommendations on the matter of loyalty oaths. They suggested that the time allowed for taking the South Carolina oath be extended and that a general pardon and amnesty be offered to those who had not yet complied with the law.[52] Both Lowndes and Gadsden were agreeable to an extension and managed to persuade the Privy Council to move the deadline forward to June 10. On June 5 Lowndes issued a proclamation giving reluctant citizens five more days to come in and sign the oath. He also promised "to apply to the legislature at their next meeting for confirmation of this "General Amnesty and Pardon" which went beyond the limitations stated in the loyalty oath law.[53]

50. Ibid., May 25, 1778.
51. Ramsay, *Revolution in South Carolina*, I, 179–80.
52. Charles Town, S. C., *Gazette of the State of South Carolina*, June 15, 1778.
53. Ibid.; Gadsden to William Henry Drayton, June 15, 1778, Walsh, ed., *Writings of Gadsden*, pp. 131–32.

President Lowndes was hardly prepared for the veritable storm of protest his proclamation drew from the more zealous patriots of Charles Town. Gadsden explained in detail the tumult it caused:

> It was hardly got into the Sheriff's Hands before some Myrmidoms Alarm'd the Town, [that President Lowndes was] Setting up a Proclamation against Law; we were going to ruin their Liberties and What not! The Proclamation I believe was never read; a Deputation was sent to the President of Doctor Budd, Capt. Mouatt, Joshua Ward and some others. His proclamation was returned to him in my presence which of itself is Insult enough but besides that the spokesman Mr. Ward told the President He thought the people were right and he would lose the last Drop of Blood to support them. This I thought so high an Insult that I immediately began with Ward, sarcastically applauded his Heroism and great Exertions for the publick Good. In return he told me I was a Madman, but first took Care to sneak out of my reach. . . . The President did all that Man could do but to no purpose. A Meeting was call'd in the Evening, Doctor Budd put in the Chair, every press prohibited from printing the proclamation and the Magistrates detered from granting Certificates to the penitent.[54]

Gadsden defied them and announced publicly that he himself would administer the oath to as many as would come in and take it by the tenth. True to his word, he administered the oath to more than thirty persons by the tenth, "which has much displeased the people, & made him very unpopular. . . ."[55]

On June 10 another mass meeting was held at the Exchange where the mob, under the influence of the Rutledge men,[56] resolved that the law "ought and shall be strictly carried into execution; and that the pains and penalties imposed in the same, shall be assuredly inflicted upon all defaulters."[57] The cry "was echoed" through the meeting that nothing of this sort would have happened had John Rutledge been president. Some urged even more radical measures; Henry Peronneau moved to petition the

54. Ibid., p. 132.
55. Ibid., pp. 132-33; Gervais to Laurens, June 26, 1778, SCHGM, LXVI (January, 1965), 31-32.
56. Gadsden to Drayton, June 15, 1778, Walsh, ed., Writings of Gadsden, pp. 132-33.
57. South Carolina and American General Gazette, June 11, 1778.

General Assembly to impeach the president and Privy Council, but the majority was content with insulting the executive and preventing his proclamation from taking effect. Afterwards the Rutledge faction attempted to brand Lowndes as a Tory, using the proclamation episode and his initial reluctance to break with Great Britain as evidence.[58]

The situation of the president following these events was unenviable, to say the least. The excessive severity of the law and his efforts to execute it had alienated a large segment of the population from him; but an even larger number had turned violently against him when he attempted to mitigate the very severity that had made the law almost impossible to enforce. Three months in office had proved sufficient to make Rawlins Lowndes the most despised man in South Carolina, with the respect and public esteem he had earned through a quarter century of devoted public service lost in rancorous controversy. For a time Gadsden feared that Lowndes might resign, an event which he felt would create great confusion if not anarchy, bringing down the government and the constitution as well.[59] But Lowndes would not so readily capitulate to popular clamor and the machinations of his political enemies. He endured the insult to his office and the vilification heaped upon himself until the matter could be turned over to the legislature in September.

In the meantime the president busied himself with a multitude of other duties. His correspondence with Laurens in Philadelphia, which sometimes found Lowndes writing "hastily by candlelight," was most gratifying. Laurens gave the beleaguered president much needed support, applauding his fiscal responsibility, approving his proclamation of June 5, and expressing an ardent wish that Lowndes could join him in the Continental Congress.[60] Their mutual diligence in discharging their public duties along with similar difficulties and frustrations attending the execution of both their offices bred a mutual respect and understanding that

58. Gadsden to Drayton, June 15, 1778, Walsh, ed., *Writings of Gadsden*, p. 133 and note.
59. Gadsden to Drayton, October 14, 1778, ibid., p. 159.
60. Laurens to Lowndes, August 5, 9, 1778, Letterbook no. 11 (March 6–September 23, 1778), SCHS.

made them friends for life. During the same period Lowndes labored to keep peace on the Cherokee frontier, repeatedly urging Governor Caswell of North Carolina to restrain his people from intruding on Cherokee lands and from taking Indian prisoners in violation of treaties. In exchange Lowndes agreed to Caswell's request to permit the recruitment of troops in South Carolina for service in her sister state, and laid plans for mutual cooperation in their common defense.[61]

The defense of his own state was Lowndes' primary concern. For her protection the president jealously guarded her limited supply of arms and war material; nor would he release any for the use of units from neighboring states. Indeed, he gave notice that he would defy any requisition of state arms, even from the Continental Congress, if in his judgment the requisition would leave his state without enough weapons to defend herself. To remove the constant threat posed by a British fort built on the St. Mary's River in Florida, Lowndes sent General Robert Howe with more than six hundred state troops to join Georgia units of similar size in a campaign to capture the garrison there. The most ambitious and the most disappointing project of his administration, though, was the effort to create a state navy. He commissioned Commodore Alexander Gillon as its commander and dispatched him to Europe in June with authorization to spend up to half a million pounds currency in building three frigates for South Carolina.[62] But a series of delays and other problems kept Gillon tied up in Europe for years, and the entire project resulted in little more than a huge addition to the state debt.

Even before Gillon departed for Europe in June, the first units of the French navy arrived in Charles Town to provide some protection for the port city. Their arrival was the occasion of much public rejoicing and lavish entertainments for the visitors.[63] A few weeks later the anniversary of the Declaration of Independence called for another round of entertainments and public

61. Lowndes to Caswell, August 6, 1778, Personal Papers, Miscellaneous, Library of Congress; Caswell to Lowndes, May 6, 1778, *North Carolina State Records*, XIII, 119–20; Lowndes to Caswell, July 2, 1778, ibid., XIII, 184–85.

62. D. E. Huger Smith, "Commodore Alexander Gillon and the Frigate South Carolina," *SCHGM*, IX (October, 1908), 189–219.

63. *South Carolina and American General Gazette*, June 18, 1778.

rejoicing. President Lowndes was the most conspicuous figure in the formal ceremonies celebrating this occasion. He concluded the festivities of the Fourth of July by giving an "elegant entertainment" and dinner for the legislature, other civil and military officers, leading members of the clergy, and the officers of the French naval vessels in the harbor.[64]

In spite of such cordial relations between the officials of South Carolina and their French allies, the continued French presence through July and August led to incidents between the men in the ranks that exploded into violence on the night of September 6. With John Lewis Gervais, President Lowndes hurried down to the bay "where the balls whisseld round us," called out the militia, and eventually restored order; but not before several had been killed and many others wounded on both sides.[65] Besides the embarrassment to international relations the incident caused, it also furnished Lowndes' enemies in the legislature with additional evidence of his inability to maintain order.

When the legislature convened on September 3, President Lowndes directed their attention to the problems they faced and reported the unhappy events of the past summer—nor was the military news encouraging. The Creeks were on the warpath in Georgia and General Howe's expedition toward Florida, having dissipated its strength in a barren country, now lay exposed to British attacks from the south. He was, however, pleased to give them official notice of the French alliance, laying the details of that agreement before them. He recommended a general amnesty and pardon for those who had failed to take the state oath, as he had promised in his controversial proclamation, and gave a full report of the riot the proclamation had provoked.[66] In general the legislators approved the measures he had taken in their absence, but when the issue of the June riot was referred to committee, Lowndes' enemies began to contrive a new insult for him.

A committee of eight, headed by Edward Rutledge and dominated by Charles Town members, conducted an investigation of

64. Ibid., July 9, 1778.
65. Ibid., September 17, 1778; Gervais to Laurens, September 9, 1778, *SCHGM*, LXVI (January, 1965), 34.
66. Ibid., pp. 33–34.

the June riot. Calling in numerous witnesses, they took testimony on the details of the episode. Observing the committee's proceedings for several days, Gervais became convinced the Rutledge faction intended to discredit the president and expressed disgust at their partisan conduct:

> The Committee on the Presidents Proclamation I believe will report tomorrow at last—never was a business carried on with more partiality, the whole aim is to censure the president & let the people get clear. Whether the house will agree with the Committee is uncertain— there is but a thin house, & the Charles Town members carry a great Sway . . . they will have it just as they please. . . . In my opinion we shall have a New President before the end of the Month, unless the house reprobate the report. We shall make a pretty figure in the eyes of the World that we can't agree 6 months with a Governor of our Own chusing.[67]

But Gervais' worst fears proved unfounded. The Assembly postponed to the next legislature consideration of the committee report and upheld Lowndes' proclamation by voting to extend further the time for complying with the law. Gadsden wanted a showdown then and there. He was so provoked at the postponment that he offered his resignation; but when the legislature refused to accept it, he agreed to continue through the remaining months of Lowndes' administration.[68]

By October 17 the legislature had completed its work. The most significant action taken was approval of the Articles of Confederation. Then fourteen bills were presented for the president's signature. The most important of these embargoed all kinds of provisions, authorizing the president to extend the embargo at his discretion, and enlarged his powers to include the impressment of horses, wagons, schooners, and other means of transport. Lowndes was given extraordinary power to enforce loyalty, by virtue of an act which gave the president authority to jail persons considered dangerous to the state. After signing the bills into law, Lowndes delivered an address to the legislature reminding them of the upcoming election and exhorting them to "stir up

---

67. Gervais to Laurens, September 21, 1778, ibid., pp. 36–37.
68. Gadsden to Thomas Bee, October 5, 1778, Walsh, ed., *Writings of Gadsden*, pp. 154–58.

in the minds of the people" a due regard for the blessings of liberty and the right to elect their representatives. He lamented the general apathy of the population, especially in view of what appeared to be an impending invasion. Earnestly soliciting their support for the government soon to be elected under the new constitution, he closed with a reference to the difficulties of his administration and the popular clamor raised against himself. He would be happy to render any service to his country, and "in all events happy in the consciousness of my own integrity, and the uprightness of my intentions." [69] Then the session adjourned and the legislators dispersed.

The country members had hardly left town before a British brig appeared off the bar and sent in a flag of truce with an offer of a separate peace based on the terms recently rejected by the Continental Congress.[70] Lowndes himself could have rejected the proposals without fear of much public criticism. The state had heartily supported the earlier rejection by the Continental Congress; but he considered it too serious a matter to be decided without consultation. The ship was detained in Rebellion Road below the harbor while President Lowndes hastily convened the Privy Council along with "the heads or leading men of the different orders of the inhabitants. . . ."[71] As soon as the president read the offer to the gentlemen assembled for the occasion, they immediately and unanimously resolved to reject the offer as highly derogatory to the Continental Congress and calculated to promote dissension and jealousy between the states. Lowndes then informed the British emissary of their decision and ordered the ship's immediate departure from Carolina waters.[72] Shortly afterwards the brig weighed anchor and sailed for New York.

Rejection of the British peace proposals by the Continental Congress signaled a change in British strategy. For the past two years they had concentrated their efforts in the middle states,

69. *South Carolina and American General Gazette*, October 22, 29, 1778.

70. McCrady, *South Carolina in the Revolution*, I, 264; Ramsay, *Revolution in South Carolina*, I, 183–84; *Gazette of the State of South Carolina*, October 21, 1778.

71. Ramsay, *Revolution in South Carolina*, I, 183–84.

72. Ibid.; McCrady, *South Carolina in the Revolution*, I, 264–65; *South Carolina and American General Gazette*, November 12, 1778.

capturing New York City in 1776 and Philadelphia in 1777. But the loss of Burgoyne's army brought the French into the war, after which the British withdrew from Philadelphia and offered peace within the empire. When the Congress, insisting on independence, refused the offer, the British shifted their attention to the southern states. First the peace feeler was made to South Carolina, and following its rejection, the British abandoned the peace offensive and began embarking troops in New York for the reduction of Georgia and South Carolina.

In mid-November President Lowndes received word that a British expedition was embarking from New York destined for an attack on South Carolina.[73] From this point forward he was convinced that the major blow would be struck at Charles Town and proved exceedingly cautious in releasing troops or supplies for use elsewhere. One week later word came to him of Colonel Alexander Prevost's invasion of Georgia from East Florida, which suggested that the enemy planned to reduce the weaker state first. But Lowndes could not be sure. On December 4 General Benjamin Lincoln arrived from Philadelphia to take charge of the continental forces and organize defensive efforts against the British, but he soon discovered that Lowndes could not be persuaded to release the continental stores in the state arsenal. When 700 poorly equipped North Carolina troops came down to help defend South Carolina and Georgia, the general proposed that the president release arms and equipment for their use. Lincoln further suggested that since it was quiet in Carolina, troops might be sent to assist Georgia against Prevost. Lowndes' reply, as reported to Lincoln, was that he could not think of releasing the stores while the state was in so precarious a situation, for to do so would be betraying at trust. They had been purchased for the defense of South Carolina and it would never do to leave themselves defenseless; "No: he would not deliver them Should he receive an order of Congress for it."[74]

Lincoln then requested that the South Carolina militia be re-

73. Ibid., November 19, 1778.
74. Ibid., November 26, December 10, 1778; Benjamin Lincoln to Rawlins Lowndes, December 13, 20, 22, 1778, Benjamin Lincoln Papers, Massachusetts Historical Society, microfilm in S.C. Archives.

leased to aid Georgia. Lowndes again refused, stating "that there was no law that obliged the militia to leave the State & if there were a law made for that purpose he was not without his doubts whether there was efficacy enough in the Government to execute it, but however he saw the necessity, & it should be the first business he would recommend to the Assembly which was soon to meet."[75] On December 24 the president justified his cautious policy, reporting that a British fleet was then on the South Carolina coast from which he expected an invasion of the state. Thus he could offer little help to Georgia, but he promised that "any assistance we can afford, either in Arms or otherwise, towards the defense of this State, and if compatible with our own safety, toward the defense of Georgia, will most readily be given you."[76] When Lincoln sent for some tents and shovels for his men, Lowndes would release nothing but cannon powder. The president did promise to consult the Privy Council on it, but offered little hope.

The president followed his parsimonious policy until he received word from Lincoln on December 26 that the British fleet had entered the Savannah River. Only then did he begin to cooperate, dispatching two regiments to Georgia and releasing the Dorchester guard to lend their assistance.[77] By then, of course, Savannah was all but lost. On December 29 the British turned General Robert Howe's flank and drove him headlong through the streets of the town. Within another fortnight the Georgia lowcountry was pacified and the British turned their attention to South Carolina.

For the disaster that befell Savannah and the reduction of Georgia which followed, an alarmed population singled out Lowndes for much of the blame. And he had the grace to admit publicly that a good deal of the blame was deserved. Few could deny, however, that defense of his own state was his first responsibility, nor did Savannah rank with the strategic importance of Charles Town. Lowndes acted on the basis of the best information

75. Lincoln to Laurens, December 31, 1778, ibid.
76. Lowndes to Lincoln, December 24, 1778, ibid.
77. Lincoln to Lowndes, December 26, 1778, ibid.; Lowndes to Lincoln, December 26, 1778, ibid.

available to him and fully in accord with the primary concern of Carolinians. Nevertheless, his conservative policy brought more criticism down on his head. Lowndes' strongest qualities, caution and moderation, were not well suited to the circumstances in which he found himself, and ironically they completed the ruin of his reputation.

The public reputation of Rawlins Lowndes was thoroughly wrecked, and no one knew it better than he. Nor could he too soon hand the reins of government to his successor. When the legislature convened in January he mustered the grace to stand with dignity before the combined House and Senate and deliver his farewell address. After congratulating them on their first meeting under the new constitution, he recounted the events that had transpired since the last legislature adjourned and recommended measures for their consideration. Then he drew to his conclusion:

> As your affairs will in all probability be now managed more by arms than with Councils, and your success in a great measure depend upon military abilities and experience, such a fitness in your choice of a chief magistrate as will answer to your present circumstances cannot escape your discernment and penetration. It is my misfortune, Gentlemen, that with the best disposition to serve my country, I have been so distressed with the sense of my own inability and incompetency to fill the high station in which I now stand, that I feel the highest pleasure and satisfaction in the hopes of a speedy dismission before a critical period may arrive, when by my insufficiency, my country may suffer.[78]

With equal grace the Senate responded, assuring him that they were impressed with "his good and steady conduct in the administration of his office," and expressed their wish that they might always be as happy in their choice of a first magistrate. Similarly the House acknowledged the purity of his intentions in discharging the duties of his office, but could not agree with him in the opinion of his supposed inability. His former colleagues declared that he neither wanted the will nor the power to conduct public affairs in such a manner as may tend to the public good. Thanking them for their gracious remarks. Lowndes said he had no hopes

<hr>

78. *South Carolina and American General Gazette,* January 21, 1779; *Gazette of the State of South Carolina,* January 20, 1779.

or expectations unconnected with the prosperity of his state and not a wish but what terminated in the public good.[79]

When Lowndes stepped down from his office, the legislature selected John Rutledge to lead the state through the difficult war years that lay ahead. A few days later the popular young governor's commission was proclaimed amid the deafening cheers of a throng that lined the way between the Senate House and the Exchange.[80] Lowndes accompanied Rutledge in the procession, then took the long ride up the road from Charles Town to Crowfield and into voluntary retirement from public life.

If Lowndes had had any way of knowing it as he contemplated over the next few years the wreck of his public career, he could have found consolation in the knowledge that his experience was not a singular one. Governor Thomas Jefferson up in Virginia was soon to endure a remarkably similar ordeal. Both had to contend with a political rival of much greater popular appeal, personal daring, and decision. Each had a fine reputation tarnished through the common misfortune of being thrust by circumstance into an office unsuited to his talents and into a role unsuited to his disposition. Both intended afterwards to withdraw from public life; yet each eventually returned to recover a measure of public esteem, Jefferson as the enduring national symbol of human rights and freedom, Lowndes as the provincial advocate of minority sectional interests.

79. Ibid., January 28, 1779; *South Carolina and American General Gazette,* January 21, 1779.
80. Ibid., February 11, 1779.

CHAPTER XI

Exile

Yielding to John Rutledge the highest office the state could give, Rawlins Lowndes withdrew from active participation in the war effort and retired to his Crowfield plantation. He left no record of his reasons for doing so nor recorded any recriminations against those who succeeded him. Elected almost immediately to the Continental Congress he declined to serve; he refused a similar election to the state legislature, only the third such refusal of his long public career.[1] His decision to retire from public life he doubtless considered satisfactory to himself, although it was certain to bring upon him the censure of some of the more zealous patriots and leave the burden of its explanation to those who concerned themselves with the matter.

Lowndes' display of personal resentment over loss of the speakership in 1765 followed by his ill-tempered reaction to being passed over for the post of chief justice four years later arouses suspicion that his withdrawal from politics in 1779 was motivated again by personal resentment toward a political rival. There were, however, other factors of more direct significance which clearly influenced his decision on this occasion. His age was certainly a contributing factor; at fifty-eight he was the oldest of the principal revolutionary leaders, being the senior of Gadsden and Laurens by three years and nearly a full generation older than John Rutledge, the

1. August 31, 1779, Journal of the House of Representatives of the State of South Carolina, 1779, p. 3, manuscript, S.C. Archives, hereafter cited House Journal. Balloting jointly, the House and Senate elected Edward Rutledge to replace Lowndes in the South Carolina delegation, September 3, 1779, ibid., p. 28.

senior member of the younger group.[2] The declining state of Lowndes' health was another consideration. Both he and Laurens were sometimes immobilized by gout so painful that their performance of public duties had to be suspended or yielded to others.[3] Moreover, while Lowndes had been occupied with an increasing burden of public responsibility his private affairs had suffered serious neglect. His annual income had exceeded £3500 sterling in 1775 but by 1779 had sunk to a small fraction of that figure.[4] The matter of paramount importance, though, appears to have been one even more personal, the health of Mrs. Lowndes. The death of both her young sons the previous summer had left her in grief so deep as to bring her for a time near to distraction.[5] The combined effect of all these circumstances drove Lowndes into retirement. Subsequent events were to reveal that he suffered from no lack of personal courage as war came to South Carolina in 1779.

With General Lincoln and the main body of South Carolina's continental troops and militia posted near Augusta, Colonel Alexander Prevost brought 2400 men of his British command across the Savannah and pushed overland toward Charles Town. William Moultrie, commanding an inferior American force in Prevost's front, could do little more than send out frantic calls for help and

2. Gadsden and Laurens were born in 1724, John Rutledge in 1739, and his brothers Hugh and Edward in 1745 and 1749, respectively. Charles Cotesworth Pinckney was the same age as Hugh Rutledge, and Thomas Pinckney, his brother, was a year younger than Edward. Their cousin Charles Pinckney, born in 1757, was the youngest member of this group, a mere stripling of twenty-two.

3. Laurens, who had suffered from periodic attacks of gout for years, described the effects of a typical attack: "I have been sitting these four days with my left leg on a Chair and Pillows, my ankle and Foot in exquisite Torture at Times, never quiet and much swell'd." Henry Laurens to William Bampfield, December 29, 1768, Henry Laurens Papers, microfilm, SCHS. The illness apparently was a factor in his petitioning for release from the Tower of London in December 1781 in terms which evoked much unfavorable comment in America, *The Papers of Henry Laurens*, eds. Philip M. Hamer and George C. Rogers, Jr. (Columbia, S.C., 1968), I, pp. xx–xxi. It will be recalled that Lowndes during his presidency was forced by the malady to yield his duties occasionally to Christopher Gadsden.

4. *See below*, at footnote eleven.

5. Ravenel, *Lowndes*, pp. 6–8.

burn bridges behind him to retard the British advance as he re-
treated into the defenses of Charles Town. Both armies passed
within three miles of Lowndes' Horseshoe plantation west of the
Edisto exposing his properties for the first time to British plunder
and confiscation. Initiating a policy of systematic appropriation
and wanton destruction of South Carolina property, Prevost apparently stripped the Horseshoe of its slave population and other
valuables but left the plantation house standing as he moved on
to the provincial capital.[6] He drew up his command before the
city's northern defenses on May 11 and sent in a demand for surrender of the garrison.

Governor Rutledge and his Privy Council seemed surprisingly
willing to give up the struggle before his limited show of British
force. Consulting the council, Rutledge secured by a vote of five
to three their approval of a proposition to surrender the capital
on terms that would have neutralized South Carolina for the remainder of the war, with determination of its independence or
retention in the empire to be settled by commissioners at the
final peace conference. If Prevost was authorized to accept such
terms, he allowed a rare opportunity to slip away by insisting on
treating only with the senior military commander there, William
Moultrie. "Bulldog" Moultrie was a man not easily intimidated.
His reply was brief: They would fight it out. This left Prevost
with the uncomfortable prospect of being "Burgoyned" between
Moultrie and Lincoln, who was approaching with all too deliberate
speed from Augusta. On the night of May 12 Prevost withdrew and
retired southward along the sea islands to Beaufort, pillaging as
he went and leaving a ravaged countryside in his wake.[7] One year
later to the very day, Charles Town was to fall.

6. By July 1780 Lowndes had lost "from various Causes" almost eighty
slaves, James Simpson to General Henry Clinton, July 1, 1780, Headquarters
Papers of the British Army in America, 107 volumes, XXIV, document no.
2877, microfilm, S.C. Archives; *Report on American Manuscripts in the Royal
Institution of Great Britain* [Calendar of Guy Carleton Papers], 4 vols., (Here-
ford, England, 1907), II, pp. 149-50 (hereafter cited Calendar of Guy Carleton
Papers).

7. A strong suspicion among Carolinians that the Continental Congress was
willing to sacrifice South Carolina and Georgia in order to gain independence
for the remaining states influenced the decision of Governor Rutledge and the
Privy Council. *See* Wallace, *South Carolina, A Short History*, pp. 290-91, who

The appearance of a French fleet under Count D'Estaing off the Georgia coast in September 1779 offered an opportunity to reverse the flow of military events. A combined Franco-American effort against Prevost in Savannah was organized. D'Estaing moved up the river to deliver a bombardment which was followed by Lincoln's abortive assault against the town. Afterwards General Lincoln returned to Charles Town while D'Estaing sailed back to the West Indies leaving the Carolina coast exposed to a massive British invasion the following spring.

In December 1779 Sir Henry Clinton left New York with a powerful fleet transporting an army numbering more than 7000 British regulars. By the following February he had picked up Prevost and was landed on Johns Island, moving unhindered up the sea islands toward the Carolina capital. Under pressure from Rutledge, Gadsden, and other civil authorities General Lincoln made the fateful decision to defend the peninsular town. By the second week in May the British fleet had entered the bay, the army had sealed off every escape route, and both were throwing a rain of shells into the city. On May 12, 1780, the greatest American military disaster of the war for independence took place when General Lincoln surrendered the city along with his army of more than 5000 men, all their weapons, transport, artillery, and military stores.[8]

Governor Rutledge had slipped the noose a few weeks earlier. When the fall of Charles Town seemed inevitable, the state legislature conferred on him such extraordinary powers that for the next two years John Rutledge was the government of South Carolina.[9] His predecessor, Rawlins Lowndes, remained behind to witness the capitulation and suffer the consequences imposed on the civilian population of the capital.

On the approach of the British, Lowndes and his son Charles had remained in the town while Mrs. Lowndes and the rest of the

refers to Moultrie as "the South Carolina bulldog"; McCrady, *South Carolina in the Revolution*, I, 357-92, 424.

8. Wallace, *South Carolina, A Short History*, pp. 291-94.

9. The broad powers extended to Governor Rutledge were similar in many respects to those conferred on Lowndes by legislative action in the Fall of 1778, *see* ibid., 290-91.

family were sent to the safety of Crowfield some twenty-five miles to the northward. Five days after the capitulation Mrs. Lowndes informed her husband that the relative safety of the plantations had evaporated:

> I have this moment received my dear Mr. Lowndes's kind, and wellcome letter of yesterdays date, and rejoice to hear you are well and have been so politely treated. . . . I am exceeding sorry you have been made uneasy on our accounts, tis true we have been often alarm'd, and sometimes a good deal frightened, but every thing considered we have done exceeding well, and I can truly say my greatest uneasiness has been on your account. I am sorry you prevented Mr. Simpson from executing his kind intentions, I am infinitely obliged to him, a visit from him would have set my heart quite at ease. I wrote him a letter last friday acquainting him with some of my distresses, but as the Negro has not returned can't tell whether he got it. . . . There are vast numbers of plunderers up this way, a large party came here yesterday, they said with orders to plunder, but told them I was convinced they had no such orders, and they should have nothing from me but what I gave them willingly, which was breakfast and a plenty of drink, and so I dismissed them.[10]

All horses on the plantation had already been taken, so she could send none down for his use in the city to replace those confiscated by the British there.

The reduced circumstances of the Lowndes family was hardly exceptional. The havoc wrought by two British invasions and the widespread disorder which followed had by July 1780 thoroughly wrecked the previous stability of Carolina life. James Simpson, who had been attorney general to the colony before the revolution and now was returned to Charles Town, explained the change to General Clinton:

> Nothing but the evidence of my senses would have convinced me that one half of the distress I am witness to could have been produced in so short a time in so rich a country as Carolina was when I left it. Numbers of families, who, four years ago, abounded in every convenience and luxury of life, are without food to live on, clothes to cover them, or the means to purchase either. It hath appeared to me the more extraordinary, because until about 12 months ago it had

10. Sarah Lowndes to Rawlins Lowndes, May 17, 1780, Henry Clinton Papers, William L. Clements Library, Ann Arbor, Michigan.

not been exposed to any other devastations of war except the captures made at sea.

Simpson quoted a report from Lowndes as a case in point:

> For several years before the troubles I annually made, at least, 1000 barrels of Rice, worth £15,000 Currency; I had as much Money at Interest as yielded £8,000 Currency more. My Houses in Town, exclusive of Repairs & the one I inhabited, brought in £3,000, so that my Annual income was £26,000 Currency, upwards of £3,799 Sterling, which I was sure to have punctually paid. But upon an Average for the last four years, my Plantations have not produced upwards of £250 Sterling a Year; my Houses have been taken from me for public Uses, and are gone so much to decay they are not fit to be let, And my Money at Interest hath been paid into the public Treasury; add to which I have from various Causes lost upwards of 80 of my best Slaves.[11]

In addition to his property losses, Lowndes had lost by July 1780 the rights of a British subject as well.

By the articles of capitulation under which Charles Town was surrendered all civilians then in town were prisoners on parole the same as the militia, who were not to be disturbed in their property and were free to go home. Subsequent proclamations on May 22 and June 1 extended these terms throughout the state to all except those still in rebellion. At this moment further resistance collapsed. Garrisons at Beaufort, Camden, Ninety Six, and elsewhere voluntarily surrendered their arms and went home on parole. Two days later on June 3 General Clinton reversed himself, abolishing the status of prisoners on parole for the population outside the city and ordering their return to Crown allegiance by June 20, which meant forced service under British arms. Clinton's reversal was a betrayal of his word, and so it was regarded by Carolinians. This aroused a new spirit of resistance and reopened the war in South Carolina. Shortly after his June 3 proclamation General Clinton sailed for New York, deputizing Lord Cornwallis to succeed him.[12]

Now a program of coercion was instituted in direct violation of

11. James Simpson to General Henry Clinton, July 1, 1780, *Calendar of Guy Carleton Papers*, II, 149–50.
12. Wallace, *South Carolina, A Short History*, pp. 296–97.

initial paroles and the terms of capitulation, to force the population of Charles Town to renew allegiance to the Crown. Instead of enjoying the status of prisoners on parole, Charlestonians suddenly found that the basic rights of British subjects had been withdrawn from them. They were denied the right to sue in court or to practice their trade or profession. Seized property could not be restored to them although systematic plundering of what they still possessed was sanctioned, troops were quartered in their homes, and their own freedom of movement was more rigidly curtailed. In a very real sense Charlestonians had become outlaws. Rights of citizenship could only be restored by petitioning the appropriate British authority for "protection" of the laws which was granted on a profession of renewed allegiance to the Crown. The laborer, artisan, or tradesman was forced to submit or starve. The more affluent such as Lowndes faced the loss of their estates along with what remained of their personal fortunes.[13]

Under the circumstances most Charlestonians had little choice in the matter and began to accept protection in June. They were spurred on by a group of 206 loyalists and vacillating Whigs who signed an address on June 5 congratulating General Clinton and Admiral Arbuthnot on their conquest of Charles Town. The more prominent political leaders led by Christopher Gadsden and Edward Rutledge steadfastly refused to accept protection and urged others to follow their example. To remove their influence and further intimidate the population Cornwallis ordered a group of forty of these men taken prisoner and sent to St. Augustine in August. This had the effect of encouraging another display of loyalty in September when 164 Charlestonians signed an address congratulating Cornwallis on his resounding victory over the Americans at Camden. Even so, resistance continued, provoking another seizure of leading political and military figures in November, who were sent down to St. Augustine bringing the number of South Carolina leaders held prisoner there to sixty-three.[14] De-

13. In effect Clinton's proclamation of June 3, 1780, turned against the Charles Town population the terms of the South Carolina loyalty oath law of 1778, adding only the quartering of troops and plundering of valuables, ibid.

14. The Charles Town, S.C., *Royal Gazette* on July 11, 1781, published a list of Charlestonians professing allegiance to the Crown. Other lists may be

prived of vigorous leadership, the resistance in Charles Town disintegrated, and by the end of the year the city was satisfactorily pacified.

Among the thousands who accepted restoration of British authority in South Carolina and acknowledged their allegiance to the king, three of the most notable were Henry Middleton, Andrew Pickens, and Andrew Williamson. Middleton, a former delegate to the Continental Congress, had served briefly as its president. Colonel Pickens had surrendered the fort at Ninety Six to accept protection, although he would later repay Clinton in kind by rejoining the war effort. General Williamson gave up his command and settled near the capital city. The dismay which their capitulations produced among those determined to hold out was nothing compared to the bitterness generated by men like Daniel Huger, Colonel Charles Pinckney, and Gabriel Manigault, the most prominent among those who congratulated Cornwallis on his Camden victory, execrating "the contemptible remains of that expiring faction" that still resisted. Huger was one of three members of the Privy Council who had escaped Charles Town with Governor Rutledge the previous April. Pinckney, the cousin of Charles Cotesworth and Thomas Pinckney, had been president of the Provincial Congress; and Manigault, the father of Peter Manigault, had held for years the lucrative post of provincial treasurer.[15]

In the various lists that identified hundreds of South Carolinians on one side or another of the issues that developed over the seven months following the fall of Charles Town, the name of Rawlins Lowndes appeared only twice. The first was on a list found in the papers of General Clinton drawn up in May 1780 naming the "People Violent in their Opposition to Government, and Persecutors of the Loyalists." High on the list, which was arranged in alphabetical order, was "Christopher Gadsden, [acting] Lieutenant Governor." A few names below Gadsden's and

---

found in Miscellaneous Proceedings of the Board of Police, Charles Town, 1780–1782, CO5/520, entries of September 19, December 19, 1780, pp. 28–29, 48–49, microfilm, S.C. Archives (hereafter cited Board of Police Proceedings); Wallace, *South Carolina, A Short History*, pp. 296–97, 304–6.

15. Ibid., pp. 297, 306; McCrady, *South Carolina in the Revolution*, II, 533–38.

well above those of Governor John Rutledge and his brothers
Hugh and Edward appeared the following entry: "Lowndes,
Laurence [Rawlins], formerly Governor, when he heard of the
Act of Independency having passed in Congress he voted that
the Delegates from this Province should be censured."[16] Seven
months later, after the principal political and military leaders
had been removed to St. Augustine, his name appeared in the
"Proceedings of the Board of Police." A few days before Christmas
1780, the petitions of eighty persons, including such prominent
names as Charles and Glen Drayton, William Heyward, Jacob
Motte, Samuel Prioleau, Thomas Osborne, John Brailsford, William Skirving, and William Roper, "praying to be restored to the
Rights of Subjects," were heard. Heading the list was the name
of Rawlins Lowndes, who had stayed within the British lines since
the fall of Charles Town.[17] When the petitions were granted
Lowndes retired once more to his Crowfield plantation. Except
for furnishing supplies to the American forces and suffering additional confiscations by British partisans, he remained inactive
through the balance of the war.[18]

In the war itself the principal theater of operations had shifted

16. Photostats of the Henry Clinton Papers from the William L. Clements
Library, filed in the South Caroliniana Library, Columbia, S.C.

17. Board of Police Proceedings, December 19, 1780, p. 48; Rawlins Lowndes
to Sir Guy Carleton, August 8, 1782, Calendar of Guy Carleton Papers, III,
pp. 59–60.

18. Lowndes was not altogether idle during his exile at Crowfield. He
corresponded with British authorities in a fruitless effort to recover some
of his slaves, many "now in New York, and in other parts beyond the Sea,
from whence I have had intelligence of them . . . ," Lowndes to Sir Guy
Carleton, August 8, 1782, Headquarters Papers of the British Army in America,
volume 43, document 5243, microfilm, S.C. Archives; Calendar of Guy Carleton Papers, III, pp. 59–60. For losses sustained at the hands of Whig partisans,
especially horses taken, see Lowndes to General Nathanael Greene, December
31, 1782, Nathanael Greene Papers, William L. Clements Library, Ann Arbor,
Michigan. During 1780, 1781, 1782, 1783 Lowndes furnished supplies to the
American military forces valued at more than £500 sterling in 1785 and 1786,
Stub Entries to Indents Issued in Payment of Claims Against South Carolina
Growing Out of the Revolution, ed. A. S. Salley, Jr. (Columbia, S.C., 1925),
Book X, Part 1, Lib. X, No. 1507; ibid., Book U–W, Lib. V, No. 590. Lowndes
also coordinated efforts in Charles Town to prevent the loss of many more
slaves toward the close of British occupation; see Lowndes to General Anthony
Wayne, October 14, 1782, Wayne Papers, XVIII, 119, The Historical Society of
Pennsylvania, Philadelphia, Pa.

to the North Carolina border by the end of 1780. In October at Kings Mountain the mountain men had avenged Banastre Tarleton's appalling slaughter of Colonel Abraham Buford's American force near the Waxhaws the previous May. General Nathanael Greene in December assumed command of American forces at Charlotte giving the southern war effort most capable leadership. In January 1781 Greene detached his cavalry westward under Daniel Morgan, who along with Andrew Pickens met Tarleton at the South Carolina "cowpens." Executing a battle plan to tactical perfection, Morgan and Pickens gave Tarleton a comeuppance so sharp as to nearly destroy the most feared of all British cavalry commands.

Advancing immediately thereafter into North Carolina, Lord Cornwallis found himself moving through a vast and hostile country with a skillful Yankee opponent employing Fabian tactics in his front while fierce guerilla bands under implacable South Carolina partisans Thomas Sumter and Francis Marion wrecked his supply lines and recovered the country in his rear. Eventually Cornwallis broke off with Greene and withdrew to coastal Wilmington for fresh supplies before pressing on to total disaster in Virginia. Greene turned southward bringing his command down against Lord Rawdon and Colonel Alexander Stewart, and more formal warfare returned to the South Carolina lowcountry where savage partisan activity between Whig and Tory had never abated.

By the middle of January 1782 the American recovery of South Carolina was all but complete. News from Virginia that Cornwallis had surrendered at Yorktown, virtually assuring American independence, was then three months old. The British force in South Carolina was confined, except for occasional forays, to a small beachhead around Charles Town, although its new commander, General Alexander Leslie, would not give up the capital until the following December.[19] Some thirty-five miles to the westward General Greene was camped at Jacksonborough on the west bank of the Edisto protecting the first meeting of the state legislature to be held since Charles Town fell. The legislators assembled

19. The issues of the *Royal Gazette* from July 1781 to September 1782 offer a fairly thorough account, from the British viewpoint, of partisan warfare in the lowcountry during the last year of British occupation.

there, all recently chosen in elections which were open only to South Carolina voters of proved loyalty to the state, included Christopher Gadsden, Edward Rutledge, Thomas Heyward, David Ramsay, and several others who had come home following an exchange of prisoners the previous summer.[20]

Seven miles farther down the Beaufort road and two miles west of it stood the Horseshoe plantation home of Rawlins Lowndes. The Lowndes family had removed to the Horseshoe probably when the British and American armies descended into the Goose Creek region near Crowfield a few months earlier. The removal was not so much influenced by the scheduled meeting of the legislature as to protect Mrs. Lowndes from sudden raids on Crowfield. Especially for her sake the drafty plantation house at the Horseshoe was kept comfortably warm during an intense cold wave that settled over the lowcountry in late January.[21] There on February 11, 1782, she was safely delivered of a child, a fine healthy boy, named William Jones Lowndes in honor of her late brother. This new addition to the family stirred the proud father to redouble efforts to recover Rynah, the family nurse who had been carried away by the British.[22]

In Jacksonborough the legislators were warmed not only by roaring fireplaces in the Masonic Hall and Tavern, the temporary capitol, but also by the main object of their deliberations, the confiscation and amercement of loyalist property. Following the recommendation of retiring Governor Rutledge, the House appointed on January 22 a committee to consider the question of loyalists and to recommend the names of those who should suffer banishment, confiscation, or amercement of their properties, as penalty for their cooperation with the British. Aedanus Burke, an outspoken member of the House who contemned the whole policy

20. Charles G. Singer, *South Carolina in the Confederation* (Philadelphia, 1941), pp. 33–34.

21. *Royal Gazette*, February 2, 1782.

22. Ravenel, *Lowndes*, 2. William Jones, the uncle and namesake of William Lowndes, had died in 1768 leaving much of his property to his sister, Sarah Jones, later the wife of Rawlins Lowndes, *see* Will of William Jones, Lowndes Papers, Southern Historical Collection; Rawlins Lowndes to Sir Guy Carleton, August 8, 1782, Headquarters Papers of the British Army in America, volume 46, document 5243, microfilm, S.C. Archives.

of retribution, reported on the partisan manner in which the names were selected:

> The Committee on this business made out a List at first about seven hundred, but before it was brought into the house the number was reduced. . . . After debating on it, the house recommited the business, and the Com[mit]tee added a further number of two hundred & forty, the Estates of Charles Pinckney, Danl. Horry, Lowndes, etc. etc. are comprehended in this list for sequestration with many more. . . . 'Twould make you laugh were you to attend this Committee, tho' the Subject is a melancholy one. Every one gives in a list of his own and the State's Enemies, and the Enquiry is not so much what he has done, as what Estate he has.[23]

The Rutledges were among the leaders of those who advocated retribution against the loyalists. One of their purposes was to raise funds for a virtually bankrupt state government by selling off the confiscated estates and heavily taxing those properties amerced.[24] But the early zeal with which this policy had been initiated was soon tempered by two factors operating on the lowcountry conscience: the discovery that the penalties would fall on many of their relatives and family connections, and the justifiable fear that the backcountry would use the program to weaken lowcountry control over the state government.[25] When the Confiscation and Amercement acts were finally passed the list of estates to be confiscated had been reduced to 232. The total number affected by all the acts has been estimated at 378. The name of Rawlins Lowndes was on neither list.[26]

The final disposition of the cases of Lowndes and Charles Pinckney illustrates the type of distinction the Assembly made on the relative gravity of offenses. That both had been prominent in the early stages of the revolution and later had returned to British allegiance or "protection" was cause enough to single them out for punishment. But Pinckney had gravely compounded his first

23. Aedanus Burke to Arthur Middleton, January 25, 1782, *SCHGM*, XXVI (October, 1925), 192–93.
24. Their purposes were common knowledge in Charles Town as elsewhere, *Royal Gazette*, February 16, 1782; Singer, *South Carolina in the Confederation*, pp. 33–34, 104–5.
25. Ibid., pp. 105–6; Zahniser, *Charles Cotesworth Pinckney*, pp. 72–73.
26. Singer, *South Carolina in the Confederation*, p. 109; *Royal Gazette*, July 13, 1782.

offense by congratulating Cornwallis on his Camden victory, an act which now subjected his estate to confiscation under the terms of the Confiscation Act. Apparently through the influence of relatives his name was later transferred to the amercement list.[27] Lowndes on the other hand had done no more than keep his word given to the British on receiving his second parole. When the House debated these two cases Christopher Gadsden criticized Pinckney's conduct but vigorously defended that of Lowndes. Charles Cotesworth Pinckney tried to explain to his cousin how his name had been left on the amercement list while Lowndes' had been removed. Of Gadsden he said, "In short I am informed he was as loud in recapitulating every thing he could recollect to your prejudice, as he was in palliating every thing alledged against Mr. Lowndes, and in trumpeting forth the praises and Services of that Gentleman."[28]

Surely Lowndes never had a better friend nor a more forceful advocate than Gadsden proved to be on this occasion. The Assembly's first choice for governor to succeed Rutledge, Gadsden had declined, citing the infirmities of age. Forty-two weeks alone in the dungeon of Fort San Marcos at St. Augustine may have weakened his health, but the ordeal had never broken his spirit nor turned him against his old friend. Actually Gadsden, Aedanus Burke, Francis Marion, Charles Cotesworth Pinckney, and several other Whigs opposed in general the program of confiscation and amercement, counseling instead "that sound policy required to forget and forgive."[29]

Although the Jacksonborough legislature left his properties untouched, Lowndes was not immediately restored to political rights. Before adjournment the Assembly passed an act "for settling the qualifications for elections and elected in the next general assembly" which had the effect of rendering ineligible for

27. Zahniser, *Charles Cotesworth Pinckney*, pp. 72–73.
28. Charles Cotesworth Pinckney to Charles Pinckney, July 24, 1782, Pinckney Family Papers, Library of Congress.
29. Christopher Gadsden to ———, November 17, 1782, Walsh, ed., *Writings of Gadsden*, pp. 193–98 is a detailed explanation of Gadsden's views; Wallace, *South Carolina, A Short History*, p. 325; Zahniser, *Charles Cotesworth Pinckney*, pp. 71–73.

another year persons who had been excluded from participation in the late elections. Burke among others charged with some truth that the Rutledge faction was attempting to establish aristocratic control over the state government. The law violated the constitution of 1778 and gave to the postwar government a decidedly conservative lowcountry tone. Nevertheless a valid case could be made for the wisdom of insuring the loyalty of the body politic while the British remained in Charles Town. For Lowndes the consequence was political exclusion beyond the British departure in December.[30]

The great day of South Carolina deliverance came on December 14, 1782. The Continental army moved slowly into town as the last British troops embarked from Gadsden's wharf. While General Greene and Governor John Matthews took possession of the city, three hundred British sail made preparations to depart, carrying with them much of the city's treasure and several thousand confiscated slaves.[31] Hundreds of loyalists also sailed away leaving behind less fortunate British partisans to face the wrath of the most bitter element among their victorious enemies. The gratification of private resentments broke out almost immediately, ranging from simple assault to premeditated murder. In addition to a number of revenge killings in the interior, four Charlestonians had been assassinated by the following June.[32] Even more alarming to government officials and lowcountry aristocracy was a new leveling spirit among the people and a movement growing out of the mob violence in Charles Town that threatened to give control of the city over to the lower classes.[33] In a summer session

30. Singer, *South Carolina in the Confederation*, pp. 34–35.
31. George C. Rogers, Jr., *Charleston in the Age of the Pinckneys* (Norman, Oklahoma, 1969), pp. 49–50.
32. Aedanus Burke stated in June 1783, "Our citizens from a habit of putting their enemies to death, have reconciled their minds to the killing of each other . . . . Not to mention the many assassinations in the country, no less than four men have been slain in Charlestown since we regained it. We see men libel and assault each other in the very face and defiance of the Magistrates . . . ." Charles Town, S.C., *Gazette and General Advertiser*, June 10, 1783.
33. Zahniser, *Charles Cotesworth Pinckney*, pp. 75–76; Singer, *South Carolina in the Confederation*, pp. 28–30.

hastily assembled and thinly attended the Assembly incorporated the city, altered its name to Charleston, and vested in an intendent and thirteen wardens more than enough power to restore order. The excessive power of the new city government, much complained of over the next few years, was not reduced until political affairs became more stabilized.[34]

The only attack of record that was made against Lowndes in the postwar years came from William Clay Snipes, a quarrelsome neighbor known as a "Terror to the Tories."[35] When Snipes impugned Lowndes' conduct during the British occupation Lowndes took him to court in 1785 on a suit for slander. Backed by Henry Laurens and Colonel Maurice Simons Lowndes won his suit and silenced "the Tongue of Slander."[36] A most unfortunate result of this suit came one month later. Snipes provoked a quarrel with Colonel Simons over the testimony he had given and killed him in a duel.[37]

Lowndes occupied most of his time after the British withdrawal stabilizing his affairs and laying foundations to rebuild his fortune. His property losses during the war and British occupation had been severe. All his horses and most of his plantation stock

34. The "Act to Incorporate Charlestown" may be seen in *Ordinances of the City Council of Charleston*, compiled by Alexander Edwards (Charleston, SC., 1802), pp. 1–6, hereafter cited Edwards, *Ordinances*. Alexander Gillon, leader of the radical Anti-Britannic Society of Charleston, stated in 1787 that the act of incorporation "was originally passed in the summer when very few members were present; the ostensible reason was that great heats and animosities prevailed amongst the people in general, so that they were divided against one another, and much mischief naturally might be expected to ensue if the city was not incorporated." Rawlins Lowndes favored incorporation but thought the powers of the city council excessive. See Charleston, S.C., *Charleston Morning Post and Daily Advertiser*, February 12, 1787. For accounts of further violence in the city, see Charleston, S.C., *State Gazette of South Carolina*, September 22, 26, October 10, 1785.

35. Beulah Glover, *Narratives of Colleton County* ([privately printed], 1963), p. 141.

36. Rawlins Lowndes to Henry Laurens, October 27, 1785; Laurens to Lowndes, October 28, 1785, Kendall Collection, South Caroliniana Library, Columbia, S.C.; "Historical Notes: 'Simons-Snipes Duel'," *SCHGM*, XII (July, 1911), 160–62.

37. Robert Bentham Simons, *Thomas Grange Simons, III, his Forebears and Relations* (Charleston, 1954), pp. 74–84; *Charleston Morning Post and Daily Advertiser*, February 21, 1786.

were gone. Of the several score of slaves who worked his two plantations before the war, census records indicate that fewer than a dozen remained.[38] His financial losses through war-time depreciation of paper currency was estimated at fifteen thousand guineas.[39] Moreover, the collection of private debts amounting to several thousand pounds owed to him was postponed by state law to 1785. On the other hand he had not suffered a great personal loss like that of his friends Henry Laurens and James Parsons whose eldest sons had died in the conflict; Rawlins, Jr., Thomas, and James, his three grown sons, had all survived.[40] Unlike many others among his friends, none of his three homes had been destroyed; and of course, his landed estate had escaped confiscation and amercement. All things considered, Lowndes emerged from the war in circumstances that were probably no worse than those of most lowcountry planters and better than many.

Lowndes began to petition the state government for restoration of citizenship early in 1783. Although he received an initial rebuff from the Privy Council, he apparently recovered his political rights without serious difficulty, probably during the August session of the legislature.[41] Turning immediately to the state commission handling the war debt, he filed for repayment of the substantial loans he had advanced early in the war. After deductions were made for depreciation and interest was added he received on

---

38. *Heads of Families At the First Census of the United States Taken in the Year 1790, South Carolina* (Baltimore, 1952), p. 42, lists eleven slaves belonging to Lowndes in the Charleston District, none elsewhere (hereafter cited *First Census, South Carolina*).

39. Elliot, *Debates*, IV, 306.

40. Singer, *South Carolina in the Confederation*, p. 20; see *Royal Gazette*, September 7, 1782, for the death of Laurens' son John; Rogers, *Charleston in the Age of the Pinckneys*, p. 26.

41. *Journals of the Privy Council*, ed. Adele Stanton Edwards (Columbia, S.C., 1971), p. 5. Explaining that only the legislature had power to restore the rights of citizenship, the council voted unanimously "that Mr. Lowndes' petition be returned to him." Although the legislative records for the summer session of 1783 are lost, Lowndes must have secured citizenship during that term, for he was exercising the rights of a citizen by August 10. His name does not appear on earlier lists, see House Journal (January 6, 1783–August 13, 1783), pp. 167, 296–97; House of Representatives Committee Book (January 19, 1782–March 7, 1783), p. 177, all in S.C. Archives.

August 10 almost £4000 sterling worth of indents.[42] The indents were essentially interest bearing promissory notes which would be redeemed when the state revenue permitted, circulating in the meantime as a form of currency. Six months later he sold Crowfield to John Middleton, "late of London but now of Charleston," for £3800 sterling cash, almost double what Lowndes had paid for the old Middleton family seat eight years earlier.[43] These transactions, supplemented by £550 sterling received in 1786 for supplies furnished the revolutionary forces, gave Lowndes financial flexibility at a time of acute economic depression. Thus he was able to invest in fresh lands west of the Edisto without having to pay the exorbitant postwar interest rates, which ran as high as fifty percent and brought other struggling planters to the brink of economic ruin after two successive crop failures.[44]

Viewed in a larger perspective, the sale of Crowfield seems to have had a deeper meaning for Lowndes. While it cannot be denied that the transaction had very practical results, he owned several other properties whose sale would have served that purpose. It seems no less true that the appearance of a buyer who had reason to prefer that particular piece of property was a fortunate happenstance, for Middleton probably paid more out of sentiment for the old family seat than another buyer would have given. Nevertheless it seems clear that Crowfield represented to Rawlins Lowndes the realization of a persistent dream of his earlier years, one that he would not likely have given up for mere financial gain unless the dream had somehow become hollow. Considered in this light the sale of Crowfield may be taken as evidence that Lowndes no longer felt the need of such an impressive symbol of aristocratic status. Nor did he fully embrace the conservative Goose Creek attitude toward government as the citadel of propertied interests

42. South Carolina Treasury Records, Audited Accounts, Revolution, No. AA 4695, Rawlins Lowndes, S.C. Archives; Salley, ed., *Stub Entries to Indents*, Book B, p. 13.

43. Charleston County Deeds, K5, pp. 390–97. John Middleton was the son of William Middleton, who had developed Crowfield into a showplace before selling it on his return to England in 1754.

44. Singer, *South Carolina in the Confederation*, p. 117; Rogers, *Evolution of a Federalist*, p. 110; Zahniser, *Charles Cotesworth Pinckney*, p. 84.

represented by the Rutledge-Pinckney faction now emerging as the dominant force in state politics.

The shift was more subtle than substantial; it did not mark a clean break with the lowcountry political perspective of state politics. Lowndes had begun to part company with the more conservative political faction when he and Gadsden brought in the moderately liberal state constitution of 1778. That his acceptance of British protection and the censure he received for it widened the rift seems hardly open to question. Having acknowledged the people's right to a larger role in state government by helping to establish the present constitution, Lowndes was now moving in the direction of Aedanus Burke and the backcountry men. Just how far he was willing to go became more evident after he entered the state legislature in 1787 as a representative from the Charleston district and came face to face with the full implications of the Constitution of the United States.[45]

45. February 5, 1787, House Journal, 1787, pp. 63–64; S.C. Archives.

CHAPTER XII

Cassandra

FOLLOWING AN ABSENCE of eight years Rawlins Lowndes returned in February 1787 to familiar political surroundings, the Assembly Chamber of the State House. His reentry into public life gave the veteran legislator an opportunity to take a public stand on several issues of current significance. But first he wanted to settle a score. As soon as balloting had elected Thomas Pinckney the new governor, Lowndes asked permission to bring in a bill to repeal the Confiscation and Amercement Acts. In his candid opinion, the acts reflected "very little honor" on the Jacksonborough Assembly; he personally found it "disgraceful . . . for a legislature composed of free men to enact such laws that punished and condemned others unheard." Edward Rutledge successfully defended the acts with eight to one support from the backcountry members.[1] Although his proposal failed of adoption, Lowndes' rebuke of the Rutledge men could not have been plainer.

On most other measures considered this session Lowndes revealed that his sentiments generally were with the conservatives. On two important issues he voted with the majority to block the importation of slaves for another three years and to extend the stay laws passed in 1784 and 1785 to relieve hard-pressed debtors in both the lowcountry and the interior.[2] Rising backcountry farmers generally favored resumption of the slave trade while the

1. Singer, *South Carolina in the Confederation*, p. 124; February 21, 1787, House Journal, 1787, pp. 159–62. Lowndes was named to a committee to revise the "charter of Charleston" this session, February 9, 1767, ibid., p. 100.

2. March 8, 17, 22, 24, 26, 1787, House Journal, 1787, pp. 241, 298–300, 331, 353–54, 364–65; October 21, November 2, 1788, ibid., 1788, pp. 345–46, 388–90. Lowndes originally opposed the installment law, Elliot, *Debates*, IV, 274.

lowcountry voting majority opposed it on the ground that it would seriously reduce the critical supply of specie in the state.[3] The votes of Lowndes here represented more public than private interest, since he then possessed only eleven slaves to operate his plantations and held long overdue notes worth more than £18,000 in undepreciated prewar currency, the collection of which was delayed by the stay laws.[4] His lowcountry conservatism was clearly demonstrated when he voted against a backcountry proposal to revise the state constitution, but the bill passed with overwhelming backcountry support. He had the satisfaction of voting with the majority to restore the citizenship of former Lieutenant Governor William Bull, Jr., disagreeing once again with representatives from the interior.[5]

But the issue which eventually drove Lowndes into an alliance with the backcountry men came as a result of the most important action taken this session, the selection of John Rutledge, Charles Pinckney, Pierce Butler, Charles Cotesworth Pinckney, and Henry Laurens to represent the state in the Constitutional Convention scheduled to meet in Philadelphia the following May. Gout prevented Laurens from going, which left South Carolina's interests completely in the hands of the Rutledge-Pinckney leadership.[6] Authorized to revise and strengthen the Articles of Confederation, they returned in the fall with an entirely new constitution for ratification. This set the stage for Lowndes to crown nearly half a century of service in public life with a valedictory no less remarkable for the singularity of his performance than for the accuracy of his predictions for the future of the South.

The proposed Constitution of the United States became the principal topic of political discussion throughout the country in

3. Rogers, *Evolution of a Federalist*, p. 136.

4. For the debts owed Lowndes see Judgement Rolls, 1789, no. 253A, no. 399A, no. 466A, no. 507A, S.C. Archives. Their collection was delayed only one more year. Lowndes filed suit for payment beginning in October 1788 and had won all four cases, with incidental damages, by October 1789.

5. March 14, 15, 26, 1787, House Journal, 1787, pp. 279–81, 287–88, 290, 361–63. The Charleston delegation split on revision of the state constitution, nine in favor of it and twenty opposed. The bill passed 71 to 64.

6. March 1, 8, 15, 1787, ibid., pp. 202–3, 245, 286. The bill appointing the deputies declared that they were being sent "for the Purpose of Revising the Federal Constitution."

the fall of 1787. The prospect of an effective federal government found strongest support among business and property interests in the northeastern states and the southern tidewater, while yeoman farmers of the interior furnished the bulk of the Antifederalist opposition. South Carolina followed the national pattern; low-country opinion favored ratification over strong opposition from the backcountry. Unanimously adopting the Federalist position, the South Carolina delegation had returned home as representatives of the convention, urging ratification without revealing that serious sectional differences had surfaced in the Philadelphia debates.[7] In these circumstances the tidewater gentry found most attractive the new plan's tendency to promote tranquillity and order at home along with renewed respect for the nation and stability of commerce abroad. Farmers in the backcountry, like their counterparts elsewhere, possessed faith in government in direct proportion to their influence upon it, highest in their immediate vicinity and diminishing with distance from home.[8]

Rawlins Lowndes was one of the few lowcountry planters of South Carolina who joined the Antifederalist cause. He had never lost touch with the people, but he was certainly no democrat, notwithstanding his support for the state constitution of 1778. A government that would protect the interests of wealth and property would bring no criticism from him on that account. He had entered the revolutionary movement with reluctance, consistently advising caution in the face of proposals for radical change, always careful to retain political control in moderately conservative hands. His lowcountry group had been successful in maintaining control over state politics through the war and resisting back-country demands for a larger share in the government since then. From his point of view the Constitution threatened to transfer most of this political power to a strong central government dominated by the northeastern states. What he feared, as indicated by the repeated objections he raised when the General Assembly took

7. Rogers, *Evolution of a Federalist*, p. 153. For a concise analysis of the sectional division of sentiment on the Constitution in South Carolina, *see* Jackson Turner Main, *The Antifederalists, Critics of the Constitution, 1781–1788* (New York, 1974), pp. 215–20.

8. *See* Richard R. Beeman, *The Old Dominion and the New Nation, 1788–1801* (Lexington, Ky., 1972), pp. 29–30.

up the question, was that the southern states under the proposed
Constitution would become the "backcountry" of the new nation,
lacking the political power necessary to protect southern interests
from the northern majority. He had no reason to expect that
northern men would be governed by altruistic motives when forty
years of experience in government had convinced him that sectional interests usually prevail. He could even point to himself as
a fair example. Applying the lessons of provincial politics to the
national political scene, Lowndes took the backcountry view of
the Constitution.

The backcountry representatives came down to Charleston for
a new session of the legislature in January 1788. Entering into
the general discussion of the Constitution,[9] they discovered that
Lowndes was no more anxious to bring in the new system than
they were. Because his long experience in government, political
stature, and prominence among the Charleston-based gentry could
be expected to give his views greater weight in the House than
any one of the backcountry men could command, a group of them
prevailed on Lowndes to speak for them when the Constitution
came up for discussion.[10] In agreeing to do so, he assumed an old
familiar role, the leader of the loyal opposition. Nor was the prospect unpleasant that he would be once more pitted against the
Rutledge men on a major issue.

On January 16, 1788, the House went into Committee of the
Whole on the matter of scheduling elections for a state convention
to consider ratification or rejection of the Federal Constitution.
Charles Pinckney opened discussion with a full review of circumstances that led to the national convention, recounted the weaknesses of the present system under the Articles of Confederation,
and outlined the basic features of this unprecedented experiment
to establish a federal republic on so large a scale. He closed by expressing his opinion that this was the best plan of government
that had ever been offered to the world although its practicability

9. The Charleston press, which generally favored ratification, carried a
number of essays on the Constitution during December 1787 and January
1788, *see* the *City Gazette and Daily Advertiser*, December 4, 18, 1787; January,
3, 5, 11, 1788.
10. Elliot, *Debates*, IV, 287.

was yet to be determined.[11] Questions immediately arose on several paragraphs of the plan which led the House, without originally intending to do so, into a full debate on the merits of the Constitution.

Henry Pendleton questioned the power of impeachment residing in the Senate along with the authority to ratify treaties for if justice called for punishment of treachery in the senators, how were they to be arraigned? Pierce Butler gave a brief explanation why these powers had not been granted to the President alone or to the House of Representatives, which Charles Cotesworth Pinckney elaborated upon for upwards of half an hour.[12] To this point Lowndes had sat quietly listening to the two Pinckney cousins and Pierce Butler deliver their optimistic expositions on the Constitution. Now Lowndes rose to offer observations to the contrary and the debate began in earnest. Over the next three days of intense debate he carried virtually alone the opposition argument to the Assembly.

Entering directly on the point under discussion, the Senate's treaty-making power, Lowndes declared inconsistent with prudence the grant of so much power to a small body of men. By the sixth article of the Constitution treaties were to be the supreme law of the land, binding on judges in every state. A two-thirds vote was required for ratification of treaties in a body where fourteen members constituted a quorum, two-thirds of which were ten. Hence a President and ten senators could "supercede every existing law in the land. . . . Now, in the history of the known world was there an instance of the rulers of a republic being allowed to go so far?" European kings, he maintained, were under greater restraints regarding treaties. Moreover, he felt the Constitution could be interpreted so as entirely to do away with South Carolina's installment law. Nor did he believe that the excessive

11. January 10, 11, 16, 1788, House Journal, 1788, pp. 5, 7–8, 19. Since discussion of the Constitution was always in Committee of the Whole, the House Journal made no record of the debates. They were, however, fully reported in the *City Gazette and Daily Advertiser* beginning with a report of preliminaries in the issue of January 15, 1788, and continuing almost daily thereafter. The following account of the debates is taken from Elliot, *Debates*, IV, 253–317. Charles Pinckney's opening speech is in ibid., 253–63.

12. Ibid., pp. 263–65.

powers of the President could ever be exercised by a South Carolinian or a Georgian, for no one was ever likely to be elected to that office from these two states. He preferred rather to strengthen the Confederation under which the five southern states could better guard their interests, since ratification of treaties presently required approval by nine of the thirteen members.[13]

General Charles Cotesworth Pinckney, whose exalted military rank belied the modesty of his military accomplishments and tended to obscure the fact he possessed one of the best legal minds in South Carolina, rose to answer Lowndes, and the debate settled down to a duel between the old veteran judge and the skillful young lawyer. Although many others contributed to the discussion, virtually all in support of ratification, the brunt of the contest was carried from this point by Lowndes and Pinckney. With provincial caution, plain speech, and hard common sense Lowndes defended what he believed to be the interests of his state and section of the country. With aristocratic confidence, legal erudition, and persuasive logic Pinckney spoke for the nation as a whole.

Pinckney attempted to discredit Lowndes by claiming that his arguments had been spoken in a manner inconsistent with his usual "fair mode of reasoning." The General denied that treaties could be so construed as to contravene previously existing state law. They must nevertheless carry the force of law paramount, for no nation would make a treaty with us if individuals or states could break treaties at their pleasure. He rejected Lowndes' contention that neither South Carolina nor Georgia would ever furnish the nation a President and stated that if senators from any state failed to attend sessions for ratification of treaties the fault would lie with the individuals or the state rather than the Constitution.[14]

Here several other lowcountry Federalists rallied behind Pinckney. John Rutledge ridiculed the notion that a President and ten senators could be such fools and knaves as to tear up liberty by the roots. Ralph Izard took a different view from Lowndes on the power of kings to make treaties. Speaker John Julius Pringle

13. Ibid., pp. 265–66.
14. Ibid., pp. 266–67.

agreed; the usually sensible Lowndes was alarmed by mere phantoms without substance and had entirely forgot that the Constitution prohibited "retrospective law." David Ramsay wondered if Lowndes meant ever to have treaties at all; nations were already complaining of America's faithlessness and dishonesty. General Pinckney contributed two points on treaties he had forgot to mention earlier, then Lowndes again took the floor.[15]

Reminding the House that most of his opponents were "gentlemen of the law, who were capable of giving ingenious explanations to such points as they wished to have adopted," Lowndes returned to the attack.[16] The security of a republic is jealousy, he said, and its ruin could be expected from unsuspecting security:

> Let us not, therefore, receive this proffered system with implicit confidence, as carrying with it the stamp of superior perfection; rather let us compare what we already possess with what we are offered for it. We are now under a government of a most excellent constitution, one that has stood the test of time, and carried us through difficulties generally supposed to be insurmountable; one that has raised us high in the eyes of all nations, and given to us the enviable blessings of liberty and independence; a constitution sent like a blessing from Heaven; yet we are impatient to change it for another that vested power in a few men to pull down that fabric, which we had raised at the expense of our blood.

The new plan of government was an experiment which he was afraid would prove fatal to the peace and happiness of the southern states. In fact, "he sincerely believed that, when this new Constitution should be adopted, the sun of the southern states would set, never to rise again."

In support of his claim that the northern states would override the interests of the southern in favor of their own, he pointed out that six eastern states, excluding Rhode Island and including Pennsylvania, could control the House of Representatives. He thought it unreasonable to suppose that the agricultural South had the smallest chance of receiving adequate advantages in a legislature dominated by a northern commercial interest group.

15. Ibid., pp. 267–71.
16. Ibid., pp. 271–74, for the entire speech.

The South Carolina delegates to the Constitutional Convention had done everything in their power to secure for their state a proportionate share in the new government; "but the very little they had gained proved what we may expect in the future—that the interest of the Northern States would so predominate as to divest us of any pretensions to the title of a Republic."

The provision which would permit federal restriction of slave importation after 1807 Lowndes considered a case in point: "What cause was there for jealousy of our importing negroes? Why confine us to twenty years, or rather why limit us at all?" For his part, the traffic was justified on principles of "religion, humanity, and justice." He did not object to the restriction of imports, for he had voted for the state law that presently prohibited imports of slaves into South Carolina. What he opposed was the grant of power over this trade to northern interest groups. Slave labor was absolutely necessary to South Carolina: "Without Negroes this state would degenerate into the most contemptible in the Union," a fact admitted by General Pinckney himself. Not only had future control over the slave trade been given up, the South was to be heavily taxed for the twenty-year indulgence:

> Negroes were our wealth, our only natural resource; yet behold how our kind friends in the north were determined soon to tie up our hands, and drain us of what we had! The Eastern states drew their means of subsistence, in a great measure, from their shipping; and, on that head, they had been particularly careful not to allow of any burdens; they were not to pay tonnage or duties; no, not even the form of clearing out; all ports were free and open to them! Why, then, call this a reciprocal bargain, which took all from one party, to bestow it on the other?"[17]

That the southern states had received too little for what they gave away in this Constitution seemed evident to Lowndes in the provision which granted the federal government power to regulate commerce "*ad infinitium.*" Here again "the Eastern States, who were governed by prejudices and ideas extremely different from ours," would predominate. The southern states were called on to pledge themselves and their posterity forever in support of northern measures. When southern legislatures had "dwindled down to

17. Ibid., p. 273.

the confined powers of a corporation," they would be liable to taxes and excise payable not in paper but in specie. However, the South need not be uneasy,

> since everything would be managed in future by great men; and great men, every body knew, were incapable of acting under mistake or prejudice; they were infallible, so that if, at any future period, we should smart under laws which bore hard upon us, and think proper to remonstrate, the answer would probably be, 'Go: you are totally incapable of managing for yourselves. Go: mind your private affairs; trouble not yourselves with public concerns—"Mind your business" '. The latter expression was already the motto of some coppers in circulation, and he thought it would soon be the style of language held out to the Southern States.[18]

That these arguments required a thoughtful response was suggested by the fact that General Pinckney kept his seat for the remainder of the day while Edward Rutledge attempted a reply, heaping ridicule on the old system and Lowndes as well in the weakest performance thus far.[19] Rutledge, of course, suffered from the disadvantage of not having heard many of these points argued through three months of debate in Philadelphia. When General Pinckney rose to resume debate the next morning the profusion of legal citations that buttressed his arguments revealed that Lowndes had sent him back to his books the night before. Nevertheless, Pinckney had known precisely what to look for, and now he delivered the most persuasive of all the speeches offered in favor of ratification in South Carolina.

For the first hour or so Pinckney occupied the House with a convincing demonstration of his knowledge of international law regarding treaties that rather thoroughly exposed Lowndes as an

18. Ibid., p. 274. Lowndes' reference to "great men" here should not be taken as a pointed allusion to George Washington. On the following day Lowndes said, "For the first President there was one man to whom all America looked up, (General Washington,) and for whom he most heartily would vote; but after that gentleman's administration ceased, where could they point out another so highly respected as to concentre a majority of ninety-one persons in his favor?" Ibid., p. 288. Lowndes' objections were typical of Antifederalist sentiment generally; cf. Cecelia M. Kenyon, "Men of Little Faith: The Anti-Federalists on the Nature of Representative Government," *William and Mary Quarterly*, 3rd Series, XII (January, 1955), 3–43.

19. Elliot, *Debates*, IV, pp. 274–77.

amateur on the subject. Pinckney then began to sap the strength of Lowndes' conclusion of the previous day. Why had he said that everything in the future would be managed by great men? The abuse of power was more effectually checked under the Constitution in the impeachment process than under the present system:

> Then why make use of arguments to occasion improper jealousies and ill-founded fears? Why is the invidious distinction of 'great men' to be reiterated in the ears of the members? Is there anything in the Constitution which prevents the President and senators from being taken from the poor as well as the rich? Is there any pecuniary qualification necessary to the holding of any office under the new Constitution? There is not. Merit and virtue, and federal principles, are the qualifications which will prefer a poor man to office before a rich man who is destitute of them.[20]

Following this effective counterpoint Pinckney proved that the northern states had indeed made a substantial concession to the South in the matter of representation based on slaves. He also felt that the population imbalance between North and South would improve; since the northern states were already full of people, the South "must necessarily increase rapidly," further enlarging southern representation in the Congress.[21]

That the southern states were weak he did not deny. In fact they were so weak that a separate union of southern states could not hope to survive. Any invading power could reduce South Carolina as easily as General Clinton had done. For this reason he believed the South should endeavor to form a closer union with the stronger northern states who could protect the nation with their ships. He felt that since the northern states were strong enough to protect their independence without southern assistance, the South was only acting with prudence in giving the North special privileges in the carrying trade of the country. Besides, the northern states had borne the brunt of the war for independence.

Turning to the restrictions laid on the slave trade, Pinckney

20. Ibid., pp. 277–81.

21. In reference to representation based on slavery Pinckney drew a parallel with the system used in South Carolina since 1778, "that both wealth and numbers should be considered in the representation," ibid., pp. 282–83. It was this dual basis of representation that gave the lowcountry a disproportionate, in terms of white population, influence in state government.

stated quite frankly that "the delegates had to contend with the religious and political prejudices of the Eastern and Middle States, and with the interested and inconsistent opinion of Virginia, who was warmly opposed to our importing more slaves." Although he was still of the opinion that, without slaves, "South Carolina would soon be a desert waste," concessions had had to be made. The delegates had insisted on the importation, and after much difficulty the terms of compromise were reached: "We would have made better if we could; but, on the whole, I do not think them bad." [22]

The remainder of the debate produced fewer new points of argument than lowcountry Federalist speakers, all of whom leveled their shot at Lowndes.[23] When he reminded them that the Articles guaranteed state sovereignty while the Constitution "at once swept those privileges away, being sovereign over all," General Pinckney condemned the doctrine of state sovereignty as "a species of political heresy, which can never benefit us, but may bring on us the most serious distresses." To Lowndes' reiterated theme that the northern majority would exploit the minority south, "It was their interest to do so, and no person could doubt but they would promote it with every means in their power," Robert Barnwell not only doubted it but pronounced the idea founded in prejudice and unsupported by fact. Lowndes called for a new national convention to meet every objection raised against the Constitution in fair and open debate; Alexander Gillon rejoined that such a suggestion was "an oblique mode of reflecting on the conduct of our delegates." Lowndes feared that the new government would need bayonets to enforce the collection of federal taxes; Edward Rutledge thought lightly of those fears, but if a spirit of resistance should appear he thought the government should have authority "to compel a coercion in the people." Remembering that South Carolina had acted with admirable restraint in its issues of currency, Lowndes wondered what harm had been done "by issuing a

22. Ibid., pp. 283–86. For an account of the South Carolina delegation's strenuous efforts to protect southern interests in the Constitutional Convention, with a balanced view of Pinckney's role, see Zahniser, *Charles Cotesworth Pinckney*, pp. 87–96.

23. For the various statements given below, see Elliot, *Debates*, IV, 286–306, *passim*.

little paper money to relieve ourselves from any exigency that pressed us?" General Pinckney answered that it had promoted speculation, destroyed credit, and "brought total ruin on number-less widows and orphans." And so it went to the last hours of the third day when Lowndes rose to deliver his closing argument against ratification.

Summarizing the various points he had previously submitted in the course of debate, Lowndes made a fervent plea for retention of the basic safeguards which protected sectional interests under the Articles of Confederation. He offered a final warning of north-ern aggrandizement of federal power to promote sectional in-terests at the expense of the South, and "ridiculed the depraved inconsistency of those who pant for change." Thus far he had stood against "formidable opposition," but "if there was such a universal propensity to set up this golden image, why delay its inauguration? Let us at once go plump into the adoration of it; let us at once surrender every right which we at present possess." With an apology to his colleagues for having taken up so much of their time, Lowndes thanked them for their patience and drew to his conclusion:

> Popularity was what he never courted; but on this point he spoke merely to point out those dangers to which his fellow-citizens were exposed—dangers that were so evident, that, when he ceased to exist, he wished for no other epitaph than to have inscribed on his tomb, 'Here lies the man that opposed the Constitution, because it was ruinous to the liberty of America.'[24]

When Lowndes took his seat the debate was all but over. He ignored John Rutledge's accusation of obstinacy and heard with satisfaction James Mason express to him the thanks of the back-country representatives. Before the debate finally ended James Lincoln of Ninety Six excoriated the lack of a bill of rights in the Constitution, then paid a remarkable tribute to the old low-country aristocrat who had championed the backcountry cause: ". . . if ever any one deserved the title of man of the people, he on this occasion, most certainly did."[25] When the final question was

24. Ibid., pp. 308–11.
25. Ibid., pp. 311–15. David Ramsay expressed a vastly different view of Lowndes' role in the debates, attributing his opposition to "a narrow illiberal

put on holding the state ratifying convention in Charleston, "the man of the people" voted consistently with his traditional role. He had had his say and now voted along with the lowcountry members in the majority.[26]

Lowndes did not attend the Charleston convention that approved the Constitution in May. He had explained during the House debate that his Charleston constituents had decided not to elect anyone opposed to ratification, so his name did not appear among the Charleston delegation. Even so he might have served, for his old constituency of St. Bartholomews elected him, but he declined to accept.[27] His reasons seem plain enough. Opponents of the Constitution, unlike its advocates, lacked the organization necessary to block ratification in South Carolina.[28] Moreover, the law providing for election of delegates to the state convention gave the lowcountry its usual preponderant influence. Finally his

jealousy of New England and the contracted notions of a planter who would sacrifice the future naval importance of America to a penny extraordinary in the freight of rice. . . . He has not one continental or federal idea in his head nor one of larger extent than that of a rice barrel." Robert L. Burnhouse, ed., "David Ramsay on the Ratification of the Constitution in South Carolina, 1787–1788," *Journal of Southern History*, IX (November, 1943), 553.

26. The measure passed by the narrowest of margins, 76 to 75, Elliot, *Debates*, IV, 317, with the unanimous Charleston delegation and most of the lowcountry in the majority. Lest too much significance be attributed to Lowndes' vote, since it gave the advocates of ratification the important advantage of location, it should not be forgotten that no important governmental proceedings had ever been transacted outside the capital except during epidemics, the British occupation, and the Beaufort Assembly. To hold the convention near the Fall Line as the backcountry men wished could strengthen the movement for transferring the capital out of Charleston, a proposal which Lowndes strongly resisted. As subsequent events were to show, he had no intention of participating in any governmental functions outside of Charleston.

27. In a manuscript list of "members of the convention," South Caroliniana Library, Columbia, S.C., Lowndes' name appears among the delegation elected from the parish of St. Bartholomew. His name was subsequently marked out and that of Edmund Bellinger substituted below and to the side of the original list.

28. The lack of organization was typical of Antifederalists everywhere. John Lamb in New York, attempting to organize interstate opposition, contacted Lowndes, Aedanus Burke, and Thomas Sumter in late May 1788, but the effort came too late to affect the decision in South Carolina. *See* Rawlins Lowndes to General John Lamb, June 21, 1788, in Isaac Q. Leake, *Memoir of the Life and Times of General John Lamb* (Albany, 1850), p. 308; Main, *Antifederalists*, p. 218.

excuse for extending the House debate to such length had been that he did not expect to attend the convention, and later to have attended he doubtless regarded as tantamount to a violation of his word.[29]

Inauguration of the new federal government coincided with the close of Rawlins Lowndes' public career. His last significant appearance in the state legislature occurred on January 7, 1789. Meeting jointly to choose presidential electors, members of the House and Senate paid Lowndes a final tribute in selecting him to preside on this auspicious occasion. Four of the seven electors chosen strikingly illustrated the passing of the old generation of leaders and the emergence of another to take its place in the new era. Christopher Gadsden and Henry Laurens joined Edward Rutledge and Charles Cotesworth Pinckney, who, along with three others, delivered South Carolina's unanimous vote for President to George Washington.[30] Two weeks later the legislature chose young Charles Pinckney and Alexander Gillon governor and lieutenant governor respectively and named Pierce Butler and Ralph Izard, two rising young lowcountry Federalists, to the United States Senate.[31]

Removal of the state capital from Charleston to Columbia after the close of this legislative session apparently was the decisive factor in Lowndes' final retirement from state politics. The struggle to increase backcountry influence in the government of South Carolina was as old as Lowndes' legislative record. Backcountry agitation had waned though it never entirely ceased following the regulator movement of the 1760s. Emerging from the war with growing strength and numbers the backcountry insurgents began to force concessions from the reluctant lowcountry planters. In 1784 a strong movement to revise the state constitution in favor of the backcountry got under way. Two years later an act to transfer the capital to a more central location resulted in the selection of the Taylor plantation on the Fall Line, present-day Columbia, as

---

29. Elliot, *Debates*, IV, 274. Lowndes had promised on this occasion that if the Constitution should be "sanctioned by the people, it would have his hearty concurrence and support."

30. January 7, 1789, House Journal, 1789, pp. 5-6.

31. January 21, 22, 1789, ibid., pp. 71-76.

the site.[32] Fate sided with the backcountry members in February 1788 when the State House burned shortly after the House debates on the Federal Constitution ended.[33] In 1790 the backcountry men were gratified with the first meeting of the state legislature in Columbia but disappointed with the revision of the state constitution which took place there in May. The lowcountry, containing only one-fifth of the white population of the state, managed to retain a narrow majority in the reapportionment of both Houses.[34]

Lowndes took almost no part in these developments, although his sentiments apparently were with the conservative lowcountry members. It will be recalled that, after returning to the House in 1787, he voted against revision of the state constitution only to see the backcountry influence carry the measure. When the state government shifted to Columbia he declined to attend its sessions and even refused election to the convention of 1790.[35] As if to say that any affairs of government that could not be conducted in the old capital would have to be managed without his assistance, he closed his political career by serving a term as intendent, or mayor, of Charleston. Probably surprised that Charlestonians should have elected him in 1788 following his vigorous attack on the Constitution, Lowndes accepted the office as a vindication of his conduct. After one term of devoting his talents to the problems of municipal administration that faced the thriving port city, he retired permanently to private life.[36]

The last decade of his life from 1790 to 1800 was rewarding to Lowndes in many respects, most especially in financial matters. Having survived the postwar depression in strong financial condition and more recently collected on the old debts due from prewar years, he invested in more lands west of the Edisto and apparently

32. Singer, *South Carolina in the Confederation*, pp. 36–37.

33. After the State House burned the Assembly met first in St. Michael's Church, then at the City Tavern, and finally in the Exchange, Charleston, S.C., *State Gazette of South Carolina*, February 7, 11, 1788.

34. Zahniser, *Charles Cotesworth Pinckney*, pp. 106–10.

35. Lowndes was elected as a delegate from Charleston, *State Gazette of South Carolina*, February 15, 1790.

36. Edwards, *Ordinances*, pp. 63–70. Ordinances approved during Lowndes' administration levied city taxes, regulated the measure of products bought and sold in the city, appointed commissioners of streets, established a municipal slave code, and even issued paper currency, ibid.

in new slaves as well. By the end of the decade he owned at least five plantations and scores of slaves to work them.[37] He had wisely resisted the temptation to sell his share of the state debt to eager speculators. As early as February 1788 he had proposed "a sort of inquisitorial authority, to inquire who were the original holders of indents, and assignees; then to allow all the original holders the full value of their indent; and to the assignees 50 per cent on the original purchase." The proposition proved as unpopular as his stand on the Constitution; the Rutledges, Butler, Matthews, and Ramsay successfully opposed it "with uncommon brilliancy of argument."[38] The unobtrusive skill with which northern speculators subsequently bought up more than a million dollars of the state debt at a fraction of its value was even more brilliant.[39] Lowndes was amply rewarded for keeping his when federal assumption of the state debt improved his position by some thirty-five thousand dollars. He promptly invested much of it in bank stock including that of Alexander Hamilton's Bank of the United States.[40] By the end of the decade Lowndes held more than $100,000 in securities alone.[41]

As an observer of the national political scene during his last years, Lowndes had small reason to celebrate developments which tended to justify his warnings of 1788. Federal authorities were

37. Between 1778 and 1791 Lowndes purchased at least 3,892 acres in six tracts west of the Edisto, *see* Charleston County Deeds, G5, p. 158; ibid., P5, pp. 392–96; ibid., E6, pp. 484–87, ibid., W–6, pp. 286–90. His treatment of slaves was relatively humane, judging from the following statement taken from an advertisement he placed in the *City Gazette and Daily Advertiser*, October 10, 1792, seeking the recovery of "Will" whom he had recently purchased: "The fellow expressing a reluctance at being removed to my plantation, so remote from his wife and children, who live at Goose Creek, Black river, and belong to Mr. Joseph Bee, I permitted him to look out for another master, and he has absconded ever since."

38. *State Gazette of South Carolina*, February 4, 1788.

39. Rogers, *Evolution of a Federalist*, pp. 198–204.

40. Ibid., pp. 203–4. In November 1783 indents for £1,839 plus interest were "Issued to Hon. Rawlins Lowndes for Messrs Martins & Eytelwein of Amsterdam," a transaction in which he acted as agent only and did not figure in the amount he received personally at the assumption of the state debt, *see* Salley, ed., *Stub Entries to Indents*, Book B, p. 23; Rogers, *Evolution of a Federalist*, p. 231, note.

41. Will of Rawlins Lowndes, Will Book D, pp. 23–36, Office of Register of Mesne Conveyance, Charleston County Court House, Charleston, S.C.

forced to bring out the bayonet as early as 1794 to collect the whiskey tax from outraged farmers in western Pennsylvania. Public anger on a grander scale boiled through the South the following year when Jay's Treaty became the law of the land, threatening the collection of old debts owed to British merchants but making no provision for reimbursement to owners of thousands of slaves carried off by the British. Even the Rutledges came out to harangue a Charleston mob that had taken to the streets in howling protest on this occasion.[42] The performance helped to prevent John Rutledge from becoming Chief Justice of the United States and contributed to the subsequent ruin of his health.[43]

Three years later in 1798 the Sedition Act sent Virginia and Kentucky into defiant repudiation of the infamous law, taking a view of state sovereignty strongly reminiscent of that expressed by Lowndes a decade earlier. South Carolina officially adopted the doctrine of state sovereignty a generation later when predominantly northern interests pressed the protective tariff and slavery issues with sufficient indifference to southern protests that South Carolina was driven into open defiance of federal law. On that occasion Henry Laurens Pinckney reminded Charlestonians how their fathers had so miscalculated the "fidelity" of their northern allies, "that he who opposed the Union, was almost regarded as an enemy to Carolina, and even the warnings of the sagacious *Lowndes*, though they have been as literally verified as the predictions of Cassandra, were still treated like hers, as the idle visions of fatuity."[44] As historian George Rogers put it, Lowndes in 1788 "saw the logic of the period from Jefferson's embargo to the Civil War."[45]

Rawlins Lowndes died on August 24, 1800, following by a few weeks the death of his old political rival, John Rutledge.[46] During his last illness Lowndes could look back over the record of his life with a sense of justifiable pride. Fatherless at fourteen, he had

42. Philadelphia, Pa., *Aurora and General Advertiser*, July 29, 31, 1795.

43. Jacob Read to Ralph Izard, December 8, 19, 1795, *Ralph Izard Papers*, South Caroliniana Library, Columbia, S.C.

44. Henry Laurens Pinckney, *An Oration, Delivered in the Independent, or Congregational Church, Charleston* (Charleston, 1833), p. 11.

45. Rogers, *Evolution of a Federalist*, p. 153.

46. *City Gazette and Daily Advertiser*, August 27, 1800.

risen from humble circumstances to a position of wealth, status and political influence strictly on the basis of personal merit, talent, character, and industry. He could take satisfaction from the fact that he had contributed substantially to the political history of his state, fully established the name of Lowndes in lowcountry society, and was leaving his numerous family in financial circumstances commensurate with their lofty social position. The old patriarch closed his life with a touch of fond remembrance that belied the sternness of his character and his usually imperious paternal manner. Shortly before he died he called in William, his favorite son, and handed him a small silver dish, a Queen Anne salver, with the request that "If he should ever marry and have a *pretty* daughter, to give it to her, for it had belonged to Amarinthia." [47]

47. Ravenel, *Lowndes*, p. 51.

Afterword

VIEWED IN A LARGER PERSPECTIVE than the fourscore years it
spanned, the life of Rawlins Lowndes represents a pattern
often repeated in the various frontier stages of America's development. Charles Town, South Carolina, during the second quarter
of the eighteenth century possessed many characteristics of a
frontier environment; most notably, a society sufficiently open
and fluid to admit newcomers who could prove themselves worthy
of recognition and status, great opportunities for acquisition of
property and economic advancement, intense, even ruthless, competition for advantage, and public honors extended to those who
proved their merit through economic success.

Entering this environment in 1730, Charles Lowndes failed because he lacked the personal character and conditioning necessary
for success. His death left his son Rawlins the advantage of a fine
name and some status as a consequence, but neither was a guarantee
that the son would do better than his father had done, as the father's failure too plainly proved. The great lesson that Rawlins
seems to have learned from the tragedy was that a society must be
dealt with on its own terms, which may be turned to advantage
when the opportunity presents itself. Hence Rawlins took a
realistic view of his circumstances and developed the character
traits demanded by them, industry, integrity, character, and ambition tempered by circumspection, always keeping a sharp eye
for the main chance. When the opportunity arrived with his
appointment to the office of provost marshal in 1745, he began
to prosper and the expected rewards quite naturally followed, including a most advantageous marriage and election to the Com-

mons House of Assembly. In the process it seems plain enough that Lowndes developed a sensitive pride along with an expectation that public men should be judged on the basis of personal merit and faithful service.

By midcentury, however, the society had begun to mature and the old traditional values were being clouded by the introduction of new factors. Evidence of a shifting attitude began to appear in the rising generation of leaders, for the most part born to wealth, educated in England, and taking on the presumptions of an aristocratic class. This coincided with a change in ministerial policy regarding South Carolina that began in the 1750s to send over English placemen to assume some of the more desirable positions in provincial government, indicating Crown recognition of the colony's maturity. The bitter result for Lowndes was that his personal merit would be disregarded both by the younger men, who maneuvered him out of the Speaker's chair in 1765, and by an arbitrary ministry, which passed him over for the post of chief justice four years later. The first event produced in Lowndes a deep resentment while the second turned him in the direction of revolution against Crown authority.

Based on the limited evidence available, it appears that Lowndes' personal and political friendships were determined in substantial degree by the circumstances of his early years. His only authenticated personal friendships were with merchants, Samuel Brailsford and John Watsone in England and Christopher Gadsden and eventually Henry Laurens at home. These were all essentially self-made men of Lowndes' generation, who knew the value of integrity from daily exposure to risk in the marketplace, while Lowndes had learned the same lessons through his intimate connection with law enforcement and the courts. This, more than any other single factor, seems to account for Lowndes' enduring friendship with Gadsden and Laurens, notwithstanding differences of opinion on the pace of revolutionary activity leading to the War for Independence.

Having grown to manhood with Lowndes in Charles Town during the second quarter of the eighteenth century, Gadsden and Laurens were well aware of the difficulties he had faced and the problems he had overcome and valued him for his character.

Moderate liberals in the eighteenth-century sense, Lowndes and Laurens developed the habitual caution of men whose fortunes represent years of patient industry and which are not to be exposed to hazard without careful consideration. Gadsden held views considerably more radical, an idealistic belief in the individual right of self-government he always considered worth losing a fortune for. All three established themselves as members of the provincial aristocracy and, following the style of their British examples, acquired mansions and manners appropriate to their station in provincial life. In short, they developed the pretensions of aristocratic status, but, never losing touch with the people nor completely forgetting their origins, none of the three ever claimed the British prerogative of aristocratic status, the right to govern.

The new generation of Rutledges, Middletons, Pinckneys, and Manigaults on the other hand were all members of the rising planter-lawyer aristocracy, many of whom would form an opposition to Gadsden and Lowndes during the latter's presidency. It seems significant that all had been born to wealth and established family status and social connections. Although these "children of privilege" united with the older men as long as the question was the familiar one of "home rule" during the 1760s and early 1770s, they began to differ when the issue changed to "who shall rule at home" during the revolution itself. Influenced to a greater degree by their British counterparts, the Rutledge-Middleton-Pinckney group assumed a similar attitude toward government, that found expression in a strong opposition toward its democratic features. The issue turned on the state constitution of 1778 which enlarged popular participation in government and produced a factional opposition led by the Rutledges that contributed to the difficulties of Lowndes' presidency and seriously damaged his reputation. Rutledge triumphed with his election to the governorship in 1779 while Lowndes withdrew for the balance of the war.

After the war when passions had begun to cool, Lowndes assumed once again the responsibilities of a man of property and reentered public life. The Rutledge-Pinckney men were firmly in control of the state government, but by now the fundamental issue of government had undergone serious changes and taken on larger dimensions. Now it was a national question involving property versus a potentially radical democracy as well as southern agricultural versus northern commercial interests. Distrusting the northern numerical majority to a far greater degree than did his peers, Lowndes took a provincial view of the Constitution and led opposition to its ratification in the state.

The sectional issues raised in these debates over the Constitution would come to haunt the next generation of South Carolinians. By an ironic stroke of fate the principal antagonists, who clashed over the fundamental question of state rights as opposed to federal authority, were two men born in the South Carolina backcountry. One, Andrew Jackson, followed a career that offers many parallels to that of Lowndes. The orphan son of an immigrant to Carolina, self-made and largely self-educated, fiercely proud, distinguished by integrity and strength of character, and trained in the law, Jackson left the Carolina piedmont and migrated to Tennessee. Settling in Nashville, he found that the frontier town for all its rudeness offered newcomers essentially the same opportunities for advancement that coastal Charles Town had presented Lowndes, exacted essentially the same demands, and held remarkably similar risks of failure. There Jackson "Got Money—Married Well—Settled Plantations—became a Planter—A Magistrate—A Senator . . . and . . . Chief Judge." He also came to be identified with the frontier aristocracy and shared their interests in state government. After his election to the Presidency, Jackson stoutly opposed entrenched privilege on the one hand and sectional division on the other.

John C. Calhoun, the son of Patrick Calhoun (whose only recorded contribution to the South Carolina debate on the Constitution was a question pertaining to religious freedom), elected to remain with his native state. As a consequence Calhoun was drawn naturally into an identification with the interests of his state and section. During the late 1820s he emerged as the most forceful spokesman of southern interests, defending his state and section from the very contingencies Rawlins Lowndes had predicted. In the process Calhoun drew upon the example provided by the South Carolina constitutions of 1778, 1790, and 1808 for his theory of the "Concurrent Majority" and expanded the view of state sovereignty, expressed by Lowndes among others during the constitutional debates and formalized in the Virginia and Kentucky Resolves of 1798–1799, to produce the Theory of Nullification. For all the sectional bitterness the controversy produced, the proof of Lowndes' foresight was complete. What Lowndes understood and Calhoun articulated with relentless logic was that the clash of interest groups competing for advantage would go on forever, just as young men would continue to learn from adversity, seize opportunity, and rise to the top as long as America remained a free and open society.

Bibliographical Note

Biographical studies of colonial South Carolinians are rarely attempted for the very sensible reason that so few of their personal papers have survived. Rawlins Lowndes offers a case in point. Lowndes compiled a substantial collection of papers relating to his private as well as public affairs through the American Revolution, the great bulk of which was accidentally destroyed by fire shortly after the restoration of peace in 1783. All but a few items of what remained were consumed along with most of the papers of his son William in the great Charleston fire of 1865. The Lowndes papers which escaped destruction eventually passed to a descendant, St. Julien Ravenel Childs of Charleston, who deposited them in two small collections, the larger in the Southern Historical Collection at Chapel Hill, North Carolina, and the smaller in the Library of Congress. Since the papers of William Lowndes comprise most of both collections, they can be supplemented by individual pieces located in the William L. Clements Library, the Historical Society of Pennsylvania, the New-York Historical Society, the New York Public Library, the Houghton Library of Harvard University, the Massachusetts Historical Society, the South Caroliniana Library of the University of South Carolina, and the Charleston Library Society. The Southern Historical Collection has made available on microfilm the William Lowndes Papers including Rawlins' important London journal of 1754–1755.

Among the collections of papers of contemporaries, who corresponded with Lowndes or mentioned him in letters written to others, the most useful to this study have been *The Writings of*

Christopher Gadsden, 1746–1805, edited by Richard Walsh (Columbia, S.C., 1966) and the microfilm edition of the Letterbooks of Henry Laurens in the South Carolina Historical Society. *The Papers of Henry Laurens*, superbly edited by the late Philip M. Hamer, George C. Rogers, Jr., and others, six volumes to date (Columbia, S.C., 1968– —), have covered Laurens' public and business affairs through the 1760s. The wealth of information provided not only by the papers themselves but also in the footnotes has already made these volumes an indispensable source on the period and promises to be the most important recent addition to the published literature of the revolutionary era in South Carolina. *The South Carolina Historical and Genealogical Magazine*, which dropped "Genealogical" from its title in 1952, is a reference work of the first importance for the study of South Carolina, containing a substantial amount of correspondence of the revolutionary generation including Lowndes, Gadsden, Laurens, John Lewis Gervais, Peter Manigault, Arthur Middleton, Aedanus Burke, and the Pinckney and Rutledge brothers. But in the printed as well as the manuscript collections of his contemporaries, even of Laurens and Gadsden, direct references to Rawlins Lowndes are disappointingly rare. Hence the reconstruction of his public career has of necessity depended primarily on public records and newspapers.

Official colony and state records in the South Carolina Department of Archives and History in Columbia, both in manuscript and microfilm copies, have been the principal source of information for this study. Of those which span the period of royal government in the colony, the Records in the British Public Record Office Relating to South Carolina, 1663–1782, thirty-six volumes, compiled and transcribed under the direction of W. Noel Sainsbury, and the Journals of the Commons House of Assembly, 1705–1775, proved absolutely essential, furnishing documentary support for most of the narrative. The former, cited SCPRO in the notes and consisting mostly of correspondence between South Carolina officials and the Lords of Trade, provide important detail on almost every aspect of provincial affairs including every major controversy which developed between the provincial government and the representatives of royal authority before the Revolution. The early history of the office of provost marshal as well as the discussion of controversies of the 1760s relating to parliamentary taxation and the provincial courts have depended in substantial degree on this source. The best method of approach was a methodical progress through the records rather than primary reliance on the index.

The same method must be employed in researching the Commons Journals, which form the backbone of this study. *The Journal of the Commons House of Assembly, 1736–1750*, 9 volumes, edited by J. H. Easterby and Ruth S. Green (Columbia, S.C., 1951–1962), were of more limited value since Lowndes did not enter the Commons House until 1749. The recent resumption of publication of this valuable series by the University of South Carolina Press for the South Carolina Department of Archives and History is welcomed by all students of colonial South Carolina. Besides the legislative proceedings, the Commons Journals contain a great deal of material on provincial affairs in the numerous petitions recorded. The usefulness of these journals is limited by the fact that speeches and individual ballots on the measures considered were not written into the legislative record. Supplementing the legislative records of the colonial era, the Council Journals, 1734–1774, are a rich source of information on original land grants. The details of land holdings and other properties held during the eighteenth century can be found in the indexed Will Books, Deed Books, Inventories of Estates, and Miscellaneous Records located in the Archives and the Office of Mesne Conveyance in the Charleston County Court House.

For the revolutionary era the legislative records are less complete. The best guide to the proceedings of the provincial congresses, the most important of the revolutionary bodies which succeeded the Commons House of Assembly, are the *Extracts from the Journals of the Provincial Congresses of South Carolina, 1775–1776*, eds. William Edwin Hemphill and Wylma Anne Wates (Columbia, S.C., 1960). The most detailed unofficial account of Lowndes' role in these proceedings is in John Drayton, *Memoirs of the American Revolution*, 2 vols. (Charleston, S.C., 1821). The *Journals of the General Assembly and House of Representatives, 1776–1780*, edited by Hemphill, Wates, and R. Nicholas Olsberg (Columbia, S.C., 1970), carry the legislative record down to the fall of Charles Town, except for a critical gap between October 1776 and September 1779 which embraces the period of Lowndes' presidency. Following the Revolution the manuscript journals of the state House of Representatives are most useful on the closing years of Lowndes' legislative career.

The laws of South Carolina for the period covered and the court records of the colonial era, although a complete compilation in neither case exists, were consulted with profit. *The Statutes at Large of South Carolina*, eds. Thomas Cooper and David J. McCord, 10 vols. (Columbia, S.C., 1836–1841), the standard legal reference work, was of particular value in discovering the powers, duties, and fees of the marshal's office. *The Records of the Court of Chancery of South Carolina, 1671–1779*, edited by Anne King Gregorie (Washington, D.C., 1950), are fuller on details of charges and court proceedings that came before the governor and Council, including the case of *Ruth Lowndes* v. *Charles Lowndes*, than the Judgement Rolls, manuscript documents pertaining to civil suits, which often present a bare outline of the case at issue along with the names of the parties at suit, opposing counsel, and the verdict. Minutes of the Court of Common Pleas, though missing for much of the period, furnished the details of the Stamp Act case, *Jordan* v. *Law*; no records exist for the 1730s when Charles Lowndes was involved in litigation. Journals for the Court of General Sessions prior to 1769, the record of criminal cases heard, were lost during the Civil War. The extant volume was especially helpful on the later stages of regulator activity when Lowndes sat on the provincial bench.

Newspapers of the colonial and revolutionary eras in South Carolina were of critical significance in tracing the life of Lowndes. By far the most important was the *South Carolina Gazette*, published in Charles Town and covering the period from 1732 to 1776. A mine of information on a variety of topics although disappointing in its usually brief treatment of local news, the *Gazette* was essential to the reconstruction of Lowndes' career as provost marshal. It also provides the most complete record of grand jury presentments and other court proceedings not available in the extant court records. From the 1760s through the remainder of the century material from the *Gazette* was supplemented by reports in roughly chronological order from the *South Carolina and American General Gazette,* the *South Carolina Gazette and Country Journal,* the *State Gazette of South Carolina,* the *Gazette of the State of South Carolina,* the *Royal Gazette,* the *Gazette and General Advertiser,* and the *City Gazette and Daily Advertiser,* all published in Charleston. The *South Carolina Gazette* is available on microfilm. Others may be seen in the Charleston Library Society, the Library of the College of Charleston, and the South Caroliniana Library in Columbia.

Secondary works have provided a good deal of connective tissue through the foregoing narrative and have been credited by citation when drawn upon directly for specific factual information. Authors of general works and specialized studies, from whose scholarship I have profited to a far greater degree than the brief citations indicate, are Charles M. Andrews, Richard Maxwell Brown, Richard B. Clow, Maurice A. Crouse, Jack P. Greene, Jackson Turner Main, Edward McCrady, David Ramsay, Mrs. St. Julien Ravenel, George C. Rogers, Jr., Charles G. Singer, M. Eugene Sirmans, W. Roy Smith, David D. Wallace, Robert M. Weir, and Marvin Zahniser. To these I must add the legion of contributors to the *South Carolina Historical and Genealogical Magazine.*

INDEX

D2